00181

Monetarist, Keynesian
and New Classical Economics

Monetarist, Keynesian and New Classical Economics

JEROME L. STEIN

New York University Press
New York *and* London

First published in the U.S.A. by
New York University Press
Washington Square
New York, NY 10003

Library of Congress Cataloging in Publication Data
Stein, Jerome L.
  Monetarist, Keynesian, and new classical
economics.

  Bibliography: p.
  Includes index.
  1. Macroeconomics.   2. Monetary policy.
3. Keynesian economics.   4. Classical school of
economics.   I. Title.   II. Title: New classical
economics.
HB172.5.S73   1983   339.5   82-12583
ISBN 0-8147-7824-0

Printed in Great Britain

To
Seth, Gil, Ilana and Carol

Contents

Preface

The paradox of "stagflation," which was first noted at the beginning of the 1970s, undermined my confidence in the dominant Keynesian economics. With the aid of a fellowship from the John Simon Guggenheim Foundation, I attempted to formulate a dynamic macroeconomic theory which could explain the paradoxical empirical phenomena. This research was published in an article "Unemployment, Inflation and Monetarism," *American Economic Review*, 1974. A conference was held at Brown University in 1974 to evaluate the "Monetarist" propositions. This conference, supported by the National Science Foundation, resulted in a book, J.L. Stein (ed.), 1976: *Monetarism* (Amsterdam: North-Holland).

In my 1974 article I noted (p. 884, note 17) that if there is no forecast error between the actual and anticipated rates of inflation, then the trajectory of the unemployment rate is independent of monetary policy. Since this scenario seemed to be inconsistent with the message in Milton Friedman and Anna Schwartz, 1963: *A Monetary History of the United States*, I did not pursue the implications of that assumption. New Classical Economics developed the implications of the joint assumptions: the forecast error is just "noise" and there is a "natural" rate of unemployment. This school of thought rejected Keynesian economics completely. By 1980, economists were polarized between the Keynesian analysis and New Classical Economics. Each school of thought has its own vocabulary, techniques of analysis, statistical tests and oral tradition. Communication between the poles is almost non-existent; and very few macroeconomists are non-aligned.

As I continued to analyze the problems of stagflation and growth dynamics, in a series of papers with Ettore F. Infante of the Division of Applied Mathematics at Brown University (published in the *Journal of Monetary Economics* and the *Journal of Political Economy*), and as a result of my statistical testing of alternative hypotheses, I was convinced that neither pole was able to explain the empirical reality. Research was directed to refining the techniques of each school rather than towards the development of a theory which could predict.

William Baumol, as President of the American Economic Association, asked me to organize a session and present a paper at the 1980 Denver meetings of the American Economic Association on the topic: the Monetarist Contribution to Macroeconomics. It provided me with an incentive to evaluate the validity of the polar points of view and to continue my research on a synthesis which could explain and predict. The resulting paper, with the title of this book, was published in the *American Economic Review*, 1981.

Basil Blackwell, Oxford, asked me to write a book on this subject. By then, "a fire was burning in my bones"; and it was an offer that I could not refuse.

Drafts of the chapters were distributed to my graduate seminar at Brown University, and the students were asked to criticize them from the viewpoint of both poles, to point out deficiencies and to suggest revisions. Much have I learned from my teachers, in particular James Tobin; but most of all I have learned from my students: David Altig, Sung Yeon Lee, Dean Leistikow, Kazuo Mino, Richard Nisenson, Robert Selvaggio, Shunichi Tsutsui and John Van Huyck. Their trenchant criticisms and suggestions were embodied in subsequent drafts. Richard Ablin, George Borts, William Haraf, Thomas Mayer and Zalman Shiffer also made excellent suggestions for improvement.

Parallel with my research in macroeconomics, I have been studying speculative markets. This research has been supported by the National Science Foundation and the Columbia University, Center for the Study of Futures Markets. This research has given me a more profound understanding of the formation of anticipations, which is of great importance in macroeconomics.

Marion A. Wathey typed this manuscript with the flawless grace and perfection that she also displays in her ballroom dancing. My wife Hadassah has given me excellent suggestions on editorial matters; and I have benefited from her wise counsel. Brown University has provided me with ideal conditions for research. I am grateful to each one.

This is a controversial book in a polarized field. I hope that the reader accepts the philosophy quoted at the very end of this book.

Jerome L. Stein

Providence, Rhode Island   February, 1982

CHAPTER 1

The Unsettled State of Macroeconomics

1 The success of, and subsequent disenchantment with, Keynesian economics

Among the casualties of the war in Vietnam was the state of macroeconomics. In 1969 Arthur Okun, who was Lyndon Johnson's Chairman of the Council of Economic Advisers, wrote a panegyric on Keynesian economics as a guide to economic policy: "More vigorous and more consistent application of the tools of economic policy contributed to the obsolescence of the business cycle pattern and refutation of the stagnation myths" (1970: 37). The innovative strategy of Keynesian economics focused upon the "Okun Gap" between potential (capacity) output and actual output[1] rather than upon the state of the business cycle, because even at the peak of the cycle in 1960 the economy was far short of full employment. Insofar as an Okun Gap exists, the economy is not realizing its potential; it is the responsibility of the government to implement demand management policies to eliminate the Okun Gap.

Adoption of this strategy led to an activist stabilization policy which "... was the key that unlocked the door to the subsequent expansion in the 1960s" (Okun, 1970: 43). Early in the 1960s the problem was diagnosed as follows. Insufficient aggregate demand produced a gap between potential output and actual output. According to Keynesian theory, the obvious remedy was to implement a stimulative fiscal and monetary policy.

This view was widely shared by the economics profession, regardless of political persuasion. Arthur Burns, who was Dwight Eisenhower's Chairman of the Council of Economic Advisers, accepted Okun's Keynesian point of view. Burns wrote:

... the vital matter is whether a gap exists between actual and potential output; that fiscal deficits and monetary tools need to be used to promote expansion

1

when a gap exists; and that the stimuli should be sufficient to close the gap — provided significant inflationary pressures are not whipped up in the process. (quoted in Okun, 1970: 43)

Keynesians acknowledged that they did not have a satisfactory solution to the problem of how to manage a full employment economy without inflation. In 1968, the economics profession generally believed that there were no difficulties involved in prescribing expansionary policies in a period of slack (see Ackley, quoted by Okun, 1970: 61). A decade later, a substantial number of economists subscribing to the New Classical Economics (NCE) totally rejected the premises and implications of Keynesian economics concerning the efficacy of demand management policy to influence the gap between potential and actual output.

Demand management policy in the 1960s was activated by an Okun Gap, and it consisted of an expansionary fiscal policy relying on tax cuts, coupled with an accommodative monetary policy.[2] Okun described the accommodative monetary policy in the following way.

The Federal Reserve allowed the demands for liquidity and credit generated by a rapidly expanding economy to be met at stable interest rates ... long-term yields were far more stable in the early sixties than in the late fifties. While the Federal Reserve obviously did not "peg" bond yields, it did aim to stabilize longer-term interest rates. (1970: 53)

To ensure that the rationale of the policy was understood, Okun described it explicitly in terms of the dominant IS−LM Keynesian model.

An accommodative or rate-oriented monetary policy fixes the interest rate and makes the LM curve horizontal in the relevant range. There is no dispute among economists that a permanent tax cut (or an increase in most types of government expenditure) shifts the IS curve. Given a horizontal LM curve, a shift in the IS curve necessarily changes the level of income .... Whether the Fed *should* pursue a rate-oriented policy that produces a horizontal LM curve is not the issue. The fact is that it *did* in 1963, 1964, and the first half of 1965. (1970: 57, note 30)

There was little doubt among the macroeconomists of the time that this "activist strategy was the key that unlocked the door to sustained expansion in the 1960s". The unemployment rate was reduced from 6.7 per cent in 1961 to 4.5 per cent in 1965. The growth rate of real GNP from 1961 to 1965 was 5.3 per cent per annum, which exceeded the trend rate of growth estimated at 3.9 per cent per annum. During the 1961–65 period, the rate of inflation of the GNP deflator was 1.8 per cent per annum. Okun noted that: "Labor costs were remarkably stable in both organized and unorganized areas" (1970: 49). Nominal unit labor costs rose at an insignificant rate of 0.5 per cent per annum during the period 1961–65.

This was the triumph and vindication of the New Economics. The spirit of Keynes was now

... scattered among a hundred cities. And wholly given over to unfamiliar affections.

Keynesian economics, which has guided demand management policy, is summarized by the propositions [K1] through [K6].

[K1] ... prices and wages respond slowly to excess demand or supply, especially slowly to excess supply. Over a long short run, ups and downs of demand register in output; they are far from completely absorbed in prices. (Tobin, 1977: 459)

A Keynesian interpretation is that prices — including money wages — are sticky in the short run, throughout those large sectors of modern economies where they are set by discrete private or public administrative decisions or negotiations.

... the speed at which prices and wages increase relative to trend depends inversely on the amounts of excess supply (of labor, commodity stocks, capital capacity) in the economy. (Tobin, 1980: 38)

[K2] The unemployment rate is a good, but imperfect, barometer of the pressure of aggregate demand on the productive resources of the economy.

[K3] In an economy with under employment of labor and capital, more labor and capital services will be supplied, if demanded, along the on-going path of wages and prices, without accelerating their increase. (Tobin, 1977: 464)

[K4] Cyclical movements of output and price, relative to their trends, are positively correlated. (Tobin, 1980: 38)

[K5] Keynes suggested ... that it was easier to stabilize real economic variables by moving aggregate money demand to a given path of

money wages than by moving wages relative to a given money
demand . . . . (Tobin, 1977: 460)

These fundamental Keynesian propositions are formally described
by the following three equations of the Keynesian system. Equation
(1.1) states that the price level p is a relatively fixed multiple k of
nominal unit labor costs W:

$$p = kW. \tag{1.1}$$

This equation is consistent with competitive pricing, where price is
equal to marginal cost, or with imperfect competition when the elasticity
of demand is relatively constant.

Equation (1.2) defines nominal income Y as the product of real
output y and the price deflator p. Alternatively, the price deflator p is
defined as the ratio of nominal to real output:

$$Y \equiv py. \tag{1.2}$$

The third equation is the IS−LM solution for nominal income Y.
Nominal income depends upon nominal government expenditures G,
nominal money stock M, nominal interest payments on the government
debt B and tax rate τ:

$$Y = F(G, M, B, \tau). \tag{1.3}$$

The function $F(G, M, B, \tau)$ is homogeneous of degree one in all
nominal variables: if G, M and B change by x per cent, then Y also
changes by x per cent. It follows that real output y depends upon the
values of G, M and B measured in wage units, as described by equation
(1.4a). It is written more simply as equation (1.4b), where the subscript
w indicates that the variable is measured in wage units.

$$y = \frac{1}{k} F(G/W, M/W, B/W, \tau). \tag{1.4a}$$

$$y = f(G_w, M_w, B_w, \tau). \tag{1.4b}$$

A crucial Keynesian proposition [K1] is " . . . that prices − including
money wages − are sticky in the short run . . . price and wage increases
relative to trend depend inversely upon excess supply of labor,
commodities . . . ."

The unemployment rate $U(t)$ is negatively related to the ratio of
actual output $y(t)$ to capacity output $q(t)$. Therefore, the deviation of
$U(t)$ from the equilibrium unemployment rate U_e and the Okun Gap
$[1 - y(t)/q(t)]$ can be used interchangeably. A Keynesian proposition

concerning the movement of unit labour costs is described by equation (1.5), which is based upon the following view.

... the historical experience clearly supports the proposition that there exists some *critical* rate of unemployment such that, as long as unemployment does not fall below it, inflation can be expected to decline .... (Modigliani and Papademos, 1976: 4)

Let the rate of inflation ω of unit labour costs W be defined by $\omega \equiv D \ln W$. The Keynesian view is that the *acceleration* of the inflation of nominal unit labor costs depends upon the ratio of actual to capacity output, that is,

$$D \ln \omega = D^2 \ln W = H(y/q); \quad D \equiv d/dt. \tag{1.5}$$

As long as there is an Okun Gap (i.e. y/q is less than unity), then the first three Keynesian propositions state that nominal unit labor costs and prices will not grow faster than the trend. In particular, when there is an Okun Gap ($y < q$), nominal wages and prices are often regarded as being fixed at the trend. Keynesian economists do not specify in any theoretical way what this trend rate is.

Demand management policy to eliminate an Okun Gap consists of: (i) raising government expenditures G or lowering tax rates τ; and (ii) following an accommodative monetary policy to stabilize the nominal rate of interest by letting the money supply M grow with the expansion of the economy, as described by equation (1.6): ·

$$M = M(y). \tag{1.6}$$

As Modigliani and Papademos phrased it:

[K6] In the initial phase of the recovery, the target should be the maintenance of current rates ... [of interest]. (1975: 165)
... our policy target is stated in terms of interest rates, not in terms of money supply. The interest rate target can be enforced by the Federal Reserve directly without any need to decide in advance what growth rate in the money supply or in reserves will be required to achieve it. (1976: 17)

By combining equations (1.4b) and (1.6), or propositions [K1] − [K6], the Keynesian demand management policy to be followed when there is an Okun Gap ($y < q$) is based upon the equation

$$q > y = f(G_w, M(y), B_w, \tau). \tag{1.7}$$

Declines in tax rates, or increases in government expenditures, produce a shift to the right of the IS curve along a relatively horizontal LM curve. Output then rises and the Okun Gap is reduced; very little of the increased demand is dissipated in price and wage increases.

Keynesian economics, which dominated academic macroeconomics in the 1960s, demonstrated to Congress and the public its ability to eliminate the gap between potential and actual output. A sustained expansion was engineered in the 1960s without any significant inflation. All this changed in the 1970s. In the aftermath of the war in Vietnam, the Keynesian propositions no longer characterized the state of macroeconomic theory. Summarized in Table 1.1 are the events which were inconsistent with the Keynesian propositions and the model described above.

TABLE 1.1 *Growth, unemployment and inflation for the period 1961 – 80.*

Period	Price inflation π (% p.a.)[1]	Labor cost inflation ω (% p.a.)[2]	Average unemployment U (%)[3]	Growth rate of real output G(y) (% p.a.)[4]
1961–68	2.5	1.9	4.85	4.9
1968–73	5.1	4.8	4.75	3.5
1973–80	7.7	8.4	6.58	2.4
1961–80	5.1	5.0	5.57	3.6

Source: [1], [2], [4]: Federal Reserve Bank of St Louis, Annual US Economic Data, May 1981; [3]: Economic Report of the President, Council of Economic Advisers.

The phenomenon of "stagflation" characterized the periods 1968–73 and 1973–80, as described in table 1.1 and figure 1.1. *Stagflation* is defined as a situation where either of the following phenomena exist: (i) a rising unemployment rate, a declining growth rate of real output and a rising inflation rate; or (ii) a "high" unemployment rate, a low growth rate of real output and a "high" or rising inflation rate.

During the last two periods, the rate of growth of output declined and the rate of inflation rose. The average unemployment rate and average annual compound rate of inflation were higher, and the growth of real output was lower, during the period 1973–80 than they were during the period 1961–68. On an even shorter-run basis (see figure 1.1 or the appendix to chapter 4): (i) the unemployment rate rose from 1969–71 and the inflation rate rose from 1967–70; (ii) the unemployment rate rose from 1973–75 and the inflation rate rose from 1972–74;

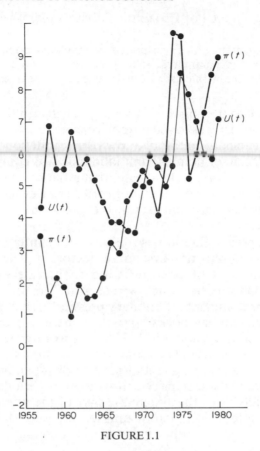

FIGURE 1.1

(iii) the unemployment rate was high or rising from 1975–80 and the inflation rate rose from 1976–80.

The post-Vietnam stagflation fundamentally contradicts the Keynesian propositions above. Cyclical movements in prices and output, relative to their trends, are not positively correlated. In the presence of excess supply, which Keynesians measure by the unemployment rate, prices and wages were rising relative to their trends. It was no longer possible to base policy upon the assumption that prices and wages are "sticky" in the presence of unemployment, and that variations in demand will be reflected primarily in output and not be dissipated by price and wage changes. The wage unit could not be regarded as a fixed point. There was no longer a consensus that the Keynesian model is an adequate guide to the formulation and execution of policies designed to eliminate a gap between potential and actual output.

In 1972, the Council of Economic Advisers plaintively wrote:

The problems of managing fiscal policy or monetary policy or both have apparently been underestimated. It may be that more has been promised than can be delivered with existing knowledge and instruments. (1972: 112)

The response to the cognitive dissonance between their theory and the post-1968 history was to focus upon price equation (1.1) and imbue it with an exogenous *ad hoc* life of its own. Price inflation was accounted for by the inflation of nominal unit labor costs. A comparison of the first two columns in table 1.1 indicates that inflation of prices is closely associated with inflation of unit labor costs. The Keynesian Council of Economic Advisers accounted for the post-1968 inflation in the following way.

The rate of price inflation π is the sum of the inflation of nominal unit labor cost ω plus non-systematic factors η. The major factor determining the rate of price inflation is the rate of inflation of nominal unit labor costs, which was termed "the underlying rate of inflation." The dominant inflationary pressures originally came from a series of large external shocks (η) to the American economy, such as the depreciation of the dollar in 1971−73, a worldwide crop shortage and the rise in oil prices. Once under way, a high rate of inflation generates responses ω and adaptations by individuals and institutions that perpetuate the wage−price spiral, even in periods of economic slack. The behavior of the systematic part of the rate of inflation is related to the rate of inflation of unit labor costs, which is not very responsive to the state of the labor market (Economic Report of the President, 1979: chapter 2, 55−7).

The Keynesian response to the cognitive dissonance between their model and the post-1968 experience is deficient in three respects.

First, inflation of prices cannot be *explained* in an epistemological sense by the inflation of unit labor costs. The price level p per unit of output is *defined* as total costs, plus profit, per unit of output. Its composition in 1970 is described as follows (Economic Report of the President, 1980: table B-12):

capital consumption allowances	9.4
indirect business taxes	11.0
compensation of employees $= W =$	67.3
net interest	3.0
corporate profits and inventory valuation adjustment	9.2
price per unit of output $= p =$	100%

Nominal unit labor costs W are about 67 per cent of price p and, from 1955–79, they ranged from 64 to 67 per cent. The value of k in equation (1.1) above is 1.5. The correlation between the inflation of prices π and the inflation of unit labor costs ω, from table 1.1, is simply a correlation between the whole (p) and 67 per cent of itself (W). One could ask *either* why the rate of price inflation accelerated *or* why the rate of inflation of unit labor costs accelerated; but it is not edifying to claim that the major part causes the whole to accelerate. There is only one degree of freedom. A theory of inflation must explain either why π or ω accelerated from 1961–68 to 1968–73 to 1973–80.

Secondly, an explanation of inflation is formally equivalent to a prediction. To provide an explanation for the inflation rate from $t-1$ to t, denoted by $\pi(t)$, or the unemployment rate at time t, denoted by $U(t)$, the dependent variable must be the mathematical expectation taken at *earlier time $t-1$* of the variable at *later date t*. The variable to be explained is a conditional expectation, denoted by $E_{t-1}\pi(t)$ or $E_{t-1}U(t)$, where E is the expectations operator, and the subscript denotes when the expectation is taken. The use of some variables at time t which are not known at $t-1$ (e.g. the inflation of unit labor costs or the rate of change of prices of food, fuel or imports) to account for other variables at time t (such as the inflation of the GNP deflator) is not an explanation — it is just a description of the phenomenon.

The following Keynesian account of the inflation of prices from 1972 to 1974 is not an explanation, but simply a description after the event. There is no hypothesis of the form: if X occurs at time $t-1$ then Y will occur at time t.

Between late 1972 and the spring of 1974 there was a rapid acceleration in the overall inflation rate, more than half of which appears to have been caused by an acceleration of food and energy prices, and the remainder by some combination of nominal demand growth and the loosening of controls. Farm prices almost doubled between early 1972 and the summer of 1973 as the result of the simultaneous occurrence of several adverse factors, including the delayed impact of the 1971 dollar devaluation, crop failures in many parts of the world combined with massive sales of United States wheat to the Soviet Union, and a peculiar disappearance of Peruvian anchovies from their normal feeding grounds. (Gordon, 1980: 142)

Thirdly, the Keynesian attempt to account for the acceleration of inflation of prices by attributing it to the inflation of nominal unit labor costs contradicts the Keynesian propositions [K1] – [K3]. The Keynesian model, as described in the propositions quoted above, requires that when there is an Okun Gap the wage unit grows below its trend rate and that it be independent of the demand management policies undertaken. Then, a rise in nominal government expenditures G or in the nominal stock of money M implies rises in real values G_w and M_w respectively in equation (1.4b). Only if real government purchases G_w, or real balances M_w, rise does fiscal or monetary policy raise real output y. If the wage unit is volatile, and especially if it is highly sensitive to the monetary and fiscal policies undertaken, then there is no presumption that demand management policies will be efficacious in raising real output and reducing the Okun Gap.

2 The polarity of views: New Classical Economics (NCE) fundamentally rejects Keynesian economics

New Classical Economics (NCE) rejects Keynesian economics completely and fundamentally. In 1969, Okun wrote that the implementation of Keynesian demand management policy contributed to the obsolescence of the business cycle and successfully eliminated the gap between potential and actual output. A decade later, Lucas and Sargent wrote that NCE theory

... predicts that there is no way that the monetary authority can follow a systematic activist policy and achieve a rate of output that is on average higher over the business cycle than would occur if it simply adopted a no feedback, x-percent rule of the kind Friedman and Simons recommended. (1978: 60–1)

NCE does not claim that a Friedman-style constant rate of growth of the money supply is preferable to a money growth rate which responds positively (or even negatively) to the unemployment rate. It claims that

... the unemployment rate [is] insensitive to demand policy choices and thereby ... [suggests] that these choices should be made on the basis of implications of alternative policy parameters for the stochastic evolution of the price level (and, therefore, the inflation rate). (McCallum, 1980: 724)

Many macroeconomic models imply that the change in the unemployment rate (or ratio of actual to capacity output) depends upon lagged values of the unemployment rate (or ratio of actual to capacity output), real shocks and the forecast error between the current price level and the value anticipated by the market on the basis of information at an earlier date, when production and spending decisions were made. A necessary condition for the validity of NCE is the Muth Rational Expectations Hypothesis (MRE) that the forecast error is a serially uncorrelated term with a zero expectation. It follows that the mathematical expectation of the change in the unemployment rate just depends upon lagged unemployment rates which reflect frictions in the economy resulting from costs of adjustment.

Formally, equations (1.8) and (1.9) are the core of New Classical Economics. Equation (1.8) states that the unemployment rate at time t, denoted by $U(t)$, depends upon its lagged values $U(t-j)$ and an "innovation" term $v(t)$. It is convenient to measure the unemployment rate as a deviation $u(t) \equiv U(t) - U_e$ from its equilibrium value U_e. Then the crucial NCE equation is

$$u(t) = \sum_{j=1} a_j u(t-j) + v(t). \tag{1.8}$$

Equation (1.9) states that the innovation term $v(t)$ is statistically independent of all past values of monetary and fiscal policies undertaken and has no structure. Let $x(t-1)$ denote a vector of monetary and fiscal policies undertaken or in force at time $t-1$. According to NCE

$$E_{t-1}[v(t) \mid x(t-1)] = 0; \qquad E[v(t), v(t-1)] = 0. \tag{1.9}$$

The mathematical expectation of the innovation of the unemployment rate is completely independent of the monetary and fiscal policies undertaken at $t-1$ or earlier. When the mathematical expectation of (1.8) is combined with (1.9) the *Policy Ineffectiveness Proposition* (1.10) can be derived, which is the fulcrum of NCE:

$$E_{t-1}u(t) = \sum_{j=1} a_j u(t-j). \tag{1.10}$$

It can be stated as proposition [NCE1].

[NCE1] On average, the unemployment rate deviation $u(t)$, or Okun Gap, is totally insensitive to demand management policies. The only systematic factor determining the evolution of the unemployment rate is its own history.

In 1961, the unemployment rate $U(t)$ was 6.7 per cent. According to NCE, its evolution from 1961−69 was statistically independent of the expansionary fiscal policy and accommodative monetary policy described by Okun. The same trajectory of the unemployment rate is expected to occur whether or not there is an activist policy. In no way was the "... activist strategy ... the key that unlocked the door to sustained expansion in the 1960s." *Equation (1.10) of NCE is the fundamental rejection of Keynesian economics.*

Major policy issues during the period 1973−81 concern the *strategies* which are efficacious in reducing the rate of inflation and the *social costs*, in terms of lost output and higher unemployment rates, associated with each strategy.

An implication of equation (1.10) is NCE proposition [NCE2]:

[NCE2]   There are no expected social costs to any feedback monetary or fiscal policy $x(t-1)$ to reduce the rate of inflation $\pi(t)$.

The expected unemployment rate $E_{t-1}u(t)$, or Okun Gap, depends only upon its own history and is independent of any monetary or fiscal policies undertaken at time $t-1$. Therefore, an anticipated monetary or fiscal policy $x(t-1)$ affects the price level $p(t)$ quickly and systematically because, in the Quantity theory equation, $x(t-1)$ has no systematic effects upon either the level of output or velocity at time t.

This view directly contradicts the Keynesian propositions [K1] − [K5]. The Keynesian view, described by equations (1.1), (1.4b) and (1.5), is that a decline in the nominal money stock M is associated with a decline in the real money stock M_w in wage units. Aggregate demand declines and real output is reduced. When Okun Gaps have been produced such that output is below capacity output, then the rate of inflation of nominal unit labor costs will be reduced. A high price must be paid if traditional monetary and fiscal policies are to be used to reduce the rate of inflation.

Tobin expressed the Keynesian view lucidly and cogently:

Must we *either* hold the real performance of the economy hostage to disinflation *or* accommodate monetary demand to the inflation that history happens to have bequeathed us? Our quandary today is a vivid example of the general dilemma ... How to a non-inflationary line of monetary demand and rely on market forces to produce a compatible and stabilization path of wages and prices? Or, as Keynes was advocating in the 1920s and 1930s, adopt the course of monetary demand to the wage−price trend. The first, experience suggests, often gives poor performance in the real payoffs of economic activity. The second leaves prices unanchored, their path the cumulative history of random shocks.

The way out, the only way out, is incomes policy .... Use corporate, personal income, and payroll taxes to reward and insure compliant employers and workers, and possibly — as Wallich and Weintraub independently proposed — to penalize violators. (1977: 467)

Disagreement between Keynesian and New Classical Economics is fundamental and complete; the profession is polarized between these two points of view. There is no longer a macroeconomic consensus theory to guide the Federal Reserves Board or Council of Economic Advisers in the formulation of economic policy.

3   Monetarism between the poles

What I *define* as the Monetarist position was considered heretical during the period of the 1960s. Twenty years later, it is intermediate between the poles of Keynesianism and New Classical Economics. Monetarism consists of a set of empirical propositions concerning the effects of a given rate of inflation and variance of the unemployment rate. Whereas Keynesian economists generally attribute the variance of the unemployment rate (or ratio of actual to capacity output) to systematic exogenous movements in the marginal efficiency of capital, Monetarists place more emphasis upon variations in the rate of monetary expansion generated by the monetary authorities as an explanation of unemployment rate variations.

The basic Monetarist proposition is that inflation is primarily a monetary phenomenon.

[M1]   Past rates of growth of the money stock are the only systematic factors determining the rate of inflation. Contrary to the Keynesian view, Monetarists claim that a restrictive fiscal policy without a reduction in the rate of monetary expansion cannot reduce the rate of inflation.

To have a significant impact upon the rate of inflation, a change in tax rates or government expenditures must be associated with a change in the rate of monetary expansion. Milton Friedman explained this proposition as follows:

Whether deficits produce inflation depends on how they are financed . . . . If, as so often happens, they are financed by creating money, they unquestionably do produce inflationary pressure . . . . If they are financed by borrowing from the public, at whatever interest rates are necessary, they may still exert some minor inflationary pressure . . . . However, their major effect will be to make interest rates higher than they would otherwise be. (1974: 140)

The reason why a money-financed fiscal policy is so powerful, according to Friedman, is that as long as the deficit continues and is financed by creating money, the LM curve keeps shifting to the right. This continuous shifting of the LM curve eventually dominates the once and for all shift of the IS curve produced by a rise in government expenditures or decline in tax rates (1974: 141).

Monetarist proposition [M1] is summarized algebraically by equation (1.11). The rate of price inflation from year $t-1$ to year t is denoted by $\pi(t)$ and the rate of monetary expansion from year $t-1$ to year t is denoted by $\mu(t)$:

$$\pi(t) = a_0 + \sum_{i=1} a_i \mu(t-i) + \varepsilon(t); \qquad \sum_{i=1} a_i = 1, \tag{1.11}$$

where $\varepsilon(t)$ is a random term with a zero expectation. The value of the constant $a_0 \leqslant 0$ depends upon which definition of the money supply is used. Figure 1.2 describes the historical relationship between the rate

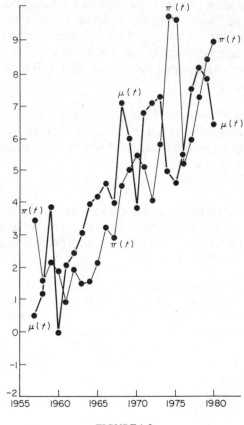

FIGURE 1.2

of inflation and the rate of monetary expansion in the United States from 1957 through 1979.

All three schools of thought agree that there is no relation between unemployment and inflation in the steady state. Contrary to NCE, Monetarists believe proposition [M2]:

[M2] There is a tradeoff between the deceleration of an inflation and a temporary rise in the unemployment rate.

Proposition [M3] differs from both these points of view:

[M3] A rise in the rate of monetary expansion temporarily reduces the unemployment rate and permanently raises the inflation rate.

For example, Karl Brunner (who coined the term "Monetarism") writes:

Monetary growth affects dominantly the price level. Monetary accelerations or decelerations, on the other hand, operate essentially on output and employment. It is, therefore, not possible to state whether a 10% annual rate of increase in the money stock is expansionary or not with respect to output. Additional information is required. We must know what happened to monetary growth previously.

The impact of monetary accelerations (or decelerations) on output and employment is essentially temporary. (1970: 13)

These three propositions can be summarized algebraically. Let $U(t)$ be the unemployment rate, $G(y(t))$ be the growth rate of real output, $\pi(t)$ be the rate of inflation and $\mu(t)$ be the rate of monetary expansion. Propositions [M2] and [M3] are summarized by equations (1.12)–(1.14).

There is no relation between a constant rate of monetary growth μ and either the unemployment rate $U(t)$ or the rate of growth of real output $G(y(t))$.

$$\text{cov}\,[U(t), \mu] = \text{cov}\,[G(y(t)), \mu] = 0. \qquad (1.12)$$

Monetary accelerations or decelerations $\Delta\mu(t)$ exert effects upon the unemployment rate and rate of growth of output:[3]

$$\text{cov}\,[\Delta U(t), \Delta\mu(t)] < 0 \qquad (1.13)$$

$$\text{cov}\,[G(y(t)), \Delta\mu(t)] > 0. \qquad (1.14)$$

A change in the rate of monetary expansion first produces changes in the real variables and later produces changes in the rate of inflation. Milton Friedman's description of this process differs fundamentally from the process implied by NCE, whereby anticipated monetary policy affects nominal, but not real, variables. Friedman writes:

If the rate of monetary growth is reduced then about six to nine months later, the rate of growth of nominal income and also of physical output will decline. However, the rate of price rise will be affected very little. There will be downward pressure on prices only as a gap emerges between actual and potential output.

On average, the effect on prices comes about six to nine months after the effect on income and output, so that the total delay between a change in money growth and a change in the rate of inflation averages something like 12−18 months. (1970: 23)

Stagflation is not inconsistent with these Monetarist propositions. Brunner perceived that

... the coexistence of permanent price inflation and fluctuations in real variables ... results from the interaction between the effects associated with high average monetary growth and large monetary accelerations or decelerations. (1970: 13)

Equation (1.11) states that the inflation rate is a linear combination of past rates of monetary expansion. A high inflation rate results from high rates of monetary expansion in the previous years. Equations (1.13) and (1.14) state that monetary decelerations $\Delta\mu(t) < 0$ are associated with rises in the unemployment rate. Monetarist propositions [M4] and [M5] can then be stated:

[M4] A deceleration of the rate of monetary expansion, following several years of high rates of monetary expansion, exerts its effects directly upon the unemployment rate. However, the rate of inflation is kept high by the inertia of past rates of monetary expansion.

[M5] Contrary to NCE, there is a significant cost in terms of unemployment and lost output to reducing the rate of inflation.

Monetarist propositions [M1] − [M5] are intermediate between the polarized Keynesian and NCE positions. See Purvis (1980) and Mayer (1978).

4 Issues to be resolved

Keynesian economists, Monetarists and New Classical economists agree that the steady state of inflation is closely related to the growth of the money supply, and that monetary policy cannot affect the equilibrium rate of unemployment or rate of growth of output. Disagreement concerns (i) the macrodynamics of unemployment, inflation and rate of growth of output between steady states, and (ii) the effects of fiscal policy upon the characteristics of the steady state. The following issues are controversial.

What are the short-run adjustments of the inflation rate and unemployment rate (or growth of output) to changes in monetary and fiscal policy? How is the current inflation rate related to the unemployment rate? What unemployment rates are consistent with decelerating an inflation? What are the social costs of reducing the rate of inflation? Are gradualist policies preferable to "bang-bang" policies? What are the characteristics of the continuous transition between the short-run situation and the long-run equilibrium, where the stocks of capital and financial assets are endogenous variables? To what extent are the IS–LM impact effects of fiscal and monetary policy, on the level of output, the real rate of interest and the price level, amplified or reversed by endogenous changes in the stocks of capital and financial assets?

My strategy is to develop a general macrodynamic model which can imply any one of the three schools of thought, depending upon the parameter specifications. My model[4] is broader than those used by the three schools of thought, since prices, quantities, the stocks of capital and of financial assets are endogenous. It is asked: to what extent do the schools of thought postulate different transmission mechanisms? Are their differences qualitative (e.g. is one based upon rational behavior and another based upon *ad hoc* equations?), or do they simply postulate different numerical values of coefficients in the same equation? I show that each school of thought is a special case of a general model, and that the disagreement among the Keynesian, NCE and Monetarist viewpoints can be resolved by testing alternative *statistical* hypotheses concerning parameter specifications.

Chapter 2 specifies the behavioral equations of the general dynamic model of a growing economy with a variable unemployment rate, inflation rate, stock of capital and stocks of financial assets. This formalistic chapter provides the structure for the subsequent economic analysis.

In chapter 3 it is shown that the three schools of thought are special cases of the general model. By specifying the values of particular parameters, the propositions of each school of thought are derived.

Hypothesis testing is the main subject of chapter 4, which discusses four issues. First, the statistical hypotheses concerning the unemployment rate or ratio of actual to capacity output are tested. The NCE hypotheses are rejected and the Monetarist hypotheses are accepted. Secondly, the Keynesian and Monetarist statistical hypotheses concerning the rate of inflation are tested against each other. The Keynesian hypotheses are rejected and the Monetarist hypotheses are accepted. Thirdly, the predictive performance of the Monetarist equations are examined for the USA, the world as a whole and for a set of 12 major countries. Fourthly, a quantitative analysis is made of demand management policies. It is shown that stagflation is produced by a demand management policy which strives to solve the *immediate* problem of *either* unemployment *or* inflation. A comparison is made of the effects of gradualist and bang-bang policies to reduce inflation.

Chapter 5 is concerned with the continuous dynamic growth path of the economy to the long-run steady state. Major attention is devoted to the study of the short- and long-run effects of money-financed fiscal policy. It is shown that government budget balance is not a condition for equilibrium. A rise in government purchases *per capita* exerts a positive impact upon output *per capita*. Steady-state output *per capita* and the capital intensity, however, decline. There is a rise in both the inflation tax on real balances and in the steady-state rate of inflation. Indeed, there is a long-run social cost involved in using fiscal policy to accelerate the return to full employment.

Chapter 6 concludes the contribution of this book to the state of macroeconomics.

> My liege, here is the strangest controversy,
> Come from the country to be judged by you
> That e'er I heard. Shall I produce the men?

Notes

1 The Okun Gap is $[(q(t)/y(t)) - 1]$, where $q(t)$ is capacity output and $y(t)$ is actual output.
2 The prescription offered by the advocates of supply side economics in 1981 was to cut tax rates without raising the rate of growth of the money supply (see R. Weintraub, 1981b). Whereas Okun advocated policies to raise the ratio of actual to capacity output, the advocates of supply side economics aim to raise capacity output.
3 See Friedman and Schwartz (1963: Table 25, 594).
4 The model is a development and synthesis of Infante and Stein (1980), Stein (1971, 1974).

CHAPTER 2

The Structural Equations of a General Macrodynamic Model

1 Introduction and outline

A general theoretical framework is developed in this chapter which can imply either the Keynesian, Monetarist or New Classical Economics. Each school of thought is shown (in chapter 3) to correspond to a particular specification of parameters. A resolution of the controversy among the three schools of thought is then reduced to an econometric debate about values of parameters.

Table 2.1 contains 11 equations which summarize the general model and a key to the symbols used. These equations are derived in this chapter and constitute a closed dynamical system. A brief description of these equations will provide a perspective of the content and organization of this chapter.

The first four equations describe the production relations and the labor market. They determine output per capita $y(t)$, the adjusted real wage $w(t)$, the unemployment rate $U(t)$ and the rent per unit of capital $r(t)$, in terms of the capital intensity $k(t)$ and the unanticipated inflation $\pi(t) - \pi^*(t)$.

Equations (2.1) and (2.2) represent production relationships. Output *per capita* $y(t)$ depends upon capital *per capita* $k(t)$, referred to as the capital intensity, the fraction of the population employed $1 - U(t)$, where $U(t)$ is defined as the unemployment rate, and the level of Hicks-neutral technology $A(t)$. The marginal product of capital $r(t)$ is a fraction of α of the average product of capital $y(t)/k(t)$.

The labor market is summarized by equations (2.3) and (2.4). There is a positive relation between the unemployment rate $U(t)$ and the real wage adjusted for the level of technology $w(t)$. A rise in the adjusted real wage raises the excess supply of labor and hence the unemployment rate. Equation (2.3), in conjunction with (2.1), is shown (in chapter 3)

TABLE 2.1   *A summary of the general macrodynamic model.*

$$y(t) = A(t)F(k(t), 1 - U(t)) \tag{2.1}$$

$$r(t) = \alpha y(t)/k(t) \tag{2.2}$$

$$U(t) = \beta_0 + \beta_1 \ln w(t) \tag{2.3}$$

$$D \ln w(t) = \pi^*(t) - h[U(t) - U_e] - \pi(t) \tag{2.4}$$

$$Dk(t) = \xi[r(t) - \delta + \pi^*(t) - \rho(t)] \tag{2.5}$$

$$\rho(t) = \rho(y(t), m(t), b(t), \pi^*(t), k(t)) \tag{2.6}$$

$$\pi(t) = \pi^*(t) - h[U(t) - U_e] + \gamma J(y(t), m(t), b(t), \rho(t), \pi^*(t), k(t), g(t)) \tag{2.7}$$

$$D \ln m(t) = \mu(t) - n - \pi(t) \tag{2.8}$$

$$\mu(t)m(t) = g(t) + b(t) - T(.) - \frac{1}{\rho(t)}\{Db(t) + [\pi(t) + n]\,b(t)\} \tag{2.9}$$

MRE $\ln p_\tau^*(t) = E_\tau[\ln p(t) \mid \phi(\tau)]$; $\ln p(t) - \ln p_\tau^*(t) = \eta(t)$;

$$E\eta(t) = E\eta(t_1)\eta(t_2) = E(\ln p_\tau^*(t), \eta(t)) = 0 \tag{2.10a}$$

ARE $D\pi^*(t) = c[\mu(t) - n - \pi^*(t)] \tag{2.10b}$

$$b(t) = \theta(t)m(t) \tag{2.11}$$

Symbols: *y* output *per capita*; *k* capital *per capita*; *U* unemployment rate; *r(t)* marginal product of capital; *w* adjusted real wage; $\pi = D \ln p$ rate of inflation of price level *p*; $D \equiv d/dt$; π^* anticipated rate of inflation; δ depreciation rate; ρ nominal rate of interest; *m* real balances *per capita* $= M/pN$ where *M* is the money stock and *N* is population; *b* real interest payments *per capita*; *g* real government purchases of goods *per capita*; $\mu \equiv D \ln M$ rate of monetary expansion; *T*(.) tax function, real *per capita*; E_τ expectations operator, where expectations are taken at time τ; $p_\tau^*(t)$ at time τ, the price anticipated to prevail at later date *t*; η noise; θ a control variable.

to be an aggregate supply equation. A feedback exists from the unemployment rate to the proportionate rate of change of the adjusted real wage. Equation (2.4) states that the proportionate rate of change of the adjusted real wage depends upon (i) the difference between the unemployment rate and its equilibrium value $U(t) - U_e$, and (ii) the unanticipated inflation $\pi(t) - \pi^*(t)$, where $\pi(t)$ is the actual and $\pi^*(t)$ the anticipated rate of inflation.

Equation (2.5) states that the rate of change of the capital intensity is positively related to the ratio of the market price of existing capital to the supply price of a unit of currently produced output. This ratio is approximately equal to the marginal net product of capital $r(t) - \delta$ less the real rate of interest $\rho(t) - \pi^*(t)$, where δ is the depreciation rate and $\rho(t)$ the nominal rate of interest on bonds. This equation describes the endogenous growth of capital and is the key to the process of economic growth.

Equations (2.6) and (2.7) are the generalizations of the LM and IS curves. The former equation states that the nominal rate of interest adjusts quickly to equilibrate the bond market. Nominal interest rate $p(t)$ depends positively upon output *per capita* $y(t)$, the anticipated rate of inflation $\pi^*(t)$ and the real stock of federal interest-bearing debt $b(t)$, and negatively upon the stock of real balances $m(t)$ and the capital intensity $k(t)$.

Equation (2.7) is extremely important. It states that the rate of inflation $\pi(t) = D \ln p(t)$ of the price level $p(t)$ depends upon the proportionate rate of change of nominal unit labor costs plus a function of the Keynesian excess demand gap $J(t)$, defined as planned consumption plus planned investment plus government purchases of goods less current output (all in real *per capita* terms). In the familiar Keynesian diagram, this Keynesian excess demand is the *vertical* distance between the aggregate demand curve and the 45° line; it is quite distinct from the Okun Gap, which is the *horizontal* distance between capacity output and current output. The determinants of aggregate demand are arguments in the excess demand for goods function. It is shown in chapter 3 that the Keynesian IS–LM analysis is a special case of these two equations.

Equation (2.8) defines the proportionate rate of change of real balances *per capita*. It is the rate of monetary expansion $\mu(t) = D \ln M(t)$ of the stock of money $M(t)$, less the growth of population $N(t)$ at rate n, less the rate of inflation $\pi(t)$.

Equations (2.9) and (2.11) describe the rates of change of the stocks of money and bonds. Government budget constraint (2.9) can be viewed in several ways. The government deficit $g(t) + b(t) - T(.)$ is the sum of real government purchases of goods $g(t)$ plus real interest payments $b(t)$ less real taxes $T(.)$, where $T(.)$ is a function of the tax rates and tax base. This deficit is financed by the issuance of new money $DM(t)/p(t)N(t) \equiv \mu(t)m(t)$ plus the issuance of new bonds, the last expression on the right-hand side of (2.9). Alternatively, the rate of monetary expansion $\mu(t)$ is the ratio of the government deficit to the money stock less the ratio of the value of new bonds issued to the stock of money.

Equation (2.11) states that the ratio of government interest payments to the money stock $\theta(t) \equiv b(t)/m(t)$ is a control variable that can be determined by open market operations or debt management policy.

Equations (2.10a) and (2.10b) describe two different ways that inflationary anticipations are formed. Muth's rational expectations hypothesis (MRE) is described by (2.10a). The forecast error between the actual price level $p(t)$ and the level anticipated on the basis of information at earlier date τ, denoted by $p_\tau^*(t)$, is a serially uncorrelated term with a zero expectation. Forecast error $\ln p(t) - \ln p_\tau^*(t)$ is pure "noise," which has no structure.

A more flexible hypothesis is the Asymptotically Rational Expectations hypothesis (ARE) described by (2.10b). It states that the market participants form an estimate of the equilibrium rate of inflation on the basis of the current monetary input. If the current ($t = 0$) rate of monetary expansion $\mu(0)$ remains constant, and there are no permanent real shocks, the price level will grow at rate $\mu(0) - n$ from the current level $p(0)$. Economic agents do not know if the current rate of monetary expansion will continue, or if real shocks affecting the price level are transitory or permanent. Consequently, they adjust their anticipated rate of inflation slowly towards the current rate of monetary expansion *per capita*, that is, the rate of inflation that will occur if the current rate of monetary expansion *per capita* were to continue. The ARE hypothesis represents behavior that is rational, when there is uncertainty and risk aversion.

Real and nominal variables are endogenous in this model. It is equally applicable in the short run and medium run as it is to a growing economy. It is shown in chapter 3 that the various schools of thought can be described as special cases of this model.

2   The labor market and production relations

In this section, three relations are derived: (i) a relation between the unemployment rate $U(t)$ and the adjusted real wage, which is approximated empirically by real unit labor cost; (ii) an equation for the proportionate rate of change of the adjusted real wage as a function both of the unemployment rate and of the unanticipated inflation; and (iii) a relation between output and unemployment.

2.1   *The unemployment rate and the adjusted real wage*

Equation (2.12) states that the unemployment rate is negatively related to the unobserved excess demand for labor. Both positive and negative excess demands for labor are associated with a positive unemployment rate. The quantity of labor demanded is denoted by N^d, the quantity of labor supplied is N^s and N is the population of working age (which is referred to as the population). The excess demand for labor is ($N^d - N^s)/N$, which is equal to zero at the equilibrium rate of unemployment, denoted by U_e:

$$U(t) = U\left(\frac{N^d(t) - N^s(t)}{N(t)}\right); \quad U' < 0; \quad 1 \geqslant U \geqslant 0; \quad U(0) = U_e.$$
$$(2.12)$$

The demand for labor $N^d(t)/N(t)$ is derived from marginal productivity theory. Denote aggregate real output produced by $Y(t)$. Aggregate production function (2.13) is homogeneous of degree one in capital $K(t)$ and employment $L(t)$. Hicks-neutral technical change is reflected by $A(t)$:

$$Y(t) = A(t)F(K(t), L(t)).$$
$$(2.13)$$

Since F is homogeneous of degree one, the production function may be expressed in terms of variables deflated by the size of the population $N(t)$. Variable $y(t) \equiv Y(t)/N(t)$ is *per capita* output and $k(t) \equiv K(t)/N(t)$ is defined as the capital intensity:

$$y(t) = A(t)F(k(t), L(t)/N(t)).$$
$$(2.14)$$

The quantity of labor demanded is determined by the condition that the marginal product of labor $A(t)F_2(k(t), L(t)/N(t))$ is equal to the real wage $W(t)/p(t)$, where $W(t)$ is the nominal wage and $p(t)$ is the price level:

$$A(t)F_2(k(t), N^d(t)/N(t)) = W(t)/p(t).$$
$$(2.15)$$

Define the adjusted real wage as the real wage $W(t)/p(t)$ deflated by the level of technology $A(t)$. Then

$$w(t) = \frac{W(t)/A(t)}{p(t)}.$$
$$(2.16)$$

This equation can be solved for the quantity of labor demanded $N^d(t)/N(t)$ to obtain equation (2.17). The quantity demanded depends upon the adjusted real wage $w(t)$ and the capital intensity:

$$N^d(t)/N(t) = N^D(w(t), k(t)).$$
$$(2.17)$$

The participation rate, or supply of labor, $N^s(t)/N(t)$ is assumed to depend on the adjusted real wage and real wealth *per capita*. The first variable reflects the view that the value of leisure or home activity rises with the general level of technology.[1] The wealth variable is reflected by the capital intensity $k(t)$ and real balances *per capita* $m(t)$. Equation (2.18) describes the labor supply equation:

$$N^s(t)/N(t) = N^s(w(t), k(t), m(t)).$$
$$(2.18)$$

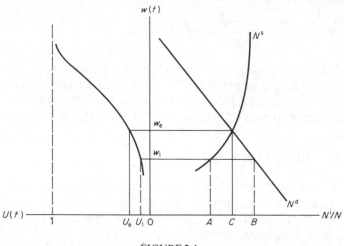

FIGURE 2.1

Figure 2.1 describes equations (2.12), (2.17) and (2.18). In the figure, at adjusted real wage w_1 there is excess demand for labor AB which is associated with an unemployment rate of U_1. At full employment $U = U_e$, the adjusted real wage is w_e. At this point, there is no excess demand for labor; unemployment is equal to vacancies and the equilibrium rate of employment is $0C$.

When equation (2.17) and (2.18) are substituted into (2.12), equation (2.19) can be derived, which states that the unemployment rate $U(t)$ is positively related to the real wage adjusted for the level of technology and the wealth variables:

$$U(t) = U(w(t), k(t), m(t)). \qquad (2.19)$$

It is convenient for subsequent analysis to write (2.19) as linear equation (2.3) in Table 2.1, repeated here, where the wealth variables are subsumed under β_0. For simplicity, assume that β_0 is relatively constant:

$$U(t) = \beta_0 + \beta_1 \ln w(t). \qquad (2.3)$$

Coefficient β_1 is the change in the unemployment rate associated with a one per cent change in the adjusted real wage. It is shown in chapter 3 that equation (2.3) is an aggregate supply equation.

Wesley C. Mitchell, in his study of business cycles, described how the cost of labor (which is associated here with $w(t)$) rises during an expansion and leads to a contraction:

During the first year or two of a trade revival the average rise in the rate of wages is slow, becoming more rapid in the later stages when employers find it hard to get a sufficient number of hands to fill their orders. Encroachments would seldom be made upon profits, however, did fluctuations in the rate of wages represent the sole changes in labor costs; for wholesale prices usually keep rising faster than wages to the very climax of prosperity. A more serious difficulty is that labor is a highly changeable commodity — its quality deteriorates as its price mounts. (1960: 31)

Among these various factors that cooperate to increase the cost of labor during prosperity — the rise in wages, the employment of undesirables, the payment of extra rates for the tired labor of overtime, and the lessening energy put into their work by old hands and new — we can approximate a quantitative estimate of the first alone. Unless employers grievously exaggerate, however, the last is the most important, and neither of the other two factors is negligible. That this combination of advancing prices of labor and declining efficiency produces a serious increase in the cost of getting work done is beyond question.

Of course, the most serious inroads are made upon profits in those industries where wages constitute a large proportion of the total outlay. (1960: 34)

The nominal wage rate, and even average hourly earnings, fail to reflect the marginal labor cost to the firm, for the reasons stressed by Mitchell. A much better index of the marginal labor cost to the firm is the nominal unit labor cost:total labor cost per unit of output. Hence, an empirical estimate of the adjusted real wage is real unit labor costs: nominal unit labor cost divided by an implicit price deflator. The adjusted real wage and real unit labor cost are used interchangeably.

A plot of the US unemployment rate $U(t)$ and of non-farm business sector real unit labor cost[2] $w_N(t)$ against time, during the period 1948 through 1979, indicates that the unemployment rate in year t is positively related to real unit labor cost in the previous year. This suggests that there is a lagged adjustment of the measured unemployment rate to the real unit labor cost. Equation (2.20) is a regression of the total unemployment rate $U(t)$ upon its lagged value $U(t-1)$ and an index of the real non-farm business sector unit labor cost $w_N(t-1)$ in year $t-1$, over the sample period for $U(t)$, 1948 through 1979:

$$U(t) = -42.2 \quad + 0.316U(t-1) + 0.45w_N(t-1) \qquad (2.20)$$
$$(t) \qquad (-4.78) \quad (2.61) \qquad\qquad (5.02)$$

$$R^2 = 0.668; \quad SE = 0.803; \quad DW = 2.38; \quad h = -1.49.$$

	$U(t)$	$w_N(t-1)$
mean	5.14%	101.61
standard deviation	1.35	1.84

SE = standard error of estimate
DW = Durbin–Watson statistic
h = standard normal deviate calculated from the DW statistic, when there are lagged dependent variables

Equation (2.20) is consistent with the view that there is a lagged response of the excess supply of labor, or the unemployment rate, to an index of real unit labor cost of the private non-farm business sector. No contemporaneous variables are used on the right-hand side of this equation. The mathematical expectation of the unemployment rate in year t, denoted by $E_{t-1}U(t)$, where E is the expectations operator and expectations are taken at $t-1$, depends upon the previous year's unemployment rate and real unit labor costs. Each coefficient is significantly different from zero at the one per cent level, and this equation explains two-thirds of the variation in the unemployment rate.

When the adjustment of the unemployment rate to the given real wage is complete, equation (2.21) can be derived:

$$U(t) = -61.7 + 0.66w(t). \tag{2.21}$$

This relation is described on the left-hand side of figure 2.1, where the function is not linear. Equation (2.3) corresponds to equation (2.21), which is an approximation of equation (2.20) designed to facilitate the analysis.

2.2 *The rate of change of the adjusted real wage*

The unemployment rate is influenced by the level of the adjusted real wage (equation (2.3)), but there is also a feedback from the state of the business cycle to the rate of change of the adjusted real wage. By definition, the adjusted real wage is the ratio of the adjusted nominal wage $W(t)/A(t)$ to an appropriate price index $p(t)$. For the reasons discussed above, it is not clear whether $W(t)/A(t)$ should be measured by average hourly earnings or by nominal unit labor costs.

There are several stylized facts about the behavior of wages, described in tables 2.2, 2.3 and 2.4 below, that should be taken into account. (i) In the prewar period, there is some evidence that *real* average hourly earnings rose during contractions and declined during expansions. (ii) *Nominal* average hourly earnings were flexible downwards during contractions and flexible upwards during expansions. (iii) Increases in *nominal* unit labor costs become more pervasive among industries during the course of an expansion. At some time after the peak, the frequency of declines in unit labor costs among industries increases. At the trough, the decline in nominal unit labor costs is most pervasive among industries.

In a period when less than 16 per cent of workers in US factories were organized in trade unions, average hourly earnings declined in contractions but by less than the decline in prices. During expansions, average hourly earnings rose, but it is not clear whether they rose by a smaller proportion than prices. Moreover, both in the US and in the UK, changes in average hourly earnings lagged behind changes in economic activity at both peaks and troughs of the business cycle.

Table 2.2 describes the movements in average hourly earnings, wholesale prices of raw materials, semi-finished and finished goods and of factory production and employment in the US from 1919 to 1939 during contractions (table 2.2a) and expansions (table 2.2b). The behavior of average weekly earnings during the recovery after 1933 was exceptional: it was caused by negotiations under the terms of the National Recovery Act (NRA) whereby the working week was shortened without reducing weekly earnings. As a matter of arithmetic, average hourly earnings rose. The changes of the variables in table 2.2 are the amplitude of cycle relatives, according to the NBER method of measurement. Table 2.3 describes the lag of factory wages behind economic activity in the UK and in the US from 1921−33.

Insofar as the "adjusted nominal wage" $W(t)/A(t)$ is reflected by labor cost per unit of output, its cyclical behavior is described by Thor Hultgren as follows.

When the national economy begins to expand, many industries expand their own production and others introduce telling technological changes. For one reason or another, hours per unit [of output] fall in most industries. As expansion unfolds, the frequency of declines diminishes. When the expansion reaches it climax, however, most industries still have lower hours per unit than they had when it began. But hourly earnings rise more or less throughout, and their advance is potent, for cost in most industries goes up in all portions of the expansion except the earliest. At the end it is higher than it was at the beginning.

When the national economy enters its declining phase, the majority of industries experience rises in hours per unit. But as the phase continues, technological improvements continue to be made, inefficient facilities are closed down, and some industries begin to expand. Hours per unit fall in most cases. Hourly earnings may continue to rise, but more slowly, and over

TABLE 2.2 *Movements of average hourly earnings, wholesale prices, factory production and employment, United States 1919−39, amplitude of cycle relatives.*

| Dates | Average hourly earnings | Wholesale prices | | | Factory | |
		Raw materials	Semi-finished goods	Finished goods	Production	Employment
(a) Contractions						
1/20− 7/21	− 24	− 71	− 104.8	− 50.1	− 39.1	− 33.9
5/23− 7/24	− 0.8	− 8.6	− 20.7	− 7.6	− 19	− 13.8
10/26−11/27	− 0.4	− 14	− 15.8	− 7.4	− 5.1	− 5.0
6/29− 3/33	− 25	− 62.4	− 47.8	− 36.9	− 69.8	− 49.9
5/37− 6/38	− 0.8	− 27.4	− 18.6	− 10.7	− 47.6	− 27.7
Mean	− 10.2	− 36.68	− 41.54	− 22.54	− 36.12	− 26.06
Standard deviation	13.06	28.41	37.63	19.74	25.15	17.51
(b) Expansions						
7/21− 5/23	15.1	20.6	33	8.7	47.4	26.2
7/24−10/26	3.3	13	6	7.2	23.3	10
11/27− 6/29	3.0	8.3	1.9	3.6	25.8	11.5
3/33− 5/37	42.1	54.2	42	27.9	80.5	54.9
Mean	15.88	24.03	20.73	11.85	44.25	25.65
Standard deviation	18.37	20.75	19.79	10.91	26.48	20.82

Source: Creamer (1950: Table 5, 37).

a narrowing industrial front. In most industries cost rises at first, but declines before the end, and is lower at the trough than at the peak. (1960: 73)

Hultgren examined 23 industries over several cycles during the post World War I period. Table 2.4 describes the number (and per cent) of the industries whose labor cost per unit of output rose or declined during the stages of the business cycle. Stage I is centered on the initial trough (T), stage V is centered on the peak (P) and stage IX is centered on the final trough (T). It is clear from table 2.4 that increases in nominal unit labor cost become more pervasive during the course of the expansion. At some time after the peak, contractions in unit labor cost become more prevalent, and at the trough (stage I) the fraction of

TABLE 2.3   *Lag of wage rates behind economic activity: UK and US, 1921–33.*

UK		US	
Date	*Lag*	*Date*	*Lag*
(a) Troughs			
6/21	26.6 months	7/21	9.0 months
8/32	23.4	3/33	2.0
(b) Peaks			
11/24	6.5	5/23	8.0
7/29	11.9	6/29	12.0

Source: Creamer (1950: 31).

TABLE 2.4   *Changes in labor cost per unit of product, in 23 industries, by stage of the business cycle.*

Stage	Observations	Number	Rises (%)	Number	Declines (%)
T: I–II	89	13	(15)	76	(85)
II–III	89	33	(37)	56	(63)
III–IV	89	52	(58)	36	(40)
IV–PV	89	57	(64)	30	(34)
P: V–VI	97	80	(82)	17	(18)
VI–VII	97	81	(84)	15	(15)
VII–VIII	97	74	(76)	22	(23)
VIII–T:IX	97	64	(66)	32	(33)

Source: Hultgren (1960: Table 15, 39). In some cases, there were no changes in nominal unit labor cost.

cases where unit labor costs are declining is at a maximum (85 per cent in table 2.4).

Equation (2.22) below models the proportionate rate of change of the macroeconomic adjusted nominal wage $D \ln W(t)/A(t)$ as depending upon: (i) the state of the labor market, measured by the deviation of the unemployment rate from its equilibrium value $U(t) - U_e$, which is not the same as the state of the NBER business cycle; and (ii) the risk-adjusted anticipated rate of price change $\pi^*(t)$, which guides supply and demand decisions (this concept is discussed in section 2.7):

$$D \ln W(t)/A(t) = \pi^*(t) - h[U(t) - U_e].$$
(2.22)

In this macroeconomic model no dichotomy is made between the anticipations of employers and of employees. Variable π^* reflects both the risk-adjusted anticipated rate of change of the price of output and of the price of goods purchased by consumers. It is assumed that the coefficient of the risk-adjusted anticipated inflation term is unity. When both employers and employees anticipate the prices of goods sold by firms and purchased by consumers to rise by one per cent net of a risk discount, there is no opposition to a one per cent rise in the nominal wage.

The term π^* represents the product of several factors, whose end result is to affect the rate of growth of nominal unit labor costs. The schematic diagram below describes the connections between the component factors:

$$DW/W \leftarrow \pi^* \leftarrow E\pi \leftarrow E\mu \leftarrow \mu.$$

At the initial stage, there are monetary policies μ which are pursued and which affect the expected growth of the money supply $E\mu$. Then there is the relation between the expected growth of the money supply and the expected rate of inflation $E\pi$. The expected rate of inflation then operates upon the risk-discounted anticipated rate of inflation π^*, which directly affects the demand and supply of labor. Finally, there may be labor contracts which affect the speed at which the risk-discounted anticipated rate of inflation affects DW/W, the growth of the nominal wage.

Different models assign different degrees of relative importance to the lags between the stages of this process. The models which use the Muth Rational Expectations Hypothesis (MRE) eliminate the lag between $E\mu$ and π^*. One subset of these models assumes a lag between μ and $E\mu$, since it takes time for the public to learn the monetary policy followed. Another subset stresses the lag between $E\pi$ and DW/W resulting from the existence of labor contracts. This lag will be short if there are staggered contracts of short duration. Moreover, when economic conditions are deemed to have changed perceptibly, contracts are revised prior to the expiration date.

The Asymptotically Rational Expectations Hypothesis (ARE), discussed in section 2.7, introduces a temporary gap between the expected inflation $E\pi$ and the risk-adjusted rate of inflation π^*, which is implied by expected utility maximization under uncertainty. In most cases, it makes no difference to the dynamics of the model where the lags are introduced in the process schematized above. The literary scenarios may differ, but the trajectories of the economically relevant variables will be the same.

One serious omission in equation (2.22) is the following. There may be a catch-up term in the wage change equation which reflects the attempt of labor to recoup declines in the real wage produced by past unanticipated inflation. In that case there will be pressure to raise the nominal wage to rectify the losses from *past* unanticipated inflation, even if no *future* inflation is anticipated and the unemployment rate is at its equilibrium level. This catch-up phenomenon increases the order of the dynamic system and causes overshooting of the equilibrium (see Stein, 1976: 264–9). For the sake of simplicity, this catch-up effect is not modelled here, but it should not be ignored in policy decisions to reduce the rate of inflation.

The growth of the adjusted real wage is $D \ln W(t)/A(t)$ less the rate of inflation $\pi(t) = D \ln p(t)$ of the price level $p(t)$, as described by equation (2.4) and repeated here:

$$D\ln w(t) = D\ln \frac{W(t)/A(t)}{p(t)} = \pi^*(t) - h[U(t) - U_e] - \pi(t). \quad (2.4)$$

Equations (2.3) and (2.4) are the key relationships which describe a feedback process in the labor market. The adjusted real wage determines the unemployment rate, and both the unemployment rate and the unanticipated inflation $\pi(t) - \pi^*(t)$ determine the rate of change of the adjusted real wage.

2.3   Output and employment

Most models focus upon the rate of output rather than upon the reported unemployment rate. There is a correspondence between these two variables which permits us to view the real sector in terms of either variable.

The unemployment rate $U(t)$, described by the model, can be defined in equation (2.23) as the complement of the employment rate, namely, the ratio of employment $L(t)$ to the population of working age $N(t)$:

$$L(t)/N(t) \equiv 1 - U(t). \quad (2.23)$$

Using this definition, equation (2.14) can be written as equation (2.1):

$$y(t) = A(t)F(k(t), 1 - U(t)). \quad (2.1)$$

If "full employment" is defined as a situation where the unemployment rate is at its equilibrium value U_e and "capacity output" *per capita* is defined as output *per capita* when the unemployment rate is at its equilibrium value, and denoted by $f(k(t), t)$ as defined by

$$f(k(t), t) = A(t)F(k(t), 1 - U_e), \tag{2.24}$$

then using equations (2.1) and (2.24), output *per capita* $y(t)$ can be written as a function of capacity output *per capita* $f(k(t), t)$ and the deviation of the unemployment rate from its equilibrium value[3]:

$$y(t) = B(U(t) - U_e) f(k(t), t); \quad B' < 0. \tag{2.25}$$

A well-known formulation of this relation is "Okun's Law," which states that the ratio of actual output $y(t)$ to potential output $f(k(t), t)$ is negatively related to the deviation of the unemployment rate from its equilibrium value.[4] Equation (2.26) is another way of writing equation (2.1):

$$\ln y(t) - \ln f(k(t), t) = - a[U(t) - U_e]. \tag{2.26}$$

If the first differences of (2.26) are taken and the rate of growth of *potential* output *per capita* is denoted by α then we obtain

$$\Delta \ln y(t) = \alpha - a\Delta U(t). \tag{2.27}$$

In the medium run α can be considered constant, although it is an endogenous variable in a growth model.

When the growth rate of real GNP from year $t - 1$ to year t, denoted by $G[Y(t)]$, is regressed upon the change in the unemployment rate $\Delta U(t)$ from year $t - 1$ to year t over the sample period for $U(t)$ 1959–77, using annual data, equation (2.28a) can be obtained. For the period for $U(t)$ 1962–80, the relation is described by equation (2.28b):

$$t: 1959-77 \quad G[Y(t)] = 3.63 \quad - 2.08\,[U(t) - U(t-1)] \tag{2.28a}$$
$$(t=) \qquad\quad (10.7) \quad (-6.22)$$

$$R^2 = 0.695; \quad SE = 1.47; \quad DW = 2.31.$$

$$t: 1962-80 \quad G[Y(t)] = 3.671 - 2.099\,[U(t) - U(t-1)] \tag{2.28b}$$
$$(t=) \qquad\qquad\qquad (-7.674)$$

$$R^2 = 0.776.$$

If the unemployment rate is constant, then real GNP grows at the growth rate of capacity output, estimated at 3.6 per cent per annum. For a percentage point rise in the unemployment rate, the growth rate of real GNP declines by two percentage points. Or, for a decline in the growth rate of real GNP by one percentage point, the unemployment rate rises by approximately one-half of a percentage point.

Equation (2.25) or (2.26) permits us to work with either real GNP *per capita* or the unemployment rate $U(t)$ in a dynamical system or econometric analysis.

3 The rate of inflation

The macroeconomic rate of inflation $\pi(t) = D \ln p(t)$ of the GNP deflator $p(t)$ is the resultant of the interaction of excess demand and cost pressures transmitted from one sector in the economy to another. Equation (2.29) below states that the aggregate rate of inflation at time t depends upon (i) the proportionate rate of growth of the adjusted nominal wage (i.e. nominal unit labor cost) $W(t)/A(t)$, plus (ii) a function of the Keynesian excess demand gap $J(t)$, defined as planned consumption plus planned investment plus government purchases of goods less current output (all in real *per capita* terms). This Keynesian excess demand gap is the *vertical* distance between the aggregate demand curve and the 45° line. It is quite distinct from the Okun Gap, which is the *horizontal* distance between capacity output and current output:

$$\pi(t) = D \ln W(t)/A(t) + \gamma J(t) \qquad \infty > \gamma > 0. \qquad (2.29)$$

In figure 2.2, let aggregate demand be $A_1 A_1'$ and current output be y_1. The Keynesian excess demand gap is $C_2 C_1$ and the Okun Gap between capacity output and current output is $f(k(t), t) - y_1$. By substituting equation (2.22) into (2.29) equation (2.30) can be derived. Prices can rise at less than full employment, if there is a Keynesian excess demand for goods $J(t) > 0$:

$$\pi(t) = \pi^*(t) - h[U(t) - U_e] + \gamma J(t). \qquad (2.30)$$

When there is a positive Keynesian excess demand for goods in the macroeconomy, the rate of price change differs by markets. In auction markets and in the markets for basic and intermediate materials (such as agricultural products and metals) supplies are relatively inelastic, and the major impact of the Keynesian excess demand is upon price. In markets for finished goods, the labor input is of relatively greater importance than it is in the markets for basic and intermediate materials, and the supply is more elastic. A positive Keynesian excess demand exerts a relatively greater effect upon output than upon price in these markets, than it does in the markets for materials. However, the output of the sector producing materials is an input to the finished goods

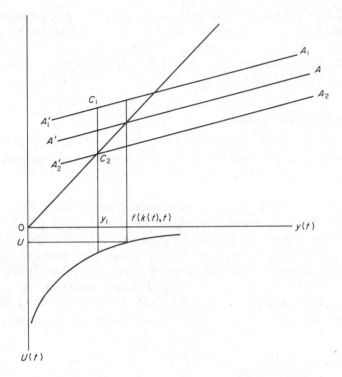

FIGURE 2.2

sector. Increases in the prices of materials are transmitted to the markets for finished goods as cost increases. Even if the mark-up over marginal cost is constant, the prices of finished goods rise in response to increases in the prices of materials.

The expansion of output at all stages, resulting from the rise in the Keynesian excess demand, leads to a tightening of the macro labor market. As a result, there is a rise in nominal unit labor cost as nominal wages rise, more overtime occurs and less efficient workers are employed (as described above). The increases in adjusted nominal wages and in the prices of raw materials and intermediate goods lead to a rise in the rate of inflation in the markets for final goods. Coefficient γ is the speed of response of prices to the state of excess demand. When there is Keynesian excess demand and γ is finite positive, then the GNP deflator rises gradually to the new equilibrium. There is a positive serial correlation of price changes in the goods market.

At any moment in time, both cost and demand pressures are simul-

TABLE 2.5 *Rates of change of wholesale prices, by subgroups, over 12 business cycles, 1913–70.*

	Expansions			Contractions		
	Basic materials	Intermediate materials	Finished goods	Basic materials	Intermediate goods	Finished goods
Mean	8.52% p.a.	15.36	9.28	−6.05	−8.77	−3.96
Standard deviation	9.62	24.12	14.95	10.16	12.0	6.74
	$F(2,33) = 0.56$			$F(2,33) = 0.72$		

Source: Derived from data in Cagan (1979: Table 3.1, 70).

taneously operative in the macroeconomy, as described by equation (2.30), although each component may affect prices in one sector differently than in another sector.

Table 2.5 describes the rate of change of wholesale prices in three subgroups — basic materials, intermediate materials and finished goods — during the expansions and contractions in 12 business cycles from 1913 through 1970. The rate of inflation in the subgroup for intermediate materials responds most strongly to expansions and contractions, and it also displays the greatest variability of rates of inflation during upswings and downswings. The rate of price inflation in the subgroup producing finished goods is less responsive to expansions and contractions than is the subgroup producing intermediate materials. Moreover, the rate of price inflation in the finished materials subgroup is less variable than in the group producing intermediate products.

An analysis of variance of the three groups, during expansions and contractions, separately, yields values of $F(2,33)$ of 0.56 and 0.72 respectively. Due to the large intragroup variances, we cannot reject the null hypothesis that there are no significant differences among the mean rates of price change of the three subgroups. In economic terms, this means that inflation is transmitted effectively from one sector to another, because the output of one sector is the input of another sector, and it is meaningful to speak of the macroeconomic rate of inflation which is generated by factors which impinge upon all the sectors, albeit at different rates.

When the Keynesian excess demand for goods and services $J(t)$ tends to zero, the rate of inflation equals the growth of the adjusted nominal wage. Then, as equation (2.30) implies, the rate of inflation depends upon the risk-adjusted anticipated rate of inflation and the deviation of the unemployment rate from its equilibrium value. It is quite possible for an inflation to continue after the Keynesian excess demand for goods has declined to zero, because the unemployment rate is not at its equilibrium value or there still remains anticipated inflation.

4   The Keynesian excess demand for goods

The next two sections discuss the determinants of the Keynesian excess demand for goods and the interaction between the markets for goods and for financial assets. Equations (2.6) and (2.7) in table 2.1 summarize this analysis. In chapter 3, it is shown that the traditional IS−LM analysis is a special case of the general analysis developed here. In the process of deriving an investment demand equation, an equation is derived for the rate of change of the capital intensity $Dk(t)$. This is the key equation for the analysis of economic growth.

Real excess demand for goods *per capita* $J(t)$ is planned investment I/N plus planned consumption c plus government purchases g less current output (in real *per capita* terms), that is,

$$J(t) = c + I/N + g - y.$$

Investment *per capita* I/N can be decomposed into two elements: $Dk(t)$, the rate of change of the capital intensity $k(t) = K(t)/N(t)$, and $(n+\delta)k(t)$, the investment *per capita* necessary to maintain the existing capital intensity when the population is growing at rate n and the depreciation rate is δ:

$$I(t)/N(t) = Dk(t) + (n+\delta)k(t). \tag{2.31}$$

Investment decisions are made by firms which are guided by the following considerations. The desired change in the capital intensity is positively related to the ratio of the market price of existing capital to the price of a unit of newly produced output. Denote this ratio by q. If q exceeds unity, it is profitable to purchase a unit of current output and use it as a capital good. This constitutes a demand for investment. If q is less than unity, it is cheaper to purchase an existing asset than to purchase a unit of newly produced output, and investment is discouraged. A general theory of investment, inspired by Keynes (1930: I, 200−9) and developed by Tobin (1969), is described by

$$Dk(t) = \phi(q-1); \qquad \phi(0) = 0, \phi' > 0. \tag{2.32}$$

Investment per worker is described by

$$I(t)/N(t) = \phi[q(t) - 1] + (n+\delta)k(t). \tag{2.33}$$

Estimates of q, the ratio of the market value of existing capital to the replacement cost of net assets, are readily available.[5] The numerator of $q(t)$ is the market value of equity plus interest-bearing debt. The capital intensity $k(t)$ cannot easily be measured, and therefore a time trend term $T = 1, 2, \ldots$ is used to approximate $(n + \delta) k(t)$ in regression equation (2.34). This regression is fitted to the data during the period 1955–79. $I(t)/N(t)$ is real private gross domestic investment divided by the non-institutional population. Equation (2.34) indicates that equation (2.33) is a plausible relation:

$$I(t)/N(t) = 542 \quad + 247q(t) + 26.8T. \tag{2.34}$$
$$(t=) \qquad (4.11) \quad (2.1) \qquad (8.6)$$

$$R^2 = 0.778; \qquad SE = 101; \qquad DW = 1.18.$$

The coefficient of $q(t)$ is significantly different from zero at the five per cent level, but the evidence for or against serial correlation of residuals is inconclusive.

Variable $q(t) - 1$ is now shown to be a function of the difference between the rent per unit of capital and the real rate of interest.

The market price of an existing asset is its present value. Let the quasi-rents expected at t units of time from the present be $p^*(t)r^*(t)$, where $p^*(t)$ is the anticipated price level $p^*(t) = p(0)\exp(\pi^* t)$ and $r^*(t)$ is the expected real rent per unit of capital $r^*(t) = r(0)\exp(-\delta t)$, where depreciation is assumed to be exponential at rate δ. The average anticipated inflation rate over the life of the asset is π^*, and the nominal long-term rate of interest used to discount the returns over the life of the asset is the current long-term rate ρ. Then, the ratio q of the market price of capital to the price of current output is described by

$$q = \int_0^\infty \frac{p^*(t)}{p(0)} r^*(t)\exp(-\rho t)dt = \frac{r}{\rho + \delta - \pi^*}. \tag{2.35}$$

Variable $(q - 1)$ can be approximated by

$$q(t) - 1 = [r(t) - \delta] - [\rho(t) - \pi^*(t)], \tag{2.36}$$

where $r(t) - \delta$ is the rent per unit of capital net of depreciation and $\rho(t) - \pi^*(t)$ is the real rate of interest. It follows that the change in the capital intensity is equation (2.5) in table 2.1 (repeated here):[6]

$$Dk(t) = \xi\{r(t) - \delta - [\rho(t) - \pi^*(t)]\}; \quad \xi > 0. \tag{2.5}$$

This is a key equation in growth theory, since it is the endogenous rate of change of the capital intensity.[7]

The resulting investment demand equation is

$$I(t)/N(t) = \xi[r(t) - \delta + \pi^*(t) - \rho(t)] + (n + \delta) k(t). \tag{2.37}$$

This is precisely Keynes' theory of investment, which is vividly described as follows:

... from the point of view of individual entrepreneurs, there will be no occasion for a reduction in the output of ... [investment] goods, unless their price is falling relatively to their cost of production, or unless the demand for them is falling off at the existing price. In what way can a rise in the bank-rate tend to bring this about?

Upon what does the demand-price of capital-goods depend? It depends on *two* things — on the estimated net prospective yield from fixed capital ... measured in money, and on the rate of interest at which this future yield is capitalized. It follows that the price of such goods can change for either of two reasons — because the prospective yield has changed or because the rate of interest has changed. And we can pursue the analysis a step further: since the prospective yield must be measured for the present purpose in terms of money, a change in it may be due either to a change in the real yield, its price remaining the same [this corresponds to $r - \delta$] or to a change in the prospective price (or money value) of the real yield [this corresponds to π^*]. (Keynes: 1930, I, 201–2)

The rent per unit of capital $r(t)$ can be expressed as a function of output *per capita* $y(t)$ and the capital intensity $k(t)$. For example, if the production function is Cobb–Douglas[8] then

$$y(t) = A(t)k^\alpha(t)(1 - U(t))^{1-\alpha}, \tag{2.38}$$

where $1 - U(t) = L(t)/N(t)$ is the employment rate. Rent per unit of capital $r(t)$ is described by equation (2.2) of table 2.1:

$$r(t) = \alpha y(t)/k(t) = R(k(t), y(t)); \quad R_1 < 0, R_2 > 0. \tag{2.2}$$

By using equation (2.2) in (2.37), the investment demand equation is

$$I(t)/N(t) = \xi[R(k(t), y(t)) - \delta + \pi^*(t) - \rho(t)] + (n+\delta)\, k(t). \tag{2.39}$$

Investment *per capita* is positively related to *per capita* output and is negatively related to the real rate of interest $\rho(t) - \pi^*(t)$.

A general consumption function which is consistent with the existing literature is specified. Consumption *per capita* $c(t)$ depends positively upon output *per capita* and real wealth *per capita* and negatively upon the real rate of interest $\rho(t) - \pi^*(t)$. Real wealth *per capita* consists of capital *per capita* $k(t)$, real balances *per capita* $m(t) = M(t)/p(t)N(t)$, where $M(t)$ is the stock of money and $p(t)$ is the price level, and real bonds *per capita* $b(t)/p(t) = (B(t)/p(t))/p(t)N(t)$, where $B(t)$ is the number of bonds outstanding each paying \$1 per year in perpetuity.

$B(t)/p(t)$ is the nominal value of the federal interest-bearing debt and $b(t)$ is the real value *per capita* of the interest payments. The consumption function is then

$$c(t) = C(y(t), k(t), m(t), b(t), p(t), \pi^*(t)). \tag{2.40}$$

The real excess demand for goods *per capita* $J(t)$ is equation (2.41a) which is simplified in (2.41b):

$$J(t) = C(y(t), k(t), m(t), b(t), p(t), \pi^*(t)) + \xi[R(k(t), y(t)) - \delta + \pi^*(t) - p(t)] + (n+\delta)k(t) + g(t) - y(t). \tag{2.41a}$$

$$J(t) = J(y(t), k(t), m(t), b(t), p(t), \pi^*(t), g(t)). \tag{2.41b}$$

Therefore, the rate of price change equation (2.30) can be written as equation (2.7) in table 2.1:

$$\pi(t) = \pi^*(t) - h[U(t) - U_e] + \gamma J(y(t), k(t), m(t), b(t), p(t), \\ \pi^*(t), g(t)), \tag{2.7}$$

where the effects of changes in unit labor costs and in the Keynesian excess demand for goods are explicitly stated.

5 The nominal interest rate and the bond market

The nominal rate of interest, which is the reciprocal of the bond price, equilibrates the bond market. Private bonds and government bonds are assumed to be perfect substitutes modulus a constant risk premium. Firms generally wish to supply a stock of bonds, and households generally provide a stock demand for bonds. Bonds, money and capital are viewed as substitutes in portfolios. The ratio of bonds to wealth that agents want to hold in their portfolios depends positively upon its own rate of return and negatively upon the rates of return on substitute assets. This view is based upon the theory of portfolio selection.

Let the $B(.)$ function in equation (2.42) below represent the real stock *excess demand* for bonds *per capita* by the private sector. Therefore, the value of B is related (i) negatively to the expected return per unit of capital $R(y(t), k(t)) + \pi^*(t)$, which is the marginal product plus the anticipated capital gain; (ii) positively to the nominal rate of interest $p(t)$, which is the own rate of return on bonds; (iii) positively to real wealth *per capita*, either in the form of real balances $m(t)$ or the capital intensity $k(t)$; and (iv) negatively to the implicit marginal convenience yield on real balances which is reflected by $y(t)/m(t)$ or velocity.

The real stock of federal interest-bearing debt *per capita* is $b(t)$. The nominal interest rate $p(t)$ adjusts quickly to equate the private stock *excess* demand for bonds to the stock of federal demand debt in existence. This is described by

$$b(t) = B(y(t), \rho(t), \pi^*(t), m(t), k(t)).$$

$$\underset{-}{} \underset{+}{} \underset{-}{} \underset{+}{} \tag{2.42}$$

By solving this equation explicitly for the nominal rate of interest which equilibrates the bond market, equation (2.6) in table 2.1 can be derived:

$$\rho(t) = \rho(y(t), m(t), \pi^*(t), b(t), k(t));$$
$$\rho_1 > 0, \rho_2 < 0, \rho_3 > 0, \rho_4 > 0, \rho_5 < 0. \tag{2.6}$$

The signs of the partial derivatives of the function of ρ on the right-hand side of this equation are explained as follows.

A rise in output *per capita* raises the rent per unit of capital and also raises the marginal convenience yield of real balances for transactions purposes. These effects increase the excess supply of bonds by the private sector. Bond prices decline, and the interest rate rises: $\rho_1 > 0$. A rise in real balances *per capita* is associated with an increase in wealth and a decrease in the marginal convenience yield from holding real balances for transactions purposes. As a result of these two effects, there is an excess demand for bonds relative to money, and the nominal rate of interest declines: $\rho_2 < 0$. A rise in the anticipated rate of inflation raises the anticipated return per unit of capital, relative to the returns on bonds and money. An excess supply of private bonds is generated, which leads to a rise in the nominal rate of interest: $\rho_3 > 0$. A rise in the stock of government bonds leads to an excess supply of bonds. The own rate of return on bonds $\rho(t)$ must rise to induce economic agents to raise the ratio of bonds to wealth in their portfolios: $\rho_4 > 0$. Finally, a rise in the capital intensity lowers the marginal product of capital and raises wealth. Both effects increase the private excess demand for bonds and lower the rate of interest: $\rho_5 < 0$.

6   Rates of change of the stocks of financial assets

6.1   *The government budget constraint*

There are two financial assets in the model — money and government bonds — whose rates of change are now derived. Real balances *per capita* $m(t) = M(t)/p(t)N(t)$ are endogenous. Its proportionate rate of change is defined in equation (2.8) in table 2.1:

$$D \ln m(t) = \mu(t) - n - \pi(t). \tag{2.8}$$

This rate of growth is endogenous because the rate of inflation is determined by the economic system and, in the general model, the rate of monetary expansion $\mu(t)$ is also endogenous.

For theoretical purposes assume that the money multiplier is unity, so that no distinction need be made between high-powered money (i.e. the monetary base) and the stock of money. The government budget deficit determines the time rate of change of the sum of money and government bonds. The term $DB(t)$ is the time rate of change of the number of bonds each paying \$1 per year in perpetuity and $1/\rho(t)$ is the price of the bond. $DM(t)$ is the time rate of change of the stock of money. The sum of $DB(t)/\rho(t)$ and $DM(t)$ finances the government deficit, which is equal to government purchases of goods plus interest payments on the debt $B(t)$ less taxes. Equation (2.43) is the government budget constraint in real *per capita* terms. The real *per capita* tax function $T(.)$ is the inner product of the vector of tax rates and the vector of the tax bases. At this point, there is no need to specify the tax function in detail, although it must be stated explicitly in the context of the growth model in chapter 5. The reader could assume that there is a completely indexed income tax so that $T(.) = \tau y$ where τ is the tax rate, but such an assumption is not required at this point.

$$g(t) + b(t) - T(.) = \frac{1}{\rho(t)} \frac{DB(t)}{p(t)N(t)} + \frac{DM(t)}{p(t)N(t)}, \qquad (2.43)$$

where $b(t) = B(t)/p(t)N(t)$ is real *per capita* interest payments on the government debt.

A trenchant description of the government budget constraint (2.43), whereby $g(t)$ represents transfers of resources from the private sector to the government sector, is contained in Keynes' *A Tract on Monetary Reform*:

It is common to speak as though, when a government pays its way by inflation, the people of the country avoid taxation. We have seen that this is not so. What is raised by printing notes is just as much taken from the public as is a beer-duty or an income-tax. What a government spends $[g(t)]$ the public pay for. There is no such thing as an uncovered deficit. But in some countries it seems possible to please and content the public, for a time at least, by giving them, in return for the taxes they pay, finely engraved acknowledgements on water-marked paper. The income-tax receipts $[T(.)]$, which we in England receive from the Surveyor, we throw into the wastepaper basket; in Germany they call them bank notes $[DM(t)/p(t)N(t)]$ and put them into their pocket books; in France they are termed Rentes $[DB(t)/\rho(t)p(t)N(t)]$ and are locked up in the family safe. (1923: 62)

The term $DM(t)/p(t)N(t)$ in equation (2.43) is the inflation tax *per capita* on real balances, since it is the purchasing power *per capita* of the newly issued money. It is identically equal to $\mu(t)m(t) \equiv (DM(t)/M(t))(M(t)/p(t)N(t))$. Equation (2.44) describes the rate of monetary expansion:

$$\mu(t)m(t) = \left(g(t) + \frac{B(t)}{p(t)N(t)} - T(.) \right) - \frac{1}{p(t)} \frac{DB(t)}{p(t)N(t)}, \qquad (2.44)$$

which consists of two parts: the real *per capita* government deficit less the value of the newly issued government bonds.

The identity (2.45) describes the time rate of change of real *per capita* interest payments on the government debt[9]:

$$Db(t) = \frac{DB(t)}{p(t)N(t)} - [\pi(t) + n]\, b\, (t). \qquad (2.45)$$

By combining equations (2.44) and (2.45) and deriving equation (2.9) in table 2.1 (repeated here), the rate of monetary expansion can be related to the government deficit and the change in real interest payments *per capita*:

$$\mu(t)m(t) = [g(t) + b(t) - T(.)] - \frac{1}{p(t)} \{ Db(t) + [\pi(t) + n]\, b(t) \}. \qquad (2.9)$$

In general, the ratio $\theta(t)$ of interest payments on the government debt $B(t)$ to the stock of money $M(t)$ is a control variable determined by open market operations and debt management policy. Equation (2.11) in table 2.1 defines the control variable $\theta(t)$:

$$\theta(t) = B(t)/M(t) = b(t)/m(t). \qquad (2.11)$$

The government budget constraint determines the sum of the new money and new bonds issued. The division between the two sources of financing is a control variable.

6.2   *The rate of monetary expansion*

There is an interesting historical relation between the rate of monetary expansion and the high employment deficit, denoted by $F^H(t)$, that reflects the autonomous component of fiscal policy. The difference between the actual deficit $F(t)$ and the high employment deficit $F^H(t)$ reflects the induced component of fiscal policy, resulting primarily from deviations of output from capacity output.

Denote the total nominal government budget deficit at time t by $F(t)$. It is financed by the change in $H(t)$ the stock of high-powered money plus the value of new bonds issued by the government, which determines the stocks of money and bonds in the next period. The bonds are sold at the market price $1/p(t+1)$ in period $t+1$. The equation

$$F(t) = [H(t+1) - H(t)] + \frac{1}{p(t+1)} [B(t+1) - B(t)] \qquad (2.46)$$

is the financing of the deficit equation in discrete time.

Consider the following control law, described by equations (2.47a) and (2.47b). Fraction $\alpha(t)$ of the *high employment deficit* $F^H(t)$ is financed by high-powered money (the monetary base), and fraction $1 - \alpha(t)$ is financed through the issuance of bonds. Fraction $\beta(t)$ of the difference between the actual $F(t)$ and the high employment deficit $F^H(t)$ is financed by high-powered money, and fraction $1 - \beta(t)$ is financed by bonds:

$$H(t+1) - H(t) = \alpha(t)F^H(t) + \beta(t)[F(t) - F^H(t)] \qquad (2.47a)$$

$$\frac{B(t+1) - B(t)}{p(t+1)} = [1 - \alpha(t)]F^H(t) + [1 - \beta(t)][F(t) - F^H(t)]. \qquad (2.47b)$$

The sum of these two equations is equation (2.46).

The money multiplier $\lambda(t)$ is the ratio of the money stock $M(t)$ to the stock of high-powered money $H(t)$. The percentage change in the money stock, equation (2.47c), can be approximated by the percentage change in high-powered money plus the percentage change in the multiplier, when the cross product terms are ignored:

$$\mu(t+1) = \frac{M(t+1) - M(t)}{M(t)} \approx \frac{\lambda(t)[H(t+1) - H(t)]}{M(t)} + \frac{1}{\lambda(t)}$$

$$[\lambda(t+1) - \lambda(t)]. \qquad (2.47c)$$

If the control law (2.47a) is substituted for the growth of high-powered money into equation (2.47c) then equation (2.47d) can be derived for the growth of the money stock $\mu(t+1)$:

$$\mu(t+1) = \lambda(t) \left(\alpha(t)\frac{F^H(t)}{M(t)} + \beta(t)\frac{[F(t) - F^H(t)]}{M(t)} \right) + \frac{1}{\lambda(t)}$$

$$[\lambda(t+1) - \lambda(t)]. \qquad (2.47d)$$

The money multiplier varies procyclically by rising during expansions and declining during contractions. Similarly, the actual deficit tends to rise above the high employment deficit during contractions and decline below the high employment deficit during expansions. When these two characteristics are combined, equation (2.47e) states that the percentage change in the money multiplier is negatively related to the difference between the actual and high employment deficit (divided by the money stock):

$$\frac{\lambda(t+1) - \lambda(t)}{\lambda(t)} = -\gamma(t)\frac{[F(t) - F^H(t)]}{M(t)}. \tag{2.47e}$$

For the rate of monetary expansion equation (2.48) can be derived by substituting equation (2.47e) into (2.47d):

$$\mu(t+1) = \alpha(t)\lambda(t)\frac{F^H(t)}{M(t)} + [\beta(t)\lambda(t) - \gamma(t)]\frac{[F(t) - F^H(t)]}{M(t)} \tag{2.48}$$

The rate of monetary expansion, from t to $t+1$, is a function of the ratio of the high employment deficit to the money stock in period t and the deviation of the actual from the high employment deficit in period t. The first determinant is based upon the fiscal policies pursued $F^H(t)$ and a control law $\alpha(t)$. The second determinant depends upon the state of the economy $[F(t) - F^H(t)]$ and a control law $\beta(t)$. Although there is no relation between the growth of the money supply and the actual deficit $F(t)$, there is a close relation between the growth of the money supply and the high employment deficit $F^H(t)$.

A regression of the rate of monetary expansion $\mu(t+1)$ on the ratio of the *high employment deficit* to the money stock $F^H(t)/M(t)$ in year t, where t ranges from 1956 through 1979, is described by equation (2.49a). The variables are measured in per cent per annum:

$$E_t\mu(t+1) = \mu(t+1) = 4.25 \quad + 0.365F^H(t)/M(t); \tag{2.49a}$$
$$(t=) \quad\quad (13.8) \quad (6.0)$$

$$R^2 = 0.632; \quad\quad SE = 1.39; \quad\quad DW = 1.58.$$

The coefficient of $F^H(t)/M(t)$ is significantly different from zero at the one per cent level. Almost two-thirds of the variation in the rate of monetary expansion is explained by the ratio of the high employment deficit to the money stock in the previous year. For this reason equation (2.49a) can be viewed as the expectation taken at time t of the rate of monetary expansion from t to $t+1$, denoted by $E_t\mu(t+1)$. In this framework, *the rate of monetary expansion is, to a large extent, jointly determined by autonomous fiscal policy $F^H(t)$ and a control law $a(t)$*

concerning the fraction of the high employment deficit which is financed by money. Variable $a(t)\lambda(t)$ is equal to one-third.

The ratio of the high employment deficit to the money stock $F^H(t)/M(t)$ is serially correlated, as described by equation (2.49b):

$$F^H(t+1)/M(t+1) = 1.07 \quad + 0.584 F^H(t)/M(t); \tag{2.49b}$$
$$(t=) \qquad\qquad\qquad (1.24) \quad (3.43)$$

$$R^2 = 0.359; \qquad SE = 3.89.$$

It is therefore no surprise that the addition of the lagged rate of monetary growth slightly increases the explanatory power of equation (2.49a), as is shown in equation (2.49c):

$$E_t\mu(t+1) = 2.92 \quad + 0.262 F^H(t)/M(t) + 0.326\mu(t); \tag{2.49c}$$
$$(t=) \qquad (4.32) \quad (3.57) \qquad\qquad (2.17)$$

$$R^2 = 0.702; \qquad SE = 1.28.$$

In forming an expectation of the rate of monetary expansion from year t to $t+1$, the *high* employment deficit in year t should not be ignored.

Table 2.6 contains the actual $\mu(t+1)$ and predicted $E_t\mu(t+1)$ rates of monetary expansion and the ratio of the high employment deficit to the money stock in the previous year $F^H(t)/M(t)$ based upon equation (2.49c). High rates of monetary expansion have been the result of large high employment deficits.

The main systematic determinant of the rate of monetary expansion can be summarized simply. The monetary authority must determine what fraction $(\alpha(t))$ of the high employment deficit $F^H(t)$, and what fraction $\beta(t)$ of the deviation of the actual deficit from the high employment deficit $[F(t) - F^H(t)]$, to finance with money. The more anxious is the monetary authority to stabilize interest rates, the larger will be fractions $\alpha(t)$ and $\beta(t)$. The values of these coefficients represent the control policies, effected through open market operations, of the monetary authority.

The theoretical equation (2.48) suggests why there is no significant relationship betwven the actual deficit $F(t)/M(t)$ and the rate of monetary growth $\mu(t+1)$; this is because expression $[\beta(t)\lambda(t) - \gamma(t)]$ is close to zero. In a recession, the induced growth of the actual deficit above the high employment deficit is offset by a decline in the money multiplier. In an expansion, the induced rise in the money multiplier is offset by an induced decline in the actual deficit below the high employment deficit. What remains is the effect of the high employment deficit.

TABLE 2.6 *Actual $\mu(t+1)$ and expected $E_t\mu(t+1)$ rates of monetary expansion and the ratio $F^H(t)/M(t)$ of the high employment deficit to the money stock in the initial year.*

t	$\mu(t+1)$	$E_t\mu(t+1)$	$F^H(t)/M(t)$
1957	1.2	2.1	-3.86
1958	3.8	3.36	0.2
1959	-0.1	3.3	-3.26
1960	2.1	0.787	-8.0
1961	2.4	2.36	-4.73
1962	3.1	3.28	-1.61
1963	3.9	2.73	-4.58
1964	4.2	4.11	-0.29
1965	4.6	4.25	-0.14
1966	3.9	5.44	3.91
1967	7.1	6.56	9.04
1968	6.0	6.91	6.39
1969	3.7	4.42	-1.72
1970	6.7	4.8	2.58
1971	7.1	6.54	5.5
1972	7.3	6.69	5.57
1973	4.9	6.45	4.38
1974	4.6	4.59	0.28
1975	5.5	7.11	10.3
1976	7.5	6.47	6.72
1977	8.2	7.25	7.2
1978	7.8	6.78	4.53
1979	6.4	5.62	0.59

Source: $F(t)/M(t)$ is from Carlson, Keith 1981: Federal Reserve Bank of St Louis, based upon data from US Department of Commerce, Bureau of Economic Analysis.

Regression equation (2.49d) is completely consistent with this view:

$$\mu(t+1) = 4.25 \quad + 0.365F^H(t)/M(t) + 0.00F(t)/M(t) \quad (2.49d)$$
$$(t=) \quad (10.98) \quad (3.85) \quad\quad\quad\quad (0.00)$$

$$R^2 = 0.63; \quad SE = 1.42; \quad DW = 1.58.$$

The coefficient of the actual deficit $F(t)/M(t)$ is zero and the coefficient of the high employment deficit $F^H(t)/M(t)$ is highly significant.

In view of the historic policies of the monetary authorities to stabilize interest rates, a credible announced change in monetary policy must bc accompanied by a change in the autonomous component of fiscal policy, namely the high employment deficit.

7 Anticipations

John Muth (1961) understood that the way anticipations are influenced by the course of events profoundly affects the dynamic processes between equilibrium points, even though the nature of the equilibrium itself is not sensitive to the way that anticipations change.[10] There is no disagreement among economists that, in a stochastic equilibrium, the average actual and anticipated prices should be equal. There is disagreement concerning the ability of the market effectively to anticipate changes in prices in an unbiased manner, when the equilibrium price is changing. Muth wrote that: "The objective of this paper is to outline a theory of expectations and to show that the implications are — as a first approximation — consistent with the relevant data."

The Muth Rational Expectations hypothesis (MRE) states that, in the aggregate, the anticipated price is an unbiased predictor of the actual price. The anticipated price is equal to the mathematical expectation of the price, conditional upon the correct model and policy inputs. In particular, the forecast error between the actual price and its expectation is a serially uncorrelated term with a zero expectation, and is independent of the anticipated price.

The MRE hypothesis (1961: equation (5.7)) is described by equation (2.10a) in table 2.1, repeated below. Let $p_\tau^*(t)$ be the price at time t that was anticipated at earlier date τ when spending and supply decisions were made, and let E be the expectations operator, $p(t)$ the realized price at time t, $\eta(t)$ the forecast error and $\phi(\tau)$ be the objective probability distribution or information set. Then

$$p_\tau^*(t) = E[p(t) \mid \phi(\tau)]; \qquad p(t) - p_\tau^*(t) = \eta(t)$$

$$E\eta(t) = E\eta(t_1)\eta(t_2) = Ep_\tau^*(t)\eta(t) = 0. \tag{2.10a}$$

An example based upon price theory clearly describes the meaning of the MRE hypothesis. Suppose that the quantity produced $q(t)$ at time t depends upon the price that was anticipated at an earlier date τ when production decisions were made $p_\tau^*(t)$, as well as upon exogenous disturbances $\eta_1(t)$. Equation (2.50) is the supply equation:

$$q(t) = Q(p_\tau^*(t), \eta_1(t)). \tag{2.50}$$

Let the quantity demanded at time t be a function of the market price $p(t)$ and exogenous disturbances $\eta_2(t)$. Equation (2.51) describes the inverse demand curve:

$$p(t) = D(q(t), \eta_2(t)).$$ (2.51)

The market-clearing price $p(t)$, as described by equation (2.52), can be derived when equation (2.50) is substituted into (2.51):

$$p(t) = D[Q(p_\tau^*(t), \eta_1(t)), \eta_2(t)].$$ (2.52)

The market-clearing price $p(t)$ is a stochastic variable. The MRE hypothesis states that the anticipated price $p_\tau^*(t)$ is an unbiased predictor of the actual price. A rational expectation price $p_\tau^*(t) = Ep(t)$ is one which satisfies equation (2.53):

$$p_\tau^*(t) = Ep(t) = ED[Q(p_\tau^*(t), \eta_1(t)), \eta_2(t)],$$ (2.53)

where E is the expectations operator and the forecast errors are independent of the anticipated price:

$$E[p(t) - p_\tau^*(t), p_\tau^*(t)] = 0.$$ (2.54)

Muth presented the MRE as an empirical proposition, and the question arises: why should equation (2.10a) be true when the equilibrium price itself is changing? Muth's rationale for his hypothesis is as follows.

If the predictions of the theory were substantially better than the expectations of the firms, then there would be opportunities for the insider to profit from the knowledge by inventory speculation if possible, by operating a firm, or by selling a price forecasting service to firms. The profit opportunities would no longer exist if the aggregate expectation of the firms is the same as the predictions of the theory. (1961: 318)

Muth was aware of the fact that there are many market participants with different-price anticipations. Supply function $Q(p_\tau^*(t), \eta_1(t))$ in equation (2.50) should be written as equation (2.55), which is the sum of the supply decision of $i = 1, 2, \ldots$, different producers with different anticipations $p_\tau^*(t;i)$:

$$q(t) = \sum_i Q_i(p_\tau^*(t;i), \eta_{1i}(t)).$$ (2.55)

He argued that, under certain conditions, the diversity of anticipations is not a problem.

... allowing for cross-sectional differences in expectations is a simple matter, because their aggregate effect is negligible as long as the deviation from the rational forecast for an individual firm is not strongly correlated with those of others. Modifications are necessary only if the correlation of the errors is large and depends systematically on other explanatory variables. (1961: 321)

Are Muth's assumptions correct descriptions of reality? When the equilibrium price is changing substantially, will the forecast errors of the individual firms be positively correlated? How quickly will firms learn the expectation of the equilibrium price $Ep(t)$ which satisfies equation (2.53)? There is no *theoretical* reason why the MRE hypothesis (2.10a) should be true as the economy moves from one equilibrium price to another. The MRE assumes that (i) learning occurs very quickly, and (ii) profit opportunities are eliminated rapidly as the firms that learn the correct model (described by the D and Q functions and exogenous disturbances η_1 and η_2) commit resources to maximize expected profits.

New Classical Economics considers the MRE as an axiom and inquires why the unemployment rate or Okun Gap is serially correlated. I consider the MRE as an empirical proposition to be tested against an alternative: the Asymptotically Rational Expectations (ARE) hypothesis. This hypothesis is in the spirit of Muth's approach. He wrote:

From a purely theoretical standpoint, there are good reasons for assuming rationality ... rationality is an assumption that can be modified. Systematic biases, incomplete or incorrect information ... can be examined with analytical methods based on rationality.

The only real test, however, is whether theories involving rationality explain observed phenomena any better than alternative theories. (1961: 330)

The *Asymptotically Rational Expectations* (ARE) hypothesis is based upon the following considerations. The crucial variable for supply and demand decisions is the expected price adjusted for risk and risk aversion, not the expected price *per se*. With uncertainty and risk aversion, there will be unexploited profit opportunities. The latter diminish as the uncertainty declines and are effectively eliminated in the steady state. Alternatively, the magnitude of a firm's commitment of resources increases as the expected price adjusted for risk converges asymptotically to the expected price. In wage change equation (2.22), for example, the relevant anticipated rate of inflation adjusted for risk π^* converges asymptotically to the expected rate of inflation as the degree of risk declines.

First, I will prove that the responsiveness of a firm's output to a change in the expected price is negatively related to risk and risk aversion, which means that there are unexploited profit opportunities that need not be eliminated quickly. Secondly, I explicitly formulate the ARE hypothesis.

7.1 The responsiveness of output to changes in the expected price

Consider a competitive firm which seeks to maximize the expected utility of profits. It produces output $q(t)$ in period t which is sold in period $t + 1$. At time t, when production decisions are made, the price $p^*(t + 1)$ is a stochastic variable (denoted by the asterisk) with a mean of $E_t p(t + 1)$ and a positive finite variance σ^2. Total costs incurred in period t are $(c/2)q(t)^2$ and marginal costs are $cq(t)$.

Equation (2.56) defines profits $Z(t + 1)$:

$$Z(t + 1) = p^*(t + 1)q(t) - \frac{c}{2}q(t)^2. \tag{2.56}$$

The utility function of profits is described by equation (2.57a). It is a second-degree approximation evaluated at expected profits of zero:

$$U(Z(t + 1)) = U(0) + U'(0)Z(t + 1) + \frac{U''(0)}{2}Z(t + 1)^2. \tag{2.57a}$$

If α is defined as absolute risk aversion, evaluated at zero expected profits

$$\alpha = -U''(0)/U'(0), \tag{2.57b}$$

then the utility function (2.57a) can be written as (2.57c), in terms of risk aversion coefficient α:

$$U(Z(t + 1)) = U(0) + U'(0)Z(t + 1) - \frac{\alpha}{2}U'(0)Z(t + 1)^2. \tag{2.57c}$$

The expected utility of profits $E_t U(Z(t + 1))$ is therefore[11] equation (2.58) which is a function of output $q(t)$, the expected price $E_t p(t + 1)$, risk measured by the variance σ^2 of price and risk aversion α:

$$E_t U(Z(t + 1)) = U(0) + U'(0)[q(t)E_t p(t + 1) - \frac{c}{2}q(t)^2]$$
$$- \frac{\alpha}{2}U'(0)\sigma^2 q(t)^2 - \alpha\frac{U'(0)}{2}[q(t)E_t p(t + 1)$$
$$- \frac{c}{2}q(t)^2]^2. \tag{2.58}$$

The firm selects quantity $q(t)$ to maximize the expected utility of profits $E_tU(Z(t+1))$ to be received in period $t+1$. The optimal output is described by equation (2.59) when the function is evaluated at expected profits of zero:[12]

$$\alpha\sigma^2 = \frac{E_tp(t+1) - cq(t)}{q(t)} = \frac{\text{expected price} - \text{marginal cost}}{\text{output}}. \tag{2.59}$$

The unexploited profit opportunities, measured by the difference between the expected price and marginal cost, per unit of output, are equal to the product of risk aversion and risk (measured by the variance of price) (see Stein, 1979). When there is neither risk nor risk aversion, then marginal cost is equal to the expected price.

Consider the response of output to a change in the expected price. Equation (2.60) is obtained by differentiating (2.59) with respect to the expected price $E_tp(t+1)$ and then solving for $dq(t)/dE_tp(t+1)$:

$$\frac{dq(t)}{dE_tp(t+1)} = \frac{1}{\alpha\sigma^2 + c}. \tag{2.60}$$

c is the slope of the marginal cost curve

It can be seen in this equation that the greater the risk and risk aversion $\alpha\sigma^2$, the smaller is the responsiveness of output to changes in the expected price.

As the degree of risk declines, output produced rises to the point where marginal cost is equal to expected price. In the steady state there is little risk, and marginal cost is equal to the expected price. When the expected price is changing, there is considerable risk and there are unexploited profit opportunities.

7.2 Asymptotic Rational Expectations (ARE)

In the above example, we can state that output is produced at the point where marginal cost $cq(t)$ is equal to the risk-adjusted price $E_tp(t+1) - \alpha\sigma^2q(t)$:

$$E_tp(t+1) - \alpha\sigma^2q(t) = cq(t). \tag{2.61}$$

As the degree of risk $\alpha\sigma^2$ diminishes to zero, the risk-adjusted price converges to the expected price. This is the logic of the ARE hypothesis.

On a macroeconomic level, the ARE hypothesis is modelled by equation (2.10b), repeated below. It is the counterpart of equation

(2.61), where μ corresponds to the expected price and π^* corresponds to the risk-adjusted price. Variable $\mu(t) - n$ is the current rate of monetary expansion *per capita*, which will be the equilibrium rate of inflation (denoted by π_e) if the current rate continues, $\pi^*(t)$ is the currently anticipated rate of inflation adjusted for risk and c is a finite speed of adjustment which reflects risk and risk aversion:

$$D\pi^*(t) = c[\mu(t) - n - \pi^*(t)].\eqno(2.10b)$$

There are several noteworthy aspects of the ARE hypothesis. First, there is an explicit use of an estimate of the steady-state rate of inflation π_e in forming anticipations of how the rate of inflation will change at every moment of time. This estimate of the steady state is implied by the model and the *current* policy input. If $\mu(t)$ is to be held constant, then the value of the steady-state rate of inflation is *not* a subject of controversy among the three schools of thought. Second, although the public knows that the *steady-state* rate of inflation π_e is equal to the steady-state rate of monetary expansion *per capita*, it does not know if the current $\mu(t) - n$ will continue. If it has been rising to its current level, the public does not know if it will remain at that level or rise further. Therefore, the public does not know the steady-state rate of inflation and is required to form an estimate.

These considerations can be modelled as follows. The anticipated rate of inflation over the planning period π^* is equal to the steady-state rate of monetary expansion *per capita* $\mu_e - n$:

$$\pi^* = \mu_e - n.\eqno(2.62)$$

At every moment of time, the public estimates the value of the steady-state rate of monetary expansion $\mu_e(t)$ according to equation (2.63a), whose solution is (2.63b):

$$D\mu_e(t) = c[\mu(t) - \mu_e(t)]\eqno(2.63a)$$

$$\mu_e(t) = \mu_e(0)\exp(-ct) + c\int^t \mu(s)\exp[-c(t-s)]\,ds.\eqno(2.63b)$$

The estimate at time t of the steady-state rate of monetary expansion $\mu_e(t)$ is a weighted average of past rates $\mu(s)$ of monetary expansion. Alternatively, the estimated steady-state rate of monetary expansion is formed adaptively.

ARE equation (2.10b) can be derived by combining equations (2.62) and (2.63a). Coefficient c reflects the uncertainties concerning future monetary policy[13] and the future non-monetary disturbances to the price level.

There are several sources of uncertainty concerning the price level, which imply a finite speed of response c of the anticipated rate of inflation to changes in the current monetary input. The equilibrium (denoted by subscript e) logarithm of the price level $\ln p_e(t)$ is described by the equation

$$\ln p_e(t) = a(t) + \pi_e t, \tag{2.64}$$

and is shown graphically in figure 2.3. The slope is the steady-state rate of inflation π_e and the intercept $a(t)$ reflects permanent factors which determine the level of real balances, but not the rate of growth of the price level.

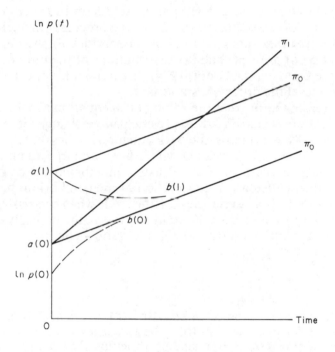

FIGURE 2.3

At every moment of time, there are shocks which change the price level but not its rate of change. Some of these shocks are transitory, while others are permanent. At $t = 0$, suppose that the price level jumps from $a(0)$ to $a(1)$ without any change in the rate of monetary expansion. If the change in the price level is due to a permanent shock, then $a(1)$ is expected to remain constant and the economy will follow trajectory $a(1)\pi_0$. If the shock is transitory, then $a(1)$ is expected to return to $a(0)$ and the price level will follow trajectory $a(1)b(1)$ back to the equilibrium price level line $a(0)\pi_0$. There is uncertainty whether the price shock, or the current rate of inflation, is permanent or transitory. Rational behavior with risk aversion induces people to wait for an accumulation of evidence, concerning the parameters of equation (2.64), before revising their risk-adjusted price anticipations and market behaviour drastically. This was the theme of section 7.1.

Firms and households form prior probability distributions of the important parameters and exogenous variables. In the example described by equation (2.52), the parameters describe functions D and Q and exogenous variables η_1, η_2. Learning proceeds through a feedback from realized market prices and quantities to the continuous modification of prior probability distributions of the unknown parameters (see Cyert and DeGroot, 1974). In this manner, the uncertainty σ^2 diminishes if the process is stationary.

These reasons imply that the value of c in equation (2.10b) is finite. Economically relevant risk-adjusted anticipations change differentially. Unlike the MRE hypothesis, the ARE equation implies that the forecast errors will be serially correlated when there are large changes in the policy inputs, because the risk-adjusted anticipated price converges slowly to the mathematical expectation of the equilibrium price. The MRE hypothesis is a special case of the ARE when the risk-adjusted anticipated price converges very rapidly to the mathematically expected price. The general macrodynamic model is now complete.

Notes

1   Let the utility function be $U(c(t), A(t), l(t))$, where $l(t)$ is leisure, $c(t)$ is consumption of goods and $A(t)$ is the general level of technology. With technical progress, a given amount of leisure time can produce more utility. For example, more distant places can be visited as the speed of travel increases or more work can be done at home with power tools. The budget constraint is $pc = W(1 - l)$, where W is the wage, p is the price level and the total time available is unity. A necessary condition for utility maximization is $U_2(.)/U_1(.) = W/A(t)p = w$. Hence, the supply of labor depends upon the *adjusted* real wage.

2   The source of the data is the Economic Report of the President, 1980: Table B-37. Variable w_N is an index of unit labor cost of the private non-farm business sector divided by its own implicit price deflator w_N (1967) = 100. The unemployment rate is the total unemployment rate.

3   If function F is Cobb–Douglas then

$$y(t) = A(t)k^\alpha(t)[1 - U(t)]^{1-\alpha}. \qquad (i)$$

Capacity output is defined as

$$f(k(t), t) = A(t)k^\alpha(t)(1 - U_e)^{1-\alpha}. \qquad (ii)$$

Divide (i) by (ii) and derive

$$\frac{y(t)}{f(k(t),\, t)} = \left(\frac{1 - U(t)}{1 - U_e}\right)^{1-\alpha} \approx 1 - \frac{(1 - \alpha)}{(1 - U_e)}\,[U(t) - U_e]$$

$$\equiv B[\,U(t) - U_e\,]. \qquad (iii)$$

The right-hand side of (iii) is the $B(.)$ function in equation (2.25). The same argument applies to any homogeneous production function.

4   Okun's preferred equation, during the period 1947–60, was

$$P = A[1 + 0.032\,(U - 4)],$$

where P is potential and A is actual output; the unemployment rate is U. He estimated a trend rate of growth of 3.9 per cent per annum which was not uniform over the period.

5   See the Economic Report of the President (1980: Table B-86).

6   It is interesting to note that along an optimal growth path, the equation for $Dk(t)$ is given by

$$Dk(t) = \frac{A(k(t))}{-f''(k(t))}\,[f'(k(t)) - (\lambda + \rho)],$$

where $f(k)$ is output per unit of effective labor, λ is the sum of the growth rate of effective labor and the depreciation rate, ρ is the social discount factor, $A(k)$ is positive and $f''(k)$ is negative. See Infante and Stein (1973).

7   Since equation (2.36) is an approximation, ξ is not necessarily constant.

8   If the elasticity of substitution differs from unity, α is not constant. Empirically, the value of α (which is the share of capital in income produced) is relatively constant.

9   From the definition $b \equiv B/pN$ we derive

$$Db/b = DB/B - \pi - n,$$

from which (2.45) follows.

10   In the steady state, every model contains the same equation for the anticipated price level: it is equal to the actual price level.

11   Note that $Z(t+1)^2 = \{ [p_i^*(t+1) - E_t p(t+1)] q(t) + [E_t p(t+1)q(t) - c/2\, q(t)^2] \}^2$. Hence: $E_t Z(t+1)^2 = \sigma^2 q(t)^2 + [q(t)E_t p(t+1) - c/2\, q(t)^2]^2$, since the expectation of the cross product terms is zero.

12   From the maximization, derive $[E_t p(t+1) - cq(t)] [1 - \alpha E_t Z(t+1)] = \alpha \sigma^2 q(t)$. At $E_t Z(t+1) = 0$, equation (2.59) is derived.

13   See Taylor (1975), Meyer and Webster (1981) and chapter 3, section 2.1.

CHAPTER 3

The Three Gospels

1 Introduction and summary

Each of the three gospels, Keynesian, Monetarist and New Classical Economics, can be viewed as a special case of the general dynamic model developed in chapter 2. There is no disagreement among them concerning the characteristics of the medium-run equilibrium, which may be viewed as the common core of macroeconomics. Fundamental differences exist concerning the dynamics of adjustment between medium-run equilibria, which is precisely the source of conflict concerning macroeconomic policy to affect the unemployment and inflation rates.

Define the medium run as a span of time where the capital intensity and ratio of government bonds to money are relatively constant. Medium-run equilibrium is defined as a situation where the unemployment rate and inflation rate are constant, and there is no forecast error between the actual and anticipated rate of inflation. The model implies that the unemployment rate is equal to its equilibrium value, the goods and bond markets clear, real balances are constant, and the rate of inflation is equal to the rate of monetary expansion. Insofar as the growth of the money supply is determined by the government deficit, the medium-run rate of inflation is the high employment deficit as a fraction of the money supply.

Two important disturbances to medium-run equilibrium are considered. (i) There is a rise in real government expenditures. (ii) An open market operation and debt management policy raise the ratio of government bonds to money. The effects of these disturbances upon the medium-run equilibrium reflect the consensus in macroeconomics.

Consider the first disturbance. A rise in real government purchases raises the excess demand for goods. Prices rise and reduce real balances. The decline in real balances leads to an excess demand for money, and

57

the rate of interest is increased. Private demand is reduced, as a result of the decline in real balances and a rise in the real rate of interest, by an amount equal to the rise in real government purchases. Aggregate demand is again equal to capacity output, but velocity and the real rate of interest have increased.

As a result of the rise in real government expenditures, the real high employment deficit has increased relative to real balances. Thereby the rate of monetary expansion has increased, which implies a higher steady-state rate of inflation.

A second disturbance is a permanent rise in the average ratio of bonds to money. To induce people to increase the ratio of bonds to money in their portfolios, the real rate of interest rises. Aggregate demand is reduced, as a result of the rise in the real rate of interest, and prices decline relative to the money stock, which raises real balances. Consumption is stimulated, and the rise in the real rate of interest is mitigated by the rise in real balances. Aggregate real demand is again equal to capacity output. Velocity has declined, and the real rate of interest has increased.

The rise in the ratio of bonds to money raises the interest payments on the government debt, and the high employment deficit is raised. Since the money supply grows as a result of budget deficits, there is a higher rate of monetary expansion and a higher rate of inflation.

Analysis of the medium-run equilibrium is of limited interest, because it cannot specify how long it takes to return to equilibrium, where output is constrained to equal capacity output. There is no way to avoid the macrodynamics described in table 2.1, if the fluctuations in the unemployment and inflation rates are to be explained. This brings us to the sources of controversy.

The New Classical Economics (NCE) gospel is summarized by the *Policy Ineffectiveness Proposition*: the mathematical expectation (at time $t-1$) of real variables (at time t), such as the unemployment rate $E_{t-1}U(t)$ or ratio of actual to capacity output $E_{t-1}y(t)$, conditional upon their past history, is independent of the monetary and fiscal policies adopted at time $t-1$ and earlier. In literary terms, it can be phrased to read: on average, the unemployment rate is insensitive to demand management policies. Another implication of the Policy Ineffectiveness Proposition is that inflation can be reduced quickly, without any social costs arising from a concomitant decline in output or rise in unemployment.

Three parameter specifications in table 2.1 are sufficient to imply NCE results: (i) Anticipations are rational in the sense of Muth. The unanticipated inflation is not serially correlated, and it has a zero expectation. (ii) Aggregate demand depends upon the real, not the nominal, rate of interest. (iii) The nominal rate of interest fully reflects the rationally anticipated inflation.

The model in table 2.1 implies that the change in the unemployment rate depends upon its lagged value, real disturbances and the difference between the current price level $p(t)$ and the value which the market anticipated on the basis of information at an earlier date $E_{t-1}p(t)$. The Muth Rational Expectations hypothesis asserts that the price forecast error $p(t) - E_{t-1}p(t)$ is a serially uncorrelated term with a zero expectation. It follows that the mathematical expectation of the unemployment rate $E_{t-1}U(t)$ just depends upon the lagged unemployment rate. Policy-makers cannot systematically affect the course of the unemployment rate through monetary or fiscal policy which would affect the price level, because the price level expected by the public would negate the effect. Alternatively, excess aggregate demand depends upon the real, not the nominal, rate of interest; and the nominal rate of interest fully reflects the rationally anticipated inflation. Demand management, which operates upon the expected price level, is therefore incapable of affecting the real excess demand for goods. This is the logic of the Policy Ineffectiveness Proposition.

The Monetarist gospel consists of three propositions. (i) A restrictive fiscal policy without a significant reduction in the rate of monetary expansion cannot significantly reduce the rate of inflation. (ii) A rise in the rate of monetary expansion above the current rate of inflation raises the rate of inflation, regardless of the slack in the economy. (iii) There is no relation between a constant rate of inflation and the unemployment rate. Nevertheless, there is a short-run trade-off between the speed at which inflation is reduced and the temporary rise in the unemployment rate.

Three parameter specifications in table 2.1 are sufficient to generate the Monetarist propositions. (i) Inflationary anticipations are generated by the Asymptotically Rational Expectations equation. (ii) A relevant variable for the rate of inflation is the Keynesian excess demand for goods, not the Okun Gap between capacity and actual output. (iii) A rising ratio of government debt to money raises the real rate of interest and lowers the excess aggregate demand for goods. Hence, bond-financed fiscal policy has a weak effect upon real aggregate demand.

A Monetarist scenario, which differs from the Keynesian and NCE, is as follows. A rise in the rate of monetary expansion initially raises real balances, since prices change differentially. The Keynesian excess demand for goods is raised and, regardless of the current value of the Okun Gap or unemployment rate, the rate of inflation is increased.

The asymptotically rational risk-adjusted anticipated rate of inflation is raised slowly because, when there is risk aversion and uncertainty, the demand for productive services responds differentially to changes in the current rate of monetary expansion.

The effective anticipated rate of inflation π^*, which affects the inflation of unit labor costs with a unitary coefficient, is the composition of several differential responses. First, there is the connection between the current rate of monetary expansion μ and the average rate of monetary expansion $E\mu$ that the public believes will be pursued by the monetary authority. It is shown that the lag between the currently announced change in monetary policy and the public's acceptance of the change depends upon (i) the previous volatility of money growth and (ii) the level of confidence required. Secondly, there is the friction between the expected rate of inflation $E\pi$ and the risk-adjusted anticipated rate of inflation π^*, which determines the demand for productive services and enters directly into the inflation of nominal unit labor costs with a unitary coefficient. The risk premium depends upon the variance of prices and the coefficient of absolute risk aversion. Thirdly, there may be frictions resulting from staggered wage contracts.

These frictions produce a differential response between the current rate of monetary expansion and the risk-adjusted anticipated rate of inflation, which is modelled by the ARE equation. The increase in the anticipated rate of inflation raises the inflation of unit labor costs and aggravates the effect of the rise in the Keynesian excess demand for goods. The net effect is that the actual rate of inflation rises faster than the anticipated rate. The decline in real unit labor costs reduces the unemployment rate. Eventually, the actual and anticipated rates of inflation catch up to the constant growth of the money supply. When that occurs, if the unemployment rate deviates from its equilibrium value, nominal wages grow at a different rate than prices. The adjustment in real unit labor costs restores the unemployment rate to its equilibrium value.

It is shown that NCE results can be obtained as a special case of the Monetarist analysis. When the coefficient c of the ARE equation tends to infinity, then the forecast error between the actual and anticipated rate of inflation tends to zero. Then the Policy Ineffectiveness Proposition occurs. However, when there is risk aversion and uncertainty, coefficient c of the ARE equation is finite. Monetarist results will be obtained, and the Policy Ineffectiveness Proposition is not valid.

Keynesian economists claim that monetary and fiscal policies affect output and employment relatively quickly through their effects upon aggregate demand. These policies, however, have weak effects upon the rate of inflation. Therefore, demand management policies are effective in affecting the real variables and are not quickly dissipated by price changes. This view is described by the IS–LM paradigm, with relatively fixed wages and prices.

To reduce the rate of inflation significantly, there must be a significant decline in the rate of inflation of nominal unit labor costs, which Keynesian economists refer to as "the underlying rate of inflation." A reduction in the rate of inflation of nominal unit labor costs requires either the creation of Okun Gaps, by any combination of fiscal and monetary policies, or an incomes policy. To be sure, the latter produces a misallocation of resources. But the social cost of the former far exceeds the sum of the Harberger triangles produced by an incomes policy, according to the Keynesians.

2   Medium-run equilibrium: the common core of macroeconomics[1]

Define the medium run as a span of time where capacity output and the capital intensity are relatively constant and where there are no significant variations in the average ratio θ of interest payments on the government debt to the stock of money. These conditions are expressed by

$$\Delta k = \Delta A = \Delta \theta = 0. \tag{3.1}$$

Define *medium-run equilibrium* as a situation where the unemployment and inflation rates are constant and there is no unanticipated inflation. Equation (3.2) expresses these conditions:

$$DU(t) = D\pi(t) = \pi(t) - \pi^*(t) = 0; \quad D \equiv d/dt. \tag{3.2}$$

Conditions (3.1) are assumed by all macroeconomic models which are not growth models. Conditions (3.2) include, as a special case, the situation where output and the price level are constant and there is no forecast error between the actual and anticipated price level. For ease of exposition, assume that the labor force is constant.

All three schools of thought can agree upon the properties of the medium-run equilibria of the general model described in table 2.1. Disagreement only concerns the speed at which the economy converges to the medium-run equilibrium. A vivid way to distinguish between NCE and Keynesian economics is that (in modulus stochastic terms) NCE views the economy as being in the neighborhood of the medium-run equilibrium, whereas the Keynesians believe that the convergence process to equilibrium is extremely slow. In this sense, NCE stresses "equilibrium" economics, and the Keynesians stress the economics of impact effects. Analysis of the medium-run equilibrium is extremely useful and necessary, since it is the common core of the various schools of thought. In particular, I examine the effects of parametric changes of (i) real government purchases of goods (g) and (ii) the ratio θ of bonds to money, upon the level of real balances (m), the interest rate (ρ), the inflation rate (π) and the endogenous rate of monetary expansion (μ). The techniques of analysis are generalizations of the familiar IS–LM curves.

2.1   Characteristics of the medium-run equilibrium

Conditions (3.1) and (3.2), applied to the equations in table 2.1, imply the following characteristics of the medium-run equilibrium. A constant unemployment rate implies that the adjusted real wage w is constant (2.3). A constant adjusted real wage and no unanticipated inflation imply (2.4) that the unemployment rate is equal to its equilibrium value U_e. These conditions imply (2.1) that output *per capita* is equal to an equilibrium value $y_e = AF(k, 1 - U_e)$.

Since there is no unanticipated inflation and the unemployment rate is at its equilibrium value, equation (2.7) implies that the real excess demand for goods is zero: $J = 0$. When there is no unanticipated inflation and the labor market clears, then the goods market clears. Aggregate demand is equal to capacity output.

When aggregate demand is equal to capacity output, then conditions (3.1) and (3.2) imply that real balances m and the nominal rate of interest ρ are constant (implied by equations (2.6) and (2.7)). Constant real balances implies that the rate of monetary expansions μ is equal to the rate of price inflation $\pi = \pi^*$.

A special case of the general model facilitates the graphic analysis of the medium-run equilibrium in terms of a generalization of the familiar IS–LM analysis. This special case, defined as the Fisher neutral case, assumes that equal changes in the anticipated rate of price change and the nominal rate of interest do not affect the excess demands for goods and for bonds. The real excess demands for goods and bonds depend upon the real, not the nominal, rate of interest. A rise in the anticipated rate of inflation, given the nominal rate of interest, increases the excess supply of bonds by firms and households who prefer to increase their holdings of capital (equity) relative to bonds. Bond prices fall and the nominal rate of interest rises until the real rate of interest is restored to its original level. Equation (3.3) below describes the bond market and equation (3.5) describes the excess demand for goods in medium-run equilibrium in the Fisher neutral case.

The real rate of interest i, defined as the nominal rate p less the anticipated rate of price change π^*, which equates the stock demand for bonds to the stock in existence is described by equation (3.3) (based upon (2.6) and (2.11)):

$$i(t) = p(t) - \pi^*(t) = p(y(t), m(t), \theta m(t), k(t)). \tag{3.3}$$

In medium-run equilibrium, the real rate of interest which equilibrates the bond market is described by

$$i = i(m; y_e, \theta, k) \qquad \text{LM.} \tag{3.4}$$

This equation is shown in figure 3.1 as the downward sloping LM curve. Its negative slope is explained as follows. Suppose that there is a rise in the price level when the stocks of money and bonds are given. Real balances are reduced. As a result of the higher price level, the transactions demand for money has increased, thereby raising the

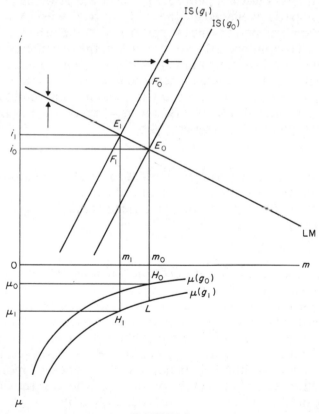

FIGURE 3.1

marginal convenience yield on money. Firms and households offer bonds in exchange for money, and the real rate of interest rises to equilibrate the bond market. Therefore, given the bond–money ratio θ, there is a negative relation between the real rate of interest i and real balances m.

Equation (3.5) describes the real excess demand for goods $J(t)$ in the Fisher neutral case. The nominal rate of interest and the anticipated rate of inflation have partial derivatives of equal but opposite sign. Consequently, the real rate of interest $i(t)$ is the appropriate argument in the real excess demand for goods function.

$$J(t) = J(y(t), m(t), \theta m(t), i(t), k(t), g(t)). \tag{3.5}$$

In medium-run equilibrium, a zero real excess demand for goods implies equation (3.6):

$$J(m, i; y_e, g, \theta, k) = 0 \quad \text{IS}. \tag{3.6}$$

This equation is shown in figure 3.1 as the upward sloping IS curve. Its positive slope is explained in the conventional way. A rise in real balances (and real bonds, since θ is given) raises the real excess demand for goods. To equilibrate the goods market, the real interest rate must rise. In this way, investment (and to a lesser extent, consumption) will be reduced to equate aggregate demand to capacity output y_e.

Since real balances are constant in medium-run equilibrium, the correctly anticipated rate of inflation $\pi = \pi^*$ is equal to the rate of monetary expansion μ, as described by

$$\pi = \pi^* = \mu. \tag{3.7}$$

According to the government budget constraint equation (2.9), the rate of monetary expansion is determined endogenously. To facilitate the analysis of the medium-run equilibria, assume that the tax function is described by

$$T(.) = \tau(y + \theta m). \tag{3.8}$$

There is a proportional income tax levied on nominal income including interest payments on the government debt, so real taxes are proportional, at tax rate τ, to real income y plus real interest payments $b = \theta m$.

Moreover, just for expositional simplicity, assume that the *marginal* deficits and surpluses are financed exclusively by money. There is an initial *average* ratio of bonds to money $\theta = B/M$. However, from then on, the number of bonds is fixed, while the stock of money varies endogenously according to the condition of the government budget deficit or surplus. This assumption is described by

$$DB = 0. \tag{3.9}$$

The same results would be obtained if it is assumed that $\theta = 0$, so that there is no government debt.

Assumptions (3.8) and (3.9), and the government budget constraint (2.9), imply equation (3.10a) for the rate of monetary expansion:

$$\mu = \theta(1 - \tau) + \frac{(g - \tau y_e)}{m}. \tag{3.10a}$$

This equation, which describes the endogenous rate of monetary expansion, is shown in the lower half of figure 3.1. It is drawn on the assumption that there is a high employment deficit net of transfer payments, that is, $g - \tau y_e$ is positive.

Medium-run equilibrium is described by equations (3.4), (3.6), (3.7) and (3.10a) which determine the real rate of interest i, real balances m, the correctly anticipated rate of inflation $\pi = \pi^*$ and the rate of monetary expansion μ. Medium-run equilibrium is at point E_0 in figure 3.1. Aggregate demand is equal to capacity output y_e. The goods and bond markets are both in equilibrium, at a real interest rate i_0 and real balances m_0. The government deficit as a fraction of the money stock is the rate of monetary expansion μ_0. Prices rise at rate $\pi_0 = \mu_0$. The nominal rate of interest is $\rho_0 = i_0 + \mu_0$, which is the sum of real rate i_0 and the correctly anticipated inflation at rate $\mu_0 = \theta(1 - \tau) + (g - \tau y_e)/m_e$:

The control variables under consideration are real government purchases g and the average ratio θ of bond interest payments to money. Characteristics of the *medium run* are that the capital intensity $k(t) \equiv K(t)/N(t)$, and that the level of technology $A(t)$ and the average ratio of government bonds to money $\theta(t) \equiv B(t)/M(t)$ are considered to be relatively constant. A good way to understand the characteristics of the medium-run equilibrium is to consider the effects of changes in control variables g and θ.

2.2   *The effect of a parametric change in real government purchases*

A rise in real government purchases of goods from g_0 to g_1 shifts the IS curve in figure 3.1 upwards from $IS(g_0)$ to $IS(g_1)$. At the initial equilibrium E_0, there is now an excess demand for goods relative to capacity output y_e. Upward pressure is exerted upon prices (denoted by the horizontal vectors) and real balances tend to decline below m_0. The rise in prices (i.e. decline in real balances) raises the transactions demand for money (marginal convenience yield on real balances) and an excess supply of bonds is generated. Real interest rate i tends to rise (denoted by the vertical vectors) which induces the private sector to economize on the use of real balances.

Both the higher real rate of interest and lower real balances reduce real private investment and consumption. At the new equilibrium E_1, real private demand for goods has declined by the amount of the rise in real government purchases. Aggregate real demand is again equal to capacity output, but the rise in the real rate of interest from i_0 to i_1 has reduced the rate of private capital formation. This rise in the real rate of interest has been produced by the decline in real balances from m_0 to m_1.

The government budget deficit as a fraction of the money stock rises from H_0 to L as a result of the rise in government expenditures. The marginal deficit is assumed (equation (3.9)) to be entirely financed by money. Therefore, the rate of monetary expansion rises from μ_0 to μ_1. Since real balances are now constant at m_1, the rate of inflation also rises to μ_1.

Figure 3.2 describes the medium-run equilibrium price level $\ln p_e(t)$, when real government expenditures rise from g_0 to g_1. There is a higher

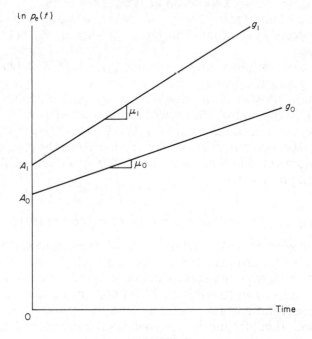

FIGURE 3.2

absolute price level, denoted by the shift in the intercept from A_0 to A_1, relative to the money stock, that is, the meaning of a lower level of real balances. Moreover, there is a higher rate of inflation, denoted by the steeper slope μ_1.

In summary, a parametric rise in the level of real government purchases has the following effects upon the medium-run equilibrium. (i) There is a rise in the real rate of interest and a reduction in the real rate of capital formation. (ii) Real balances decline, so that the income velocity of money is raised. (iii) There is a larger government deficit, which is assumed to be financed on the margin by money. (iv) Hence, there is a higher rate of monetary expansion. (v) The higher correctly anticipated rate of inflation is equal to the higher rate of monetary expansion.

2.3   The effect of a parametric change in the ratio of bonds to money

Open market operations can change the initial average ratio θ of bonds to money. Suppose that an open market sale raises the bond—money ratio from θ_0 to θ_1. Continue to assume, however, that subsequent government budget deficits are financed entirely by money. What are the effects of this open market sale?

The LM curve (figure 3.3) shifts upwards from $LM(\theta_0)$ to $LM(\theta_1)$. To induce the public to hold a larger ratio of bonds to money in their portfolios, they must be offered a higher real rate of interest. If real balances were at m_0, then the real rate of interest would have to rise from i_0 to $m_0 F_0$ to induce the public to increase the ratio of bonds to money in their portfolios.

It is convenient for graphic analysis to assume that the open market sale *per se* has no significant effect upon the excess aggregate demand for goods, given the rate of interest. At real rate of interest i_0, the open market exchange of assets of equal value (bonds for money) is assumed to exert no perceptible effect upon aggregate demand. No shift occurs in the IS curve, when the LM curve rises.

Medium-run equilibrium shifts from E_0 to E_1. The rise in the real rate of interest, necessary to induce the public to increase the ratio of bonds to money held in portfolios, reduces aggregate demand. Prices fall relative to the money stock, and real balances are raised. This resulting rise in real balances raises consumption and mitigates the adverse effects (particularly on investment) of the initial increase in the real rate of interest resulting from the open market sale.

At the new medium-run equilibrium E_1, there is a higher real rate of interest ($i_1 > i_0$) and a higher level of real balances ($m_1 > m_0$). Velocity

declines, since real balances rise relative to output. Real capital formation is discouraged, but real consumption is encouraged. Aggregate
demand is again equal to capacity output.

Consider the effects of the open market sale upon the government
budget deficit and rate of monetary expansion. Unambiguous results
are obtained in the case where the high employment budget, net of
interest payments on the government debt, is in balance, that is, $g = \tau y_e$.
Then, the rate of monetary expansion is described by

$$\mu = \theta(1 - \tau), \tag{3.10b}$$

which is the horizontal line in the lower half of figure 3.3. The deficit
as a fraction of the money stock $\theta(1 - \tau)$ rises, since the ratio of interest
payments on the debt to the money stock rises as a result of the open
market sale. The rise in the rate of monetary expansion from μ_0 to μ_1
produces an equal change in the rate of inflation.

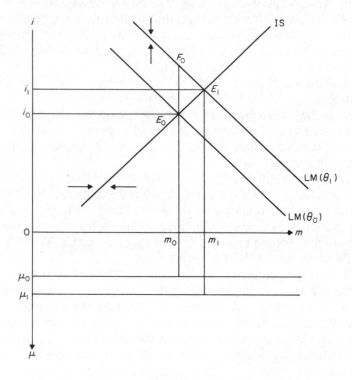

FIGURE 3.3

Figure 3.4 describes the path of the price level. The open market sale *per se*, which raises real balances from m_0 to m_1, lowers the price level from A_0 to A_1. When the government budget constraint is taken into account, then the resulting higher interest payments generate deficits which are assumed to be financed on the margin by money. An increase in the resulting rate of monetary expansion increases the steady-state rate of inflation. Therefore, the resulting path of the price level $\ln p_e(t)$ is described by the line $A_1\theta_1$ when there is an open market sale.

In summary, a parametric rise in the ratio of government bonds to money has the following effects upon the medium-run equilibrium. (i) There is a rise in the real rate of interest and a decline in the rate of capital formation. (ii) Real balances rise, so that the income velocity of money is reduced. (iii) There is a larger deficit, due to the greater interest payments, which are assumed to be financed on the margin by money. (iv) Consequently, there is a higher rate of monetary expansion. (v) The higher correctly anticipated rate of inflation is equal to the higher rate of monetary expansion.

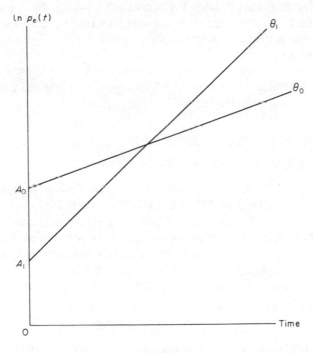

FIGURE 3.4

2.4   *The importance of a dynamic analysis*

The analysis of changes in medium-run equilibria, resulting from parametric changes in control variables, are not the subject of controversy among the Monetarists, Keynesians and New Classical Economists. To understand the divergence of views, consider the following situation. Suppose that the economy is not in medium-run equilibrium: the unemployment rate is not at its equilibrium value, the rate of inflation is not fully anticipated and differs from the rate of monetary expansion.

What are the trajectories of the economy to the medium-run equilibrium? To what extent can demand management policies accelerate the return of the unemployment rate to its equilibrium value? If the rate of monetary expansion is raised when the unemployment rate exceeds its equilibrium value, to what extent will the rate of inflation increase and to what extent will output be stimulated? Can a restrictive fiscal policy, unaccompanied by a reduction in the rate of monetary expansion, reduce the rate of inflation? If the monetary authority wishes to decelerate an existing inflation, what will be the consequences for the unemployment rate? How can the phenomenon of "stagflation" be explained: the simultaneous existence of high inflation and high unemployment?

Each school of thought offers different answers to these questions. I will now examine each school of thought as a special case of the general model summarized in table 2.1.

3   New Classical Economics (NCE)

3.1   *The Policy Ineffectiveness Proposition*

The essence of NCE is summarized by the *Policy Ineffectiveness Proposition*[2] equation (3.11). Let $X(t)$ be a vector of real variables, such as the unemployment rate $U(t)$ or ratio of actual to capacity output, and let $G(t)$ be a vector of monetary and fiscal variables at time t. Then the mathematical expectation of $X(t)$, conditional upon its past history $X(t-1)$, $X(t-2)$, ..., is independent of the monetary and fiscal policies $G(t-1)$, $G(t-2)$, ..., adopted through time $t-1$:

$$E_{t-1}[X(t); X(t-1), X(t-2), \ldots; G(t-1), G(t-2), \ldots]$$
$$= E_{t-1}[X(t); X(t-1), X(t-2), \ldots]. \qquad (3.11)$$

This unambiguous proposition is directly contradictory to Keynesian economics, and has the following implications. (i) "... there is *no* way that the government can operate so that it can expect to depress

the unemployment rate below the natural rate even in the short run . . . "
(Sargent, 1976a: 213–14). (ii) On average, the unemployment rate is
insensitive to demand management policies (McCallum, 1980: 724).
(iii) On average, it makes no difference for the trajectory of the
unemployment rate (or ratio of actual to capacity output) if the rate of
monetary expansion is typically increased rapidly, slowly, or not at
all, when high unemployment rates are observed.

The Policy Ineffectiveness Proposition is inconsistent with both the
Brunner–Meltzer and Friedman–Schwartz critique of Federal Reserve
policy during the Great Depression. Friedman argues, in the quotations
below, that the Federal Reserve actions which allowed the stock of
money to decline rapidly over a sustained period of time exacerbated
the severity of the depression (which contradicts point iii above). Moreover, the Federal Reserve followed a consistent and known policy rule
during that period.

Despite the decline in Federal Reserve credit outstanding, the Board described
its policy for the year 1930 as one of "monetary ease . . . expressed through
purchases at intervals of additional United States Government securities and
in progressive reductions of reserve bank discount and acceptance rates".
This is a striking illustration of the ambiguity of the terms "monetary ease"
and "tightness" and of the need stressed above . . . to interpret Federal
Reserve actions in light of all the forces affecting the stock of money and
credit conditions. It seems paradoxical to describe as "monetary ease" a
policy which permitted the stock of money to decline in fourteen months by a
percentage exceeded only four times in the preceding fifty-four years and
then only during extremely severe business-cycle contractions. And those
words seem especially paradoxical when other factors were tending to expand
the money stock, so that a potential expansion was converted into an actual
contraction entirely by the decline in Federal Reserve credit outstanding.
(Friedman and Schwartz, 1963: 374–5)

Friedman and Schwartz's main theme, concerning the Great
Depression, is as follows.

The failure of the Federal Reserve System to prevent the collapse reflected
not the impotence of monetary policy but rather the particular policies
followed by the monetary authorities and, in smaller degree, the particular
monetary arrangements in existence. (1963: 300)

In their discussion of the period January to the end of October 1930,
they write:

None of the arguments later advanced in support of the view that expansionary monetary measures by the Federal Reserve System might have been ineffective [in lessening the severity of the economic contraction] or undesirable applies to this period .... (1963: 392)

Brunner and Meltzer (1971, 1964) argue that the Federal Reserve System followed a consistent and known monetary policy during the period 1929–33. This policy was responsible for the failure to engage in open market operations when the money stock declined, and thereby prolonged the Great Depression. According to NCE, a known policy rule should not have any effects upon output and employment.

The policy guiding the Federal Reserve was the Riefler–Burgess doctrine, which they described as follows:

... the Riefler–Burgess analysis presupposed a one-way causal relation running from the volume of member bank borrowing to the level of market rates. A main purpose of open market purchases and sales was to change the volume of member bank borrowing. This was viewed as the principal means by which policy affected short-term market interest rates. The rise or fall in short-term rates was expected to change long-term rates and increase the quantity of bank loans demanded by domestic and foreign borrowers; the change in loans and market interest rates were taken as an indicator that policy action was effective. There is no evidence that the particular level of interest rates used to identify "easy" or "tight" policy depended on the rate of inflation or deflation.

The minutes of the Open Market Investment Committee, of the Federal Reserve Board and of the Conference of Governors of the reserve banks provide a considerable amount of evidence showing that most of the policy decisions are consistent with the Riefler–Burgess framework. (1963: 4)

When nominal rates of interest were "low," or when bank borrowings were "low," the Federal Reserve System inferred that money was "easy;" and they were not inclined to engage in open market purchases. The Riefler–Burgess policy implied that money was "easy" and there was no need to engage in open market purchases, even though there was a drastic decline in the money stock.

Another aspect of the known monetary policy was that discount rates would be raised whenever the dollar was under attack in the foreign exchange market. Consider the events that occurred when the United Kingdom left the Gold Standard in 1931. There was an internal rise in the ratio of currency to deposits which aggravated the effect of the gold outflow upon bank reserves. The Federal Reserve System did not take measures to offset the currency drain.

The sharp rises in discount rates were widely supported not only within the system but also outside. The maintenance of the gold standard was accepted as an objective in support of which men of a broad range of views were ready to rally. (Friedman and Schwartz, 1963: 382)

Consequently:

The System took no active measures to ease the internal drain, as it could have done through open-market purchases. (1963: 395)

Monetary policy during the 1929–33 period was guided by the Riefler–Burgess doctrine and the defense of the dollar. The policies were known to the public; and, contrary to NCE, the authors claimed they had real effects.

Therefore, Friedman and Schwartz and Brunner and Meltzer argue that the course of the unemployment rate during the Great Depression was profoundly affected by the known monetary policies followed by the Federal Reserve Board. Thereby, they do not accept equation (3.11) and its implications. Given a deviation of the unemployment rate from its equilibrium value $U(t) - U_e$, monetary policy $G(t)$ can indeed be expected to affect $U(t+1) - U_e$, contrary to the Policy Ineffectiveness Proposition of NCE.

A second implication of NCE is that the mathematical expectation of the price level $E_{t-1} \ln p(t)$ can be changed quickly by varying the mathematical expectation of the money stock $E_{t-1} \ln M(t)$, without any effects upon the expected values of the unemployment rate or level of output.

3.2 Derivation of the NCE Policy Ineffectiveness Proposition from the general model

In this section, the propositions of NCE are derived as a special case of the model in table 2.1. To be faithful to the spirit and letter of NCE, discrete rather than continuous time is used. Equations (2.1), (2.3), (2.4) and (2.10a) are written as equations (3.12)–(3.15) below.

$$\ln y(t) - \ln y(t-1) = -a[U(t) - U(t-1)] \qquad (3.12)$$

$$U(t) - U_e = \beta \ln w(t) \qquad (3.13)$$

$$\ln w(t) - \ln w(t-1) = -h[U(t-1) - U_e] + \ln p^*_{t-1}(t) - \ln p(t) \qquad (3.14)$$

$$\ln p^*_{t-1}(t) = E_{t-1}\ln p(t); \quad E_{t-1}\,\eta(t) = E\eta(t_1)\eta(t_2) = 0;$$
$$\ln p(t) - E_{t-1}\ln p(t) = \eta(t). \tag{3.15}$$

Equation (3.12) is (2.1) when changes in *capacity* output are ignored; the growth rate of the ratio of actual to capacity output is negatively related to the change in the unemployment rate.[3] Equation (3.13) is (2.3) which relates the unemployment rate to the adjusted real wage $w(t)$. For notational simplicity, the equilibrium real wage w_e associated with the equilibrium unemployment rate U_e is defined as unity. Equation (3.14) is (2.4). Coefficient h represents the flexibility of the nominal wage to deviations of the unemployment rate from its equilibrium value. The term $\ln p^*_{t-1}(t) - \ln p(t)$ is the difference between the anticipated and actual rates of inflation $\pi^*_{t-1}(t) - \pi(t)$. Equation (3.15) is the Muth Rational Expectations (MRE) hypothesis (2.10a). The forecast error $\eta(t)$, between the actual price level $\ln p(t)$ and the level anticipated $\ln p^*_{t-1}(t)$, is a serially uncorrelated term with a zero expectation.

It follows[4] that the deviation of the unemployment rate from its equilibrium value $U(t) - U_e$ is described by

$$U(t) - U_e = (1-\beta h)[U(t-1) - U_e] - \beta[\ln p(t) - E_{t-1}\ln p(t)]. \tag{3.16}$$

The first term reflects the speed at which the unemployment rate returns to its equilibrium value, as a result of frictions β and h. The second term reflects the effects of unanticipated price changes, which affect the real wage.

When Okun's Law (equation 2.26) is used to relate output and employment, then (2.26) and (3.16) imply the well-known NCE supply equation

$$\ln y(t) = (1-\beta h)\ln y(t-1) + \alpha\beta[\ln p(t) - E_{t-1}\ln p(t)]. \tag{3.17}$$

That is why equation (2.3) or (3.13) is a supply equation.

The Policy Ineffectiveness Proposition is an immediate consequence. The forecast error η in equation (3.15) can be substituted into unemployment rate equation (3.16) to derive equation (3.18a). It is convenient to write $u(t)$ for the deviation $U(t) - U_e$ of the unemployment rate from its equilibrium value. This is described in equation (3.18b):

$$U(t) - U_e = (1-\beta h)[U(t-1) - U_e] - \beta\eta(t). \tag{3.18a}$$

$$u(t) = (1-\beta h)u(t-1) - \beta\eta(t). \tag{3.18b}$$

The mathematical expectation E_{t-1} taken at time $t-1$ of the unemployment rate deviation is described by equation (3.19a). It only depends upon its past value $u(t-1)$ and is independent of any monetary or fiscal policies taken at $t-1$ or earlier, since the expectation of the forecast error $E_{t-1}\eta(t)$ is zero:

$$E_{t-1}u(t) = (1 - \beta h)u(t-1). \tag{3.19a}$$

Similarly, the expectation of the ratio of actual to capacity output $E_{t-1}\ln y(t)$ is described by equation (3.19b) using equations (3.17) and (3.15):

$$E_{t-1}\ln y(t) = (1 - \beta h)\ln y(t-1). \tag{3.19b}$$

This is exactly the content of the Policy Ineffectiveness Proposition, equation (3.11) above.

There is a simple explanation of equations (3.18) and (3.19a, b), the essence of NCE. Wage bargains, which determine the unemployment rate (equation (3.14)), concern the real wage and not the nominal wage. If, on average, there is no forecast error of the price level ($E\eta(t) = 0$), then the real wage declines when there is a positive unemployment rate deviation $u(t)$ and rises when there is a negative deviation. Government demand management policies affect the price level, but they can only affect the real wage, and hence the unemployment rate, by producing a forecast error of the price level. The MRE hypothesis states that the mathematical expectation of the price forecast error $E_{t-1}\eta(t)$ is zero, and it is not serially correlated. Consequently, on average, demand management policies cannot be expected to affect the unemployment rate. It does not matter what are the magnitudes of $u(t-1)$ or $\ln y(t-1)$. *Demand management policies cannot be expected to accelerate the return to full employment or capacity output.* In reference to the quotations from Friedman and Schwartz, NCE claims that the path of the recovery of the economy starting in mid-1930 could be expected to be the same whether Federal Reserve policy raised, lowered or kept the money stock constant.

At any time t, the unemployment rate deviation $u(t) \equiv U(t) - U_e$ is described by equation (3.20), which is the solution of (3.18b):

$$u(t) = (1 - \beta h)^t u(0) - \beta \sum_{s=1}^{t} (1 - \beta h)^{t-s}\eta(s). \tag{3.20}$$

In a stable dynamic system, the absolute value of $(1 - \beta h)$ must be less than unity, since too much nominal wage flexibility is a destabilizing influence. However, the magnitude and duration of deviations from the equilibrium rate of unemployment depend upon the time pattern of the random price forecast errors $\eta(s)$. The greater the variance of the price forecast errors, the greater is the variance of the deviation from full employment.

3.3 *Price level forecast errors as sources of unemployment rate deviations*

The price forecast error $\eta(t) = \ln p(t) - \ln p_{t-1}^*(t)$ is the factor which leads to the deviation of the unemployment rate from its equilibrium rate. It is now shown to be a function of three variables: (i) the unanticipated growth of the money stock; (ii) the unanticipated fiscal and real exogenous disturbances; and (iii) the structure of the economic system. There is, however, no relation between the deviation of the unemployment rate from its equilibrium value and either monetary or fiscal variables *per se*. Only *unanticipated* disturbances have effects upon these variables, and these disturbances have no structure. Although monetary or fiscal policy cannot affect the speed at which the unemployment rate returns to its equilibrium value, there are policies which can conceivably diminish the sensitivity of the real variables to unanticipated disturbances.

To complete the analysis of NCE, the rate of price change equation (2.7) and the nominal interest rate equation (2.6) should satisfy two conditions. Then real variables are independent of nominal variables. First, aggregate real excess demand for goods $J(t)$ depends upon the real, rather than upon the nominal, rate of interest. Secondly, the nominal rate of interest (in equation (2.6)) fully reflects the rationally anticipated inflation.

Specifically, we write the real Keynesian excess demand for goods equation $J(t)$ as

$$J(t) = J(U(t) - U_e, \ln m(t), \rho(t) - E\pi^*; z(t)), \tag{3.21}$$

where $U(t) - U_e$ corresponds to $y(t)$, the ratio of actual to capacity output, $\ln m(t) = \ln M(t) - \ln p(t)$ is the logarithm of real balances, and $\rho(t) - E\pi^*$ is the real rate of interest, the nominal rate $\rho(t)$ less the rationally anticipated rate of inflation $E\pi^*$ over the relevant time period. Variable $z(t)$ subsumes fiscal policy variables, such as real government purchases of goods and tax rates, and exogenous disturbances, such as foreign demand for our exports and foreign prices measured in domestic currency.

Interest rate equation (2.6) is specified as

$$\rho(t) = E\pi^* + i(U(t) - U_e, \ln m(t); z(t)). \tag{3.22}$$

By substituting (3.22) into (3.21), a real excess demand for goods can be derived which just depends upon real variables. This is

$$J(t) = J^*[U(t) - U_e, \ln m(t); z(t)]. \tag{3.23}$$

If (3.23) is substituted into price change equation (2.7), and this equation is written as $\pi(t) = \pi^* - hu(t) + \gamma J(t) \equiv \pi^* + P(u, m; z)$, then the linearized result is equation (3.24). The price level is

$$\ln p(t) = E_{t-1} \ln p(t) + P_1 u(t) + P_2 [\ln M(t) - \ln p(t)] + z(t), \tag{3.24}$$

where $u(t) \equiv U(t) - U_e$. The mathematical expectation of the price level $E_{t-1} \ln p(t)$ is immediately derived from (3.24) by taking expectations E_{t-1}:

$$E_{t-1} \ln p(t) = E_{t-1} \ln M(t) + \frac{P_1}{P_2} E_{t-1} u(t) + \frac{1}{P_2} E_{t-1} z(t). \tag{3.25}$$

The expectation of the unemployment rate deviation $u(t)$ is described by equation (3.19a) above. Therefore, the mathematical expectation of the price level is

$$E_{t-1} \ln p(t) = E_{t-1} \ln M(t) + \frac{P_1}{P_2} (1 - \beta h) u(t-1) + \frac{1}{P_2} E_{t-1} z(t). \tag{3.26}$$

Alternatively, the expected rate of inflation $E_{t-1}\pi(t)$ is derived from (3.26) by subtracting $\ln p(t-1)$ from both sides. It is described by equation (3.27) below[5] which states that the expected rate of inflation $E_{t-1}\pi(t)$ changes by the same amount as the expected rate of monetary expansion $E_{t-1}\mu(t)$, given: (i) the previous period's values of real balances $\ln m(t-1)$ and the unemployment rate deviation $u(t-1)$; and (ii) the expected fiscal and real disturbances $E_{t-1}z(t)$.

$$E_{t-1}\pi(t) = E_{t-1}\mu(t) + \ln m(t-1) + \frac{P_1}{P_2}(1 - \beta h)u(t-1) + \frac{1}{P_2} E_{t-1} z(t). \tag{3.27}$$

Equations (3.16) and (3.24) permit us to solve for the unemployment rate and the price level. The method of solution is important in understanding the content and significance of NCE. The expectation E_{t-1} of (3.16) is taken and subtracted from (3.16) to obtain equation (3.28). The expectation E_{t-1} of (3.24) is taken and subtracted from (3.24) to obtain equation (3.29). Variable $\mu(t) - E_{t-1}\mu(t) \equiv \ln M(t) - E_{t-1} \ln M(t)$ is unanticipated money growth and $z(t) - E_{t-1}z(t)$ represents unanticipated fiscal and real disturbances:

$$[u(t) - E_{t-1}u(t)] + \beta[\ln p(t) - E_{t-1} \ln p(t)] = 0. \tag{3.28}$$

$$\begin{aligned} -P_1[u(t) - E_{t-1}u(t)] + (1+P_2)[\ln p(t) - E_{t-1} \ln p(t)] \\ = P_2[\mu(t) - E_{t-1}\mu(t)] + [z(t) - E_{t-1}z(t)]. \end{aligned} \tag{3.29}$$

These equations are solved for the unanticipated price level, or unanticipated inflation, to derive equation (3.30). This is precisely the forecast error $\eta(t)$ that produces the deviation of the unemployment rate from the equilibrium level:

$$\ln p(t) - E_{t-1} \ln p(t) \equiv \pi(t) - E_{t-1}\pi(t)$$
$$= (1 + P_2 + \beta P_1)^{-1}\{P_2[\mu(t) - E_{t-1}\mu(t)]$$
$$+ [z(t) - E_{t-1}z(t)]\} = \eta(t). \qquad (3.30)$$

It has been shown that the forecast error $\eta(t)$ is a function of three variables: unanticipated money growth $\mu(t) - E_{t-1}\mu(t)$; unanticipated fiscal policy and real disturbances $z(t) - E_{t-1}z(t)$; and the structure of the economy described by coefficients P_2 and $(1 + P_2 + \beta P_1)$.

By using equation (3.30) explicitly in (3.16), the unemployment rate deviation $u(t)$ is written as

$$u(t) = (1 - \beta h)u(t-1) - \frac{\beta}{(1 + P_2 + P_1\beta)}\{P_2[\mu(t) - E_{t-1}\mu(t)]$$
$$+ [z(t) - E_{t-1}z(t)]\}. \qquad (3.31)$$

Policy Ineffectiveness Proposition (3.11) is an immediate consequence of (3.31). There is no way that monetary or fiscal policy can affect the speed at which the unemployment rate returns to its equilibrium value. The *policies* are defined as $E_{t-1}\mu(t)$ and $E_{t-1}z(t)$ respectively; only the unanticipated changes have real effects. Therefore, *NCE claims that the expectation of the unemployment rate $E_{t-1}u(t)$ is insensitive to demand management policies.*

3.4   The transmission mechanism

The essence of NCE is fully described by equations (3.31) and (3.26). Figure 3.5 is a graphic portrayal of the dynamics of the unemployment rate deviation, equation (3.31), whose closed form solution is equation (3.20). When $\eta(t) = 0$, equation (3.31) is described by the curve $E_{t-1}u(t)$ in figure 3.5, which is equation (3.19a).

Suppose that the unemployment rate were substantially above the equilibrium rate, $u(t-1) = 0A$, in figure 3.5. On average, there will be no forecast error of the price level. Hence, due to the excess unemployment $u(t-1) > 0$, nominal wages are expected to rise less rapidly than prices. The real wage is expected to decline, and the expected unemployment rate $E_{t-1}u(t)$ is $AB = 0C$. Unemployment is expected to decline by AC.

An announced rise in the rate of monetary expansion raises the expected rate of inflation by the same amount, as described by equation

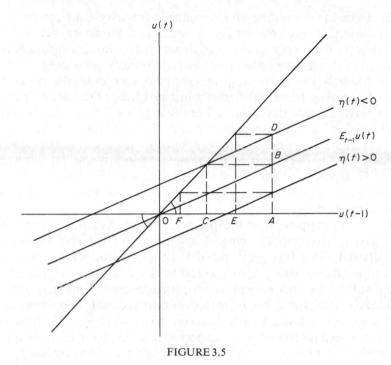

FIGURE 3.5

(3.27). Since wage bargains are over the real wage, the anticipation of more inflation simply raises the growth of the nominal wage by the same amount. No further change occurs in the real wage $w(t)$. Nominal wages and prices rise by the same amount as the higher rate of monetary expansion. Line $E_{t-1}u(t)$, the expected unemployment rate deviation, is unaffected by the anticipated monetary policy.

If the rise in the rate of monetary expansion were less than anticipated, then $\eta(t)$ is negative. The unemployment curve in figure 3.5 is the line labelled $\eta(t) < 0$. As equation (3.30) indicates, prices rise by less than were expected when wage bargains were made, and employers find that the real wage is higher than anticipated. In this case, the unemployment rate would decline to $0E$ which exceeds $0C$, the rate that would have occurred had there been no unanticipated demand management policy. To be sure, if the money growth were in excess of the anticipated rate, then $\eta(t)$ would be positive. Prices would rise by more than was anticipated in the wage bargains. The real wage would decline by more than the amount produced by the excess unemployment, and unemployment rate deviation would decline to $0F$.

By deceiving the public, the monetary authority is able to lower the unemployment rate below its expected value. However, according to NCE people learn very quickly and do not make the same mistake twice in succession, thus forecast errors are not serially correlated. Over the cycle, the policy of producing forecast errors increases the variance of $\eta(t)$. According to closed form solution (3.20), the variance of the unemployment rate deviation is thereby increased. Graphically, a non-predictable monetary policy means that there are parallel shifts of the curve in figure 3.5 about the curve labelled $E_{t-1}u(t)$. Instead of expecting deviation $0A$ to decline to $0C$ in the next period, it could decline to $0F$ or to $0E$, depending upon the realized forecast error. A non-systematic monetary policy does not change the average unemployment rate — it just raises its variance.[6]

Similarly, suppose that the foreign demand for our exports were expected to rise steadily, when the unemployment rate deviation is initially $0A$. This foreign demand is subsumed under $E_{t-1}z(t)$ in the equations above. Prices are expected to rise (equations (3.25), (3.27)) as a result of the greater expected foreign demand. The wage bargains will take this higher expected inflation into account, and the resulting real wage $w(t)$ will not be any different from what it would have been had there been no change in the expected foreign demand. The expected unemployment rate deviation would be fully described by line $E_{t-1}u(t)$ in figure 3.5 or equation (3.19a).

3.5 *Stabilization policies implied by NCE*

Stagflation is a term describing the situation where high unemployment rates coexist with high inflation rates. According to the logic of NCE, what produces stagflation and how can it be reduced at minimum social cost?

According to equation (3.31) or (3.20), high deviations of the unemployment rate from its equilibrium value are due to a run of rates of monetary expansion $\mu(t)$ *below* their expected values $E_{t-1}\mu(t)$, or to a run of fiscal policy inputs or real disturbances *below* their expected values. Formally, there must have been a run of negative values of $\eta(s)$. Consequently, the anticipated price level used in wage negotiations must have exceeded the realized price level. The real wage was unduly high, thereby raising the unemployment ratio, as described by the curve labelled $\eta(t) < 0$ in figure 3.5.

On average, high inflation rates (according to equation (3.27)) are produced by high rates of monetary expansion and also possibly by large fiscal and real disturbances. Nevertheless, the economy must have anticipated even higher rates of monetary expansion than were realized, in order to produce high unemployment rate deviations. Therefore, the logic of NCE implies that stagflation is produced by *high* and *overanticipated* rates of monetary expansion and real disturbances.

Anticipated monetary policy can reduce the rate of inflation quickly and significantly, without any social cost in terms of increases in the unemployment rate deviation. It has already been shown that correctly anticipated money growth, $\mu(t) - E_{t-1}\mu(t) = 0$ in equation (3.31), has no effect upon the unemployment rate. Unemployment rate deviation $u(t)$ will converge asymptotically to zero, as long as there are no unanticipated monetary and fiscal disturbances, as described by equation (3.20) when $\eta(s) = 0$.

Moreover, a one percentage point change in the expected rate of monetary expansion changes the expected rate of inflation by one percentage point, as described by equation (3.27). Therefore, the monetary authority should commit itself to a constant rate of monetary expansion μ equal to the target rate of inflation. Then the rate of inflation will converge to this rate of monetary expansion without any adverse effects upon the unemployment rate. For this reason, NCE claims that: "... policy makers face no 'cruel choice' between inflation and unemployment over any time frame" (Sargent, 1976a: 213–14).

There is no reason why a "gradual" reduction in the rate of monetary expansion is preferable to a drastic reduction, as long as the policy is communicated to the public in advance so that there are no forecast errors. In fact, there may be less uncertainty about monetary policy if the monetary authority announces a target rate of monetary expansion and adheres to it than if the rate of monetary expansion is lowered gradually to the ultimate target.

Policy can also be formulated to keep the economy near the equilibrium rate of unemployment with a minimum of inflation. First, the monetary growth rate should be easily predictable. Secondly, at the equilibrium rate of unemployment, the monetary growth rate should equal the long-term growth of the economy so that there will be no inflation. Thirdly, if possible the current monetary growth rate should be a built-in stabilizer which varies positively with the current employment rate deviation.[7]

Specifically, let the current rate of monetary expansion $\mu(t)$ be described by equation (3.32) (when the long-term growth rate of the economy is zero). It is positively related to the current unemployment rate deviation:

$$\mu(t) = c_1 u(t). \tag{3.32}$$

In the control theory literature, this is called a "direct control." It can be implemented if all government budget deficits or surpluses are financed by money, and taxes net of transfers are proportional to nominal income. In equation (2.9), let the number of bonds be zero $DB = b = 0$ and real taxes per capita $T(.) = \tau y$. Then the rate of monetary expansion $\mu(t)$ is

$$\mu(t) = \frac{g - \tau y(t)}{m(t)} \tag{3.33}$$

As the unemployment rate rises, output *per capita* $y(t)$ declines, and the rate of monetary expansion rises automatically.

Under these conditions, the anticipated money growth $\mu(t) - E_{t-1} \mu(t)$ is a multiple c_1 of the unanticipated unemployment rate deviation:

$$\mu(t) - E_{t-1}\mu(t) = c_1 [u(t) - E_{t-1}u(t)]. \tag{3.34}$$

By substituting (3.34) into (3.29) and using (3.28), the unanticipated rate of inflation or unanticipated price level can be derived:

$$\ln p(t) - E_{t-1} \ln p(t) \equiv \pi(t) - E_{t-1} \pi(t)$$

$$= \frac{z(t) - E_{t-1}z(t)}{(1 + P_2) + \beta(P_1 + c_1 P_2)}. \tag{3.35}$$

Unanticipated disturbances to the price level only arise from fiscal policy and exogenous variables, since the rate of monetary expansion is determined by control law (3.32). Therefore, the unemployment rate deviation (3.31) can be written as

$$u(t) = (1 - \beta h)u(t - 1) - \frac{\beta}{(1 + P_2) + \beta(P_1 + c_1 P_2)}$$
$$[z(t) - E_{t-1} z(t)]. \tag{3.36}$$

The greater is the "built-in stabilizer" c_1, the smaller are the effects of unanticipated disturbances $z(t) - E_{t-1}z(t)$ upon the employment rate deviation. The reason is that, in formulation (3.32), there is no "lag" between the state of the economy $u(t)$ and the control input $\mu(t)$. Disturbances $z(t) - E_{t-1}z(t)$ tend to affect unemployment rate deviation $u(t)$ immediately. But as soon as $u(t)$ varies, the rate of monetary expansion $\mu(t)$ also changes, and the counterbalancing effect of unanticipated money growth $\mu(t) - E_{t-1}\mu(t) = c_1 [u(t) - E_{t-1}u(t)]$ is also immediate.[8]

This argument breaks down completely is there is a lag between the rate of monetary expansion $\mu(t)$ and the state of the economy. For example, if the control law were

$$\mu(t) = c_0 u(t - 1),\tag{3.37}$$

then there would be no unanticipated monetary changes because[9]

$$\mu(t) - E_{t-1}\mu(t) = c_0 u(t - 1) - E_{t-1}c_0 u(t - 1) = 0.\tag{3.38}$$

When the rate of monetary expansion responds to the state of the economy with a lag, it is not possible (in equation (3.31)) for unanticipated monetary changes to offset unanticipated fiscal policy and exogenous disturbances.

In that case, the best that policymakers can do is to follow an easily predictable money growth rule that produces a rate of monetary expansion equal to the long-term growth in the economy, when the unemployment rate is at its equilibrium value. A constant rate of monetary expansion equal to the long-term growth rate is a special case of this policy. The value of c_0 in equation (3.37) could be any fixed number. Demand management policy can only increase the variance of the unemployment rate deviation. Policy makers should select a monetary policy which is easily predictable, and, in order to avoid inflation, it should produce a rate of monetary expansion equal to the long-term growth of the economy.

3.6 "Market clearing" is not necessary for the Policy Ineffectiveness Proposition

Both NCE and its critics emphasize the importance of "market clearing" for NCE policy conclusions. Tobin writes

Of course, the twin assumptions — market clearing and rational expectations — are essential [for NCE policy conclusions]. (1980: 42)

Equation (3.31) above, which characterizes NCE, was *not* derived on the assumption of market clearing, namely, that there are zero excess demands for goods and labor. Nevertheless, the Policy Ineffectiveness Proposition is derived, along with the implication that there never is a trade-off between unemployment and inflation over any time span. My analysis above, therefore, proves that the market-clearing assumption is not necessary for NCE.

My analysis is based upon a complex model. Consider a very simple model, which is NCE in spirit. I show very simply that the market-clearing assumption is not necessary for NCE results.

Equation (3.39) is the supply equation. The logarithm of output supplied relative to capacity output, $y^s(t)$, is a function of the unanticipated price level, where $p(t)$ is the logarithm of the price level and disturbances $\varepsilon(t)$ which have zero expectations:

$$y^s(t) = \gamma[p(t) - E_{t-1}p(t)] + \varepsilon(t). \tag{3.39}$$

Equation (3.40) is the demand equation. The logarithm of output demanded relative to capacity output, $y^d(t)$, is a function of the logarithm of real balances $m(t) - p(t)$ and disturbance term $v(t)$. This equation is a simple money demand equation solved for the output demanded:

$$y^d(t) = m(t) - p(t) + v(t). \tag{3.40}$$

Equation (3.41) determines the price level $p(t)$ as the sum of the anticipated price level $E_{t-1}p(t)$ and a constant α times the excess demand for goods $y^d(t) - y^s(t)$. If market clearing always occurred, α would be infinite, and $y^d(t) = y^s(t)$. Insofar as $\infty > \alpha > 0$, markets are not always in equilibrium:

$$p(t) = E_{t-1}p(t) + \alpha [y^d(t) - y^s(t)]. \tag{3.41}$$

By solving for the unanticipated price level,[10] equation (3.42) can be derived:

$$[p(t) - E_{t-1}p(t)] = \frac{\alpha}{1 + \alpha(1 + \gamma)} \{ [m(t) - E_{t-1}m(t)] + [v(t) - \varepsilon(t)] \}. \tag{3.42}$$

Equation (3.42) can be substituted into (3.39) to derive the ratio of actual to capacity output, which corresponds to the unemployment rate:

$$y^s(t) = \frac{\alpha\gamma}{1 + \alpha(1 + \gamma)} \{ [m(t) - E_{t-1}m(t)] + [v(t) - \varepsilon(t)] \} + \varepsilon(t). \tag{3.43}$$

The Policy Ineffectiveness Proposition, the Policy Evaluation Proposition and the other basic NCE propositions follow immediately from equation (3.43), even though ($\infty > \alpha > 0$) markets are not always in equilibrium. The mathematical expectation of the Okun Gap is independent of demand management policy $E_{t-1}m(t)$. Therefore, the market-clearing assumption is not necessary to derive the NCE propositions.

4 Monetarism

4.1 *Sufficient conditions for Monetarist propositions*

The main tenets of what I define as Monetarism are summarized by a series of empirical propositions.

[M1] Inflation is primarily a monetary phenomenon. Contrary to the Keynesian view, a restrictive fiscal policy without a reduction in the rate of monetary expansion cannot significantly reduce the rate of inflation.

[M2] Stagflation results from a policy whereby the rate of monetary expansion is raised when the unemployment rate is too high and is lowered when the rate of inflation is too high.

[M3] A rise in the rate of monetary expansion above the current rate of inflation raises the rate of inflation, even when the unemployment rate exceeds the equilibrium rate. This is contrary to the Keynesian view.

[M4] There is no relation between a constant rate of inflation and the unemployment rate. Contrary to NCE, there is a short-run trade-off between the speed at which inflation is reduced and the temporary rise in the unemployment rate. A decline in the rate of monetary expansion below the current rate of inflation temporarily raises the unemployment rate relative to the equilibrium rate, by lowering real aggregate demand and by producing forecast errors between the actual and anticipated rates of inflation. Even an anticipated rise in the growth of monetary aggregates over the next few years (e.g. due to a war) leads to a temporary decline in the unemployment rate. Similarly, an announced program of monetary deceleration below the current rate of inflation (e.g. by the newly elected Conservative government in the UK) leads to a temporary rise in the unemployment rate. This proposition contradicts the NCE Policy Ineffectiveness Proposition (equation (3.11) above), whereby there is no trade-off *at any time* between the deceleration of an inflation and the trajectory of the unemployment rate. There is a social cost to reducing the rate of inflation, which is less than the Keynesians estimate and more than the NCE asserts.

These propositions can be derived from the general dynamic model, summarized in table 2.1, by imposing certain parameter specifications. The Monetarist specification is described by three equations in table 3.1 below, which are now derived.

Equation (3.44) describes the rate of change of the unemployment rate. It is the continuous time counterpart of the discrete time equation (3.16) used in connection with NCE. By differentiating the unemployment rate equation (2.3) with respect to time and substituting (2.4) for the proportionate rate of change of the adjusted real wage, we obtain

$$DU(t) = -\beta h[U(t) - U_e] - \beta[\pi(t) - \pi^*(t)]; \quad D \equiv d/dt.$$
(3.44)

The first term on the right-hand side represents the adjustment of the aggregate unemployment rate to its equilibrium value, when there are no forecast errors of the price level in the wage bargaining process. The speed of response is reflected by ccoefficient βh. If the nominal wage is not very responsive to deviations of the unemployment rate from its equilibrium value (i.e. h is small), then the convergence to equilibrium is very slow. A typical Keynesian argument is that βh is small, so that demand management policy should be used to accelerate the convergence to the equilibrium rate of unemployment. The second term represents the forecast error between the realized price level and the level that was anticipated in the wage bargaining process. Insofar as $\pi(t) - \pi^*(t)$ is not zero, the ex-post real wage differs from the level that was anticipated. This term reflects the unanticipated changes in the demand for labor.

There is no theoretical reason why equation (3.44) cannot be accepted by all three schools of thought. Moreover, it was shown in equation (2.20) that the evidence from 1948 through 1979 is consistent with the hypothesis that the unemployment rate responds to real unit labor costs, which is the empirical counterpart of the adjusted real wage.

Disagreement among the schools of thought is focused upon the actual and anticipated rates of price change, that is, equations (2.7) and (2.10a, b). This is reflected in a quasi-reduced form of the rate of price change equation. By substituting the interest rate equation (2.6) into the rate of inflation equation (2.7) we obtain

$$\pi(t) = \pi^*(t) + P[U(t) - U_e, m(t), \pi^*(t); k(t), g(t), \theta(t)], \quad (3.45a)$$
where $P(.) \equiv -h[U(t) - U_e] + \gamma J(.)$.

A convenient linear version of (3.45a) is (3.45b), where real balances $m(t)$ enter in logarithmic form and $u(t)$ is $U(t) - U_e$. (In this chapter and the next, $k(t)$ will be treated as a constant and ignored. It is the focus of our attention in chapter 5.)

$$\pi(t) = \pi^*(t) + P_1 u(t) + P_2 \ln m(t) + P_3 \pi^*(t) + P_4 g(t)$$
$$+ P_5 \theta(t). \tag{3.45b}$$

Several parameter specifications are sufficient to generate Monetarist results [M1] – [M4] above.

[A1] Inflationary anticipations adjusted for risk are generated by ARE equation (2.10b), where coefficient c is positive and finite. NCE results tend to occur as c approaches infinity; Keynesian results tend to occur as c approaches zero.

[A2] Given the height of the aggregate demand function, the level of unemployment *per se* has a weak effect upon the rate of inflation. The relevant variable for the rate of inflation is the Keynesian excess demand gap, not the Okun Gap between actual and capacity output. Formally, coefficient $P_1 \equiv \partial P/\partial U$ is assumed to be small in absolute value.

[A3] A rising ratio of debt to money, resulting from continuing budget deficits, raises real rates of interest and adversely affects investment. This is the crowding-out effect, which dominates the wealth effect in the consumption function. Eventually, excess aggregate demand is lowered by the rise in the debt–money ratio. Formally, $P_5 \equiv \partial P/\partial \theta$ is assumed to be negative. Keynesians assume that P_5 is positive, so that a growing debt (given the money stock) raises excess aggregate demand.

[A4] It is convenient, but not necessary, to assume that there is a Fisher effect whereby a unit rise in the (risk-adjusted) anticipated rate of inflation raises the relevant nominal rate of interest by the same amount. Formally, $P_3 = 0$.

The rationale for these parameter specifications is now discussed.

Asymptotically Rational Expectations[11]
The effective anticipated rate of inflation π^*, which affects the inflation of nominal unit labor costs DW/W with a unitary coefficient, is the composition of several functions. In chapter 2 the relation between the current rate of monetary expansion $\mu(t)$ and the effective anticipated rate of inflation was described schematically as

$$DW/W \leftarrow \pi^* \leftarrow E\pi \leftarrow E\mu \leftarrow \mu.$$

There are frictions in each link, thereby producing a differential response of the effective anticipated rate of inflation to the current rate of monetary expansion. Each friction is discussed in turn.

First, there is the connection between the current rate of monetary expansion $\mu(t)$ and the average rate of monetary expansion $E\mu$ that the public believes will be pursued by the monetary authorities. This lag is often referred to as the credibility problem.

Suppose that the monetary authority has produced quarterly changes in the rate of monetary expansion, with a mean $E\mu_1$ and a standard deviation of σ_1. At time $t = 0$, it announces that it is pursuing a less expansionary monetary policy. In view of past experience, the public is skeptical. How long will it take for the public to accept the opinion that a new and lower mean rate of monetary expansion $E\mu_2 < E\mu_1$ is being pursued? How long will it take for the new policy to be credible? Meyer and Webster (1981) approached this problem by using a Bayesian framework. I suggest a simpler approach which yields approximately the same results.

Consider the problem in terms of statistical inference. From $t = 0$, $1, 2, \ldots, n$, there will be observed n quarterly rates of monetary expansion $\mu(t)$. How large a sample size n (i.e. how many quarters) is required for the public to be able to estimate the new mean rate of monetary expansion $E\mu_2$ with a given degree of confidence, denoted by Pr?

The solution is quite simple. The public considers a sample of $\mu(t)$ over n quarters, which has a mean of $\bar{\mu}$, and it desires to estimate the new population mean $E\mu$. The distribution of sample means around the population mean $E\mu$ is

$$t(Pr) = \frac{\bar{\mu} - E\mu}{\sigma/\sqrt{n}}. \tag{3.46a}$$

According to the Central Limit Theorem, the distribution of the sample means approaches the normal distribution as the sample size n increases. For $n > 10$, the approximation is nearly normal.

The required sample size n, that is, the number of quarters, is

$$n = \frac{\sigma^2 t(Pr)^2}{(\bar{\mu} - E\mu)^2}. \tag{3.46b}$$

There are three components of the required sample size n. (i) What accuracy, or distance between the sample mean $\bar{\mu}$ and the unknown population mean $E\mu$, is desired? The closer the estimate, that is, the smaller the distance $(\bar{\mu} - E\mu)^2$, the larger is the necessary sample size.

(ii) What confidence interval does the public desire? The higher the probability that the unknown population mean is a given distancce from the sample mean, the larger is the required sample size. (iii) The greater is the standard deviation of the rate of money growth, the larger is the required sample size.

Consider the following example. From the last quarter of 1976 through the last quarter of 1979, the *quarterly* rate of M1B monetary expansion (expressed as a per cent per annum) had the following mean and standard deviation:

mean   7.96
standard deviation 1.69.

From February 1980 through August 1981, the *monthly* rate of monetary expansion (expressed as a per cent per annum) had the following mean and standard deviation:

mean   6.742
standard deviation 11.135.

It can be seen immediately that monthly data have very high coefficients of variation, and reasonable estimates of population means require many months of observations.[12] Quarterly, rather than monthly, observations should be used.

Suppose that a new policy is announced at the end of 1979 that a more restrictive monetary policy is to be followed. Suppose that the public assumes that the same standard deviation $\sigma = 1.69$ characterizes the new population, and it wants to estimate the new mean rate of monetary expansion $E\mu_2$ within one or two percentage points. Then the following sample size or number of quarterly observations is required for the 95% and 99% confidence intervals.

$\bar{\mu} - E\mu$	$t(95\%) = 1.96$	$t(99\%) = 2.576$
1	$n = 10.97$ quarters	18.95 quarters
2	2.74	4.74

If the public wants to be 95 per cent sure that the unknown population mean is within 2 percentage points of the sample mean, it is required to sample 3 quarters of observations. If it insists on being 99 per cent sure that the unknown population mean is within one percentage point of the sample mean, it must have a sample size of 19 quarters. Therefore, the lag between the currently announced change in policy and the public's acceptance of the change depends upon (i) the previous volatility of monetary growth σ, and (ii) the level of confidence required $t(Pr)$.

The degree of confidence required should be related to the consistency of the new policy with the relation described in (2.49) that the mathematical expectation of the rate of monetary expansion $E_t\mu(t + 1)$ is directly related to the ratio of the *high* employment deficit to the money stock in the previous year $F^H(t)/M(t)$. This relation explains 63 per cent of the variance of the annual rate of monetary expansion. If there has been no reduction in $F^H(t)/M(t)$, then an announced restrictive monetary policy is not too credible. The public would then require a high degree of probability $t(Pr)$ that there has indeed been a change in policy. Consequently, a larger sample size is required to induce the public to alter its evaluation of monetary policy. The required sample size n is the lag $\mu \rightarrow E\mu$ described above.

Secondly, there is a lag $(E\mu \rightarrow E\pi)$ between the expected rate of inflation and the expected rate of monetary expansion because economic agents consist of Keynesians, Monetarists and New Classical economists (among others), with different models concerning the speed at which the economy converges to a commonly accepted steady state. Keynesians look at the "underlying rate of inflation," which is the rate of inflation of unit labor costs, and regard the inflation of material prices as exogenous and transitory. Since the inflation of nominal unit labor costs lags behind the expansion of the economy (see table 2.4), the Keynesians among economic agents do not raise their anticipated rate of inflation quickly to correspond with the higher rate of monetary expansion. They attribute the price rises to exogenous, and possible ephemeral, rises in raw material prices. Others rely on the historical evidence concerning the long lags between changes in the rate of monetary expansion and the rate of inflation. Most economic agents probably share Modigliani's view that the relation between money and prices is only valid in the long run. In the short run, it is affected by the rate of capacity utilization and is dominated by special factors such as exogenous shocks to the prices of domestically produced raw materials and imports.

Since the unemployment rate $U(76) = 7.7$ per cent exceeded the Keynesian estimate of a non-inflationary equilibrium rate of unemployment of 5.5 per cent, they did not expect inflation to accelerate in 1977. The Carter Council of Economic Advisers, in their Report transmitted in January 1978, explained the inflation at the time as follows.

After initial moderation in 1975, the rate of inflation remains high and relatively stable. The rate of increase of consumer prices fell from 1975 to

1976, but then rose again in 1977. These fluctuations were principally due to erratic variations in food and energy prices. Excluding those two categories, consumer prices rose at almost the same 6 to $6\frac{1}{2}$ percent rate in each year from 1975 through 1977 . . . .

Even allowing for delays in the response of wages and prices to underlying changes in demand, the failure of prices and wages to decelerate over the past several years starkly illustrates the strength of the forces that support inflation in the face of substantial economic slack. (1978: 142)

The second lag would not exist if there were a commonly accepted dynamic model of the economy.

Thirdly there is the lag $E\pi \rightarrow \pi^*$ between the expected rate of inflation $E\pi$ and the effective risk-adjusted anticipated rate of inflation π^* which affects the growth of nominal unit labor costs, with a coefficient of unity. In Chapter 2, equation (2.60), it was proved that, when there is risk aversion in an uncertain world $\alpha\sigma^2 > 0$, the response of output $q(t)$ to a change in expected price $E_t p(t + 1)$ is reduced. The equation is

$$\frac{dq(t)}{dE_t p \, (t + 1)} = \frac{1}{\alpha\sigma^2 + c}. \tag{2.60}$$

When the expected price rises, the demand for labor and other inputs rises by less than would occur if there were certainty. Consequently, there is less upward pressure upon nominal wages than would occur if firms were risk neutral. This is the friction between the expected rate of inflation $E\pi$ and the risk-adjusted anticipated rate of inflation π^* which enters directly into the inflation of nominal unit labor costs. In the steady state, the gap between $E\pi$ and π^* tends to zero.

Fourthly, Taylor (1979) and others have argued that the adjustment of nominal wages to anticipated inflation depends upon the staggered wage contract mechanism. To what extent are wage contracts forward looking and to what extent are they backward looking? The more forward looking is the contract determination, the smaller is the lag between π^* and DW/W.

All these lags are subsumed under ARE equation (2.10b), repeated here:

$$D\pi^*(t) = c[\mu(t) - \pi^*(t)]. \tag{2.10b}$$

The speed of response c, which is inversely related to the length of the four lags, depends upon the predictability of the relation between current monetary input and the rate of inflation.

Inflation is not closely related to the Okun Gap

A second Monetarist assumption [A2] is that the rate of inflation is significantly related to the Keynesian excess demand for goods and the state of the labor market. But there is no clear relation between the rate of inflation and the Okun Gap.

Consider figure 2.2 when the economy is producing output y_1 which is below capacity output $f(k(t), t) \equiv 1$. Distance $1 - y_1 > 0$ is the Okun Gap. Suppose that the aggregate demand curve is currently at $A_1 A_1'$. A Keynesian excess demand gap of $C_2 C_1 > 0$ coexists with an Okun Gap of $1 - y_1 > 0$.

Given the height of the aggregate demand curve, for example $A_1 A_1'$, the level of output or unemployment *per se* has a weak effect upon the rate of inflation for the following reason. At output y_1 there is an unemployment rate U_1 which exceeds the equilibrium rate U_e, but there is also a Keynesian excess demand for goods $C_2 C_1 > 0$. The excess unemployment $U_1 - U_e > 0$ reduces the cost-push pressure from nominal unit labor costs. However, the Keynesian excess demand for goods $C_2 C_1 > 0$ is a source of demand-pull pressures. These two forces tend to counterbalance each other. Formally, this view is summarized by the assumption that P_1 is approximately zero, where

$$P_1 = - h + \gamma \frac{\partial J}{\partial y} \frac{\mathrm{d}y}{\mathrm{d}U} \approx 0,$$

which is based upon inflation equation (2.7) or (3.45a) and Okun's Law. The first term on the right-hand side reflects the labor market and the second term reflects the product market.

Upward and downward *shifts* of the aggregate demand curve are produced by changes in real balances. When the latter rises, the aggregate demand curve associated with any level of output or unemployment rate rises, and the inflation rate tends to accelerate. This parameter specification concerning the shift of the aggregate demand curve is summarized by the assumption that P_2 in equation (3.45b) is significantly positive.

The effect of the debt – money ratio

Assumption [A3] is that bond-financed fiscal policy has a positive *impact* effect upon aggregate demand. If the resulting deficits are allowed to continue, however, then the *cumulative* effect upon aggregate demand eventually becomes negative.[13]

This "crowding-out" assumption is seen very clearly through the IS – LM paradigm in the real interest rate-output space. A unit rise in real government purchases initially shifts the IS curve upwards to the right. Given the real rate of interest, a higher level of output is produced. This is the *impact* effect of a rise in government expenditures.

When government expenditures are financed by bonds, the bond – money ratio θ rises. Two counterbalancing effects are produced: (i) the increase in private wealth raises to IS curve further to the right; (ii) to induce the public to absorb a higher ratio of bonds to money in their portfolios, the real rate of interest must rise — the LM curve shifts upwards. However, the rise in the real rate of interest reduces real aggregate demand. Monetarist assumption [A3] states that the net effect of (i) and (ii) is negative. The secondary shifts of the IS – LM curves resulting from the rise in the debt, given the stock of money, reduces the level of income.[14]

The accumulation of debt, resulting from continuing government deficits which are financed by bonds, continues to depress the level of income. Formally, the argument is as follows. A unit step rise in real government purchases at $t = 0$ initially raises real excess aggregate demand $J(.)$ by $\partial J/\partial g$. When government expenditures are financed by bonds, the bond – money ratio θ rises and produces two countervailing effects. The increase in private wealth further raises aggregate demand by $\partial J/\partial \theta$. The nominal rate of interest rises by $\partial p/\partial \theta$ to induce the public to alter its portfolio composition. A rise in the nominal rate of interest tends to reduce excess demand by $\partial J/\partial p$. The net effect of the bond-financed rise in real government expenditure upon excess aggregate demand is the sum of the conventional Keynesian multiplier $\partial J/\partial g$ and the effect of a cumulative change in the bond – money ratio:

$$\frac{\Delta J(t)}{\Delta g} = \frac{\partial J}{\partial g} + \left(\frac{\partial J}{\partial \theta} + \frac{\partial J}{\partial p} \frac{\partial p}{\partial \theta} \right) \frac{\Delta \theta(t)}{\Delta g}. \tag{3.47}$$

Specification [A3] states that the term in parentheses describing the stock effect is negative. As long as there is a bond-financed government deficit, $\Delta \theta(t)/\Delta g$ is positive and increases with time. Initially, impact effect $\Delta J/\Delta g$ is positive. As $\theta(t)$ rises, the second term on the right-hand side tends to dominate and $\Delta J(t)/\Delta g$ declines to zero. If the rise in $\theta(t)$ were allowed to continue, $\Delta J(t)/\Delta g$ would become negative.

It is shown in chapter 5 that bond-financed fiscal policy cannot be expected to be compatible with economic stability.[15] Consequently, $\theta(t)$ cannot be considered to be a state variable in a stable dynamic process.[16] Sooner or later, either the high employment deficit must be reduced, or some of the deficit must be financed with money. Monetarist specification [A3] states that the bond-financed fiscal policy effect $\Delta J(t)/\Delta g$ is approximately zero during a time span of one year. Specifically, *specification* [A3] *assumes that over a year* $\Delta[P_4 g(t) + P_5 \theta(t)]$ *is close to zero.*[17]

The Fisher Effect

It is convenient, but not necessary, to assume [A4] that there is a Fisher Effect in the interest rate equation. The Fisher Effect is defined as a situation where a unit rise in the (risk-adjusted) anticipated rate of inflation π^* raises the nominal rate of interest by approximately the same amount. In that case, the interest rate equation is of the form

$$i(t) \equiv \rho(t) - \pi^*(t) = i(y(t), m(t), k(t), \theta(t))$$
$$i_y > 0, i_m < 0, i_\theta > 0, \tag{3.48a}$$

which is a special case of equation (2.6). The *real rate of interest* $i(t)$ is independent of the anticipated rate of inflation.

Insofar as the excess demand for goods $J(t)$ depends upon the real rate of interest $i(t)$ and the real rate of interest is described by equation (3.48a), then $J(t)$ is independent of π^*. Formally, this means that P_3 in equation (3.45b) is assumed to be approximately equal to zero.

Assumption [A4] does not state that changes in the current or recent past rate of inflation $\pi(t)$ or $\pi(t - j)$ changes the nominal rate of interest by the same amount.[18] It is exclusively a relation between the anticipated rate of inflation π^* and the nominal rate of interest.

Specifications [A2] – [A4] imply that the time rate of change of the rate of inflation $D\pi(t)$, that is the acceleration of inflation, derived by differentiating equation (3.45b) with respect to time, is described by

$$D\pi(t) = D\pi^*(t) + P_2 D \ln m(t). \tag{3.48b}$$

It is assumed that P_1 and P_3 are zero, and that $\Delta[P_4 g(t) + P_5 \theta(t)]$ is also zero.

4.2   The Monetarist dynamical system and its graphic representation

The equations in table 3.1 summarize the Monetarist specification. Equation (3.49) is equation (3.44), where $u(t)$ is the unemployment rate deviation $U(t) - U_e$. Equation (3.51) is the ARE equation (2.10b), where the anticipated rate of inflation is measured as a deviation from the estimated steady-state value μ, the current rate of monetary expansion. Inflationary anticipations are adjusted differentially (i.e., not instantaneously) towards the current rate of monetary expansion. Equation (3.50) is equation (3.48b) when (i) equation (2.8) is substituted for $D\ln m(t)$; (ii) ARE equation (3.51) describes inflationary anticipations; and (iii) the rate of inflation is measured as a deviation from its estimated steady-state value μ, the constant rate of monetary expansion.[19]

TABLE 3.1   *The Monetarist specification of the general dynamic model.*

$$Du(t) = -\beta h u(t) - \beta[\pi(t) - \mu] + \beta[\pi^*(t) - \mu] \qquad (3.49)$$
$$D[\pi(t) - \mu] = -P_2[\pi(t) - \mu] - c[\pi^*(t) - \mu] \qquad (3.50)$$
$$D[\pi^*(t) - \mu] = \qquad\qquad\quad -c[\pi^*(t) - \mu] \qquad (3.51)$$

Symbols: $u(t) = U(t) - U_e$ is the deviation of unemployment rate from its equilibrium value; $\pi(t)$ is the rate of price inflation; $\pi^*(t)$ is the anticipated rate of inflation; μ is a constant rate of monetary expansion; and $D = d/dt$.

The eigenvalues λ_i are real and negative, so the system is dynamically stable:

$$\lambda_1 = -\beta h; \qquad \lambda_2 = -P_2; \qquad \lambda_3 = -c. \qquad (3.52)$$

The system converges to equilibrium along the slowest eigenvector. An analytic solution of the equations in table 3.1 is contained in the appendix to this chapter. The text analyzes the system graphically and in literary terms. If, as Keynesians and Monetarists believe, the labor market adjusts slowly, then the convergence to equilibrium along the eigenvector associated with $\lambda_1 = -\beta h$ takes a long time.

The dynamical system equations (3.49) – (3.51) in table 3.1 imply the Monetarist propositions. It is also shown that variations in the parameters of the Monetarist equations can produce NCE or Keynesian conclusions.

Define the medium-run equilibrium as a situation where the unemployment rate and inflation are constant, and there is no forecast error between the actual and anticipated rate of inflation. Then table 3.1 implies that (i) the unemployment rate is at its equilibrium value and (ii) the rate of inflation is equal to the rate of monetary expansion. Section 2 of this chapter describes in detail the medium-run equilibrium of this model.

It must be repeated that there are no disagreements among the three schools of thought concerning the steady-state properties of the economy. All the disagreement concerns the dynamic processes between steady states.

Monetarist table 3.1 describes a triangular dynamical system. If equation (3.51) is solved for the anticipated rate of price change, then, with the use of equation (3.50), the actual rate of price change can be determined. The implied forecast error between the actual and anticipated rate of price change is then used in equation (3.49) to determine the unemployment rate.

Figure 3.6 describes the unemployment rate equation, where the rate of change of the unemployment rate deviation $Du(t)$ is plotted against the current value of the unemployment role deviation $u(t)$. Slope $-\beta h$ represents the speed of adjustment as a function of nominal wage flexibility (h) and the response ($-\beta$) of the excess demand for labor to changes in the adjusted real wage. A steep curve reflects a fast adjustment, and a flat curve reflects a slow adjustment. The intercept term reflects the difference between the anticipated and the actual rate of inflation $\pi^*(t) - \pi(t)$. When there is no forecast error, the unemployment rate deviation converges to $u(t) = 0$. If there is unanticipated inflation, the unemployment rate tends towards point a; and, if the inflation is overanticipated, the unemployment rate tends towards point b.

The unanticipated inflation is derived by solving equations (3.50) and (3.51) and is described in figure 3.7. No change occurs in the

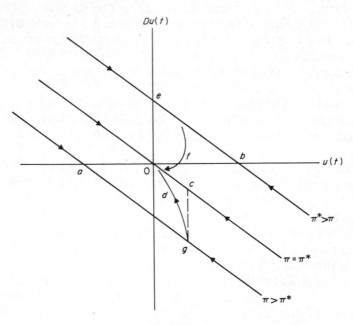

FIGURE 3.6

anticipated rate of inflation ($D\pi^* = 0$) when it is equal to its equilibrium value, the rate of monetary expansion μ. Therefore, along the horizontal axis where $\pi^* - \mu = 0$, there is no change in the anticipated rate of inflation. Insofar as $\pi^*(t)$ deviates from its steady-state value, the anticipated rate converges at rate c to the rate of monetary expansion. Vertical vectors describe the direction of movement of the anticipated rate of inflation to the rate of monetary expansion.

Equation (3.53) describes the line $D\pi = 0$. which is the locus of points where the rate of inflation is not changing. It is derived from equation (3.50) by equating $D[\pi(t) - \mu(t)]$ to zero:

$$[\pi^*(t) - \mu(t)] = \frac{-P_2}{c}[\pi(t) - \mu(t)]. \tag{3.53}$$

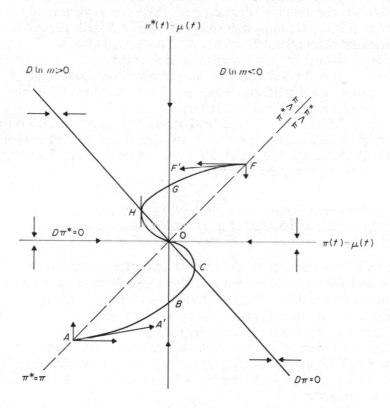

FIGURE 3.7

The change in the rate of inflation $D\pi(t)$ in equation (3.48b) is a combination of two elements: the change in real balances, which shifts the aggregate demand curve $P_2 D \ln m(t) = -P_2[\pi(t) - \mu(t)]$; and the change in anticipated rate of inflation $D\pi^*(t) = -c[\pi^*(t) - \mu(t)]$. Along line $D\pi = 0$, described by equation (3.53), these two effects cancel each other.

In the right half plane of figure 3.7 (quadrants I and IV), the rate of inflation exceeds the rate of monetary expansion, and hence $D \ln m < 0$ real balances decline. If the anticipated rate of inflation is equal to the rate of monetary expansion, there is no change in the anticipated rate of inflation. Therefore, the decline in real balances lowers aggregate demand and reduces the rate of inflation. The vectors along the horizontal axis describe this movement.

On the other hand, suppose that the rate of inflation is equal to the rate of monetary expansion so that $D \ln m = 0$ real balances are constant. If the anticipated rate of inflation is below the rate of monetary expansion, the anticipated rate rises. The vertical vectors along the vertical axis describe this movement. At point B both the actual and anticipated rates of inflation rise.

The horizontal vectors describe the movement of the actual rate of inflation, and the vertical vectors describe the movement of the anticipated rate of inflation. Along the 45° broken line, the actual and anticipated rates of inflation are equal.

Figures 3.6 and 3.7 describe the dynamics of the Monetarist model, whereby the unemployment rate converges to its equilibrium value, and both the actual and anticipated rates of price change converge to the rate of monetary expansion.

4.3   Monetarist propositions concerning demand management policies, the paradox of stagflation and the deceleration of inflation

The basic Monetarist propositions, which differentiate this view from NCE and Keynesian economics, emerge clearly from an analysis of figures 3.6 and 3.7. Although hypothesis testing and quantitative analysis are the subjects of chapter 4, actual examples are used to illustrate the implied trajectories of the dynamical system.

The phenomenon of "stagflation," namely high unemployment coexisting with high and rising inflation, cannot be explained (objectively and logically) within either a Keynesian or NCE framework. James Tobin wrote:

It is indeed difficult to give a rationale for the observed persistence of rising wages and prices coexisting with excess supply. It is difficult to give a convincing rationale with the paradigm of [NCE] utility and profit-maximizing behaviour in competitive models. (1980: 43)

The Monetarist analysis is that stagflation is the result of a policy which (i) substantially raises the rate of monetary expansion above the rate of inflation, when the unemployment rate is too high, and (ii) substantially lowers the rate of monetary expansion below the rate of inflation, when the rate of inflation is too high.

Figures 3.6 and 3.7 are used to show that stagflation can easily be explained within the Monetarist system. Let us start with a situation where: (i) the unemployment rate exceeds its equilibrium value $u(0) = 0b > 0$ in figure 3.6; (ii) both the actual and anticipated rates of inflation are equal $\pi^*(0) = \pi(0)$ in figure 3.7; and (iii) these inflation rates are equal to the rate of monetary expansion. The situation in 1976 would roughly correspond to these points. The unemployment rate was 7.7 per cent, the inflation rate of the GNP deflator was 5.2 per cent per annum, which is assumed to be the anticipated rate, and the rate of monetary expansion was 5.5 per cent per annum. For the purposes of explaining the Monetarist dynamics, consider the 1976 situation to be close to the origin in figure 3.7.

Let the rate of monetary expansion rise substantially (for example) from 5.5 per cent per annum in 1976 to 8.2 per cent per annum in 1978. The economy is displaced to point A in figure 3.7. The actual and anticipated rates of inflation are equal, but they are below the rate of monetary expansion. This is the initial condition. The following Monetarist dynamic process differs fundamentally from the Keynesian analysis. A rise in the rate of monetary expansion raises the rate of inflation while the unemployment rate is "high." This is one aspect of stagflation.

The rise in the rate of monetary expansion initially raises real balances, since prices change differentially ($\infty > P_2 > 0$). The Keynesian excess demand for goods is raised because the rise in real balances shifts the aggregate demand curve upwards from (A_2 to A in figure 2.2). Prices of raw and intermediate materials respond quickly to the excess demand (see table 2.2 for the characteristic behavior) and these are passed on gradually to the finished goods sectors as cost increases. This is one force raising the rate of inflation.

In addition, the asymptotically rational (risk-adjusted) rate of inflation is raised differentially towards the higher rate of monetary expansion for the reasons developed in section 4.1 above. There is a lag between the current rate of monetary expansion $\mu(t)$ and the expected rate of monetary expansion $E\mu$, which determines the expected steady-state rate of inflation $E\pi$. The length of this lag depends upon the variance of the rate of monetary expansion and the confidence level that the public requires before it revises its estimate of the expected rate of monetarry expansion.

There is also a lag between the expected rate of inflation $E\pi$ and the risk-adjusted rate π^*, which guides firms' input and output decisions. The length of this lag depends upon the variance of the distribution of prices and the public's aversion to risk. Insofar as the monetary policy continues and the economy converges to the steady state, the uncertainty declines, and the risk-adjusted anticipated rate of inflation converges to the rate of monetary expansion.

Both the effect of the rise in the Keynesian excess demand upon prices $P_2[\mu(t) - \pi(t)]$ and the anticipations effect $D\pi^*(t) = c[\mu(t) - \pi^*(t)]$ raise the rate of inflation. Therefore, the actual rate of inflation rises by more than the anticipated rate. The slope of the trajectory of the anticipated and actual rates of inflation, as the economy departs from point A at time $t = 1$, is described by equation (3.54) and is the vector AA' in figure 3.7. The anticipated rate rises by less than the actual rate of inflation:[20]

$$\frac{d\pi^*(1)}{d\pi(1)} = \frac{c}{c + P_2} = \frac{1}{1 + (P_2/c)} < 1. \tag{3.54}$$

Real unit labor costs decline, since the growth of nominal unit labor cost is less than the actual rate of inflation. The excess demand for labor rises in response to the decline in real unit labor costs, and the unemployment rate declines as described by figure 2.1. In terms of the phase diagram figure 3.6, there is unanticipated inflation $\pi > \pi^*$. Therefore, the decline in real unit labor costs drives the unemployment rate deviation from point c to point g and then in the direction of the origin.

Empirically, equation (2.20) describes the lagged adjustment between the unemployment rate $U(t)$ and the real non-farm business sector unit labor costs $w_N(t-1)$ in the previous year. A comparison of the actual unemployment rate $U(t)$ with the rate predicted $E_{t-1}U(t)$ on the basis of equation (2.20) repeated here, during this 1976–78 period, is as follows. Note that no contemporaneous data are used to predict $U(t)$. The rate of inflation of the GNP deflator $\pi(t)$ and the rate of M1B monetary expansion $\mu(t)$ are also given.

$$E_{t-1}U(t) = -42.2 + 0.316U(t-1) + 0.45w_N(t-1). \qquad (2.20)$$

t	$U(t)$ (%)	$E_{t-1}U(t)$ (%)	$\pi(t)$ (% p.a.)	$\mu(t)$ (% p.a.)
1976	7.7	7.1	5.2	5.5
1977	7.0	6.5	6.0	7.5
1978	6.0	6.5	7.3	8.2

The rate of inflation continues to rise for two reasons: real balances are rising, and hence the aggregate demand for goods is rising; and the anticipated rate of inflation rises towards the rate of monetary expansion. In figure 3.7 the actual and anticipated rates of inflation rise from point A to point B. When the economy reaches point B, the rate of inflation has caught up to the rate of monetary expansion, and real balances no longer rise. However, there is still unanticipated inflation equal to distance $0B$.

From point B in figure 3.7, the anticipated rate of inflation becomes the dominant force driving the economy. Insofar as the anticipated rate of inflation is less than the rate of monetary expansion, the anticipated rate continues to rise. The inflation rate of nominal unit labor costs increases and, as table 2.4 indicates, becomes more pervasive among industries. This acceleration in the inflation of unit labor costs is due to two factors: (i) the unemployment rate has declined, thereby increasing pressure in the labor market; and (ii) the higher anticipated rate of inflation is taken into account in the wage bargaining process. Therefore, the actual rate of inflation rises due to the cost-push effects, and the economy is driven along trajectory BC in figure 3.7. Along BC, real balances decline since the rate of inflation exceeds the rate of monetary expansion. As a result, the aggregate demand curve begins to shift downwards.

The forecast error between the actual rate of inflation and the anticipated rate of inflation is described by equation (3.55). It is a closed form solution (see the appendix to this chapter) of the equations in table 3.1:

$$\pi(t) - \pi^*(t) = \frac{\mu(0) - \pi(0)}{(P_2 - c)} P_2 [\exp(-ct) - \exp(-P_2 t)]. \quad (3.55)$$

At time $t = 1$, the forecast error is described by equation (3.56) derived from a linear approximation of (3.55):

$$\pi(1) - \pi^*(1) = [\mu(0) - \pi(0)]P_2. \qquad (3.56)$$

The forecast error, that is, unanticipated inflation, never changes sign, and goes monotonically to zero. The trajectory ABC ... 0 (in figure 3.7) never rises above the 45° line.

In figure 3.6, the decline in unanticipated inflation is described by the shifting of the curve from $\pi > \pi^*$ to the curve through the origin $\pi = \pi^*$. As the unanticipated inflation declines, the excess unemployment ($u > 0$) at point d (figure 3.6) produces a smaller inflation of nominal unit labor costs than of prices. Real unit labor costs decline, and the unemployment rate is reduced.

At point C in figure 3.7, the rate of inflation exceeds the rate of monetary expansion, but the anticipated rate of inflation is less than the rate of monetary expansion. The continued rise in the anticipated rate of inflation is counterbalanced by the decline in real balances, which depresses the aggregate demand curve. As a result of the decline in aggregate demand, from point C to the origin, the rate of inflation decelerates towards the rate of monetary expansion, and the anticipated rate of inflation continues to rise towards the higher rate of monetary expansion. Segment $C0$ of the trajectory describes this process.

As the unanticipated inflation (forecast error) converges to zero, nominal unit labor costs decline relative to prices. Therefore, the trajectory of the unemployment rate is $d0$ in figure 3.6.

This Monetarist analysis of the movement of the inflation and unemployment rates resulting from a rise in the rate of monetary expansion is totally at variance with the Keynesian view, summarized by the Carter Council of Economic Advisers (1978: 142) quoted above. Keynesians believe that demand management can accelerate the return to full employment without an acceleration of inflation. When inflation accelerated from 1976 to 1978, Keynesians were unable to explain it and were forced to attribute it to exogenous, unpredictable forces.

The Monetarist analysis is that stagflation is the result of a substantial rise in the rate of monetary expansion above the rate of inflation (segment AB of the trajectory in figure 3.7) when the initial unemployment rate is substantially above its equilibrium value: $u(0) = 0b$ (in figure 3.6). The 1976−78 stagflation can be explained under the Monetarist system.

Monetarists would not that the rate of monetary expansion is omitted from the Carter Council's discussion of the causes of inflation and unemployment.[21] Their reaction to the Carter Council's Report could and should be the following:

This is the excellent foppery of the world, that when we are sick in fortune, often the surfeit of our own behavior, we make guilty of our disasters the sun, the moon, and the stars: as if we were villains by necessity, fools by heavenly compulsion . . . .

The second aspect of stagflation is that the unemployment rate can rise while the inflation rate is still "high." Let us continue with the previous example, where the economy returns to a medium-run equilibrium at the equilibrium rate of unemployment but with a high rate of inflation equal to the rate of monetary expansion. Appalled by the inflation, the monetary authority announces and implements a policy to reduce the rate of monetary expansion. Graphically, the economy is now at point F in figure 3.7. The actual and anticipated rates of inflation are equal, but exceed the new lower rate of monetary expansion. The scenario is the negative of the one previously described. The unemployment rate follows trajectory ef0 in figure 3.6, and the inflation rates follow trajectory FGH0 in figure 3.7.

The decline in the rate of monetary expansion reduces the level of real balances. Aggregate demand curve A (figure 2.2) declines to A_2, and a Keynesian excess supply is produced. The impact effect is greatest upon the prices of raw materials and intermediate goods, and consumer goods prices respond with a lag (see table 2.2). The asymptotically rational anticipated rate of inflation responds slowly to the decline in the rate of monetary expansion.

The economy moves along vector FF' (figure 3.7), described by equation (3.54), since the anticipated rate of inflation declines by less than the actual rate (as described by equation (3.56)). As a result, the unemployment rate dynamics start at point e in figure 3.6 and move towards point b. Nominal unit labor costs rise at a faster rate than prices, because: (i) the wage bargaining process is more closely geared to the recent history of inflation than to the current rate of monetary expansion; and (ii) real aggregate demand is declining. Unemployment rises as a result of the rise in real unit labor cost, as described by the vector from point e in the direction of point b in figure 3.6.

Real balances continue to decline, as the economy travels along segment FG in figure 3.7. Aggregate demand curve A (figure 2.2) continues to shift downwards, as a result of the decline in real balances, and the Keynesian excess demand is reduced. Both the decline in the Keynesian excess demand and the gradual decline in the anticipated rate of price change serve to reduce the rate of inflation.

The forecast error between the anticipated and actual rate of inflation continues to decline, and the excess unemployment rate declines along trajectory f0 in figure 3.6. Real unit labor costs decline as a result of the excess unemployment, and the unemployment rate declines. At the new medium-run equilibrium, unemployment has returned to the equilibrium rate, and both the actual and anticipated rates of price change are equal to the lower rate of monetary expansion.

Stagflation has been generated in a dynamic adjustment process. Initially, the unemployment rate was high and the inflation rate was rising. Then the inflation rate was high and the unemployment rate was rising. A quantitative analysis of the theory developed here is contained in chapter 4 and is based upon statistical estimates of the relevant parameters.

The main difference between the Monetarist and NCE analysis concerns the social costs involved in decelerating an inflation. The magnitude of the social cost of reducing inflation depends upon the speed at which the forecast error $\pi(t) - \pi^*(t)$ tends to zero. NCE claims that the forecast error tends to zero very quickly, whereas the Monetarist view is that it may take a couple of years. (See the quantitative analysis in table 4.15.)

Formally, the NCE view is a special case of the Monetarist analysis when the coefficient c of the ARE equation is infinite. As is shown in the appendix to this chapter, if $c \to \infty$ then: (i) the anticipated rate of inflation π^* converges infinitely quickly to the current rate of monetary expansion μ; and (ii) the forecast error is zero. Graphically the vectors from points A and F in figure 3.7, described by equation (3.54), have unitary slopes:

$$\lim_{c \to \infty} \frac{d\pi^*(1)}{d\pi(1)} = \frac{1}{1 + (P_2/c)} \to 1. \tag{3.57}$$

The differential equation for the unemployment rate is then always described by the curve, labelled $\pi = \pi^*$, through the origin in figure 3.6. Inflation can be reduced without any social cost, in the special case where coefficient c of the ARE equation is infinite. When there is risk aversion and uncertainty, coefficient c will be finite, and Monetarist results will be obtained.

5   The Keynesian specification

There is a spectrum of Keynesian, just as there is of non-Keynesian, views. A Keynesian view could also be described by figures 3.6 and 3.7. Suppose that there is very little nominal wage flexibility, that is, h is small (in equation 2.4). Then the curves in figure 3.6 would be near horizontal, and it would take a long time to restore full employment. Moreover, anticipations can be claimed to change very slowly when the rate of monetary expansion is varied. In equation (2.10b), coefficient c is small, and it would then take a long time for the forecast error $\pi(t) - \pi^*(t)$ to go to zero, when there is a monetary deceleration (point F in figure 3.7). The trajectory of the unemployment rate would be eb in figure 3.6, and it would take a long time for the economy to move from point b to point c and then return to the origin. Such a scenario would be faithful to the spirit of Keynesian economics.

Keynesians can accept the formulation of the unemployment rate (equation (2.3)) even though they prefer to emphasize the goods market rather than the labor market. The change in the unemployment rate equation (3.44) can be written in a Keynesian manner on the basis of the following reasoning. The change in the unemployment rate is a function of the growth of the adjusted nominal wage $D \ln W(t)$ (i.e. nominal unit labor costs) less the rate of inflation, where $W(t)$ represents nominal unit labor costs:

$$DU(t) = \beta [D \ln W(t) - \pi(t)]. \tag{3.58}$$

The rate of inflation equation (2.29) (repeated here as equation (3.59)) states that the rate of inflation $\pi(t)$ is the sum of the growth of nominal unit labor costs $D \ln W(t)$ and a function of the Keynesian excess demand $J(t)$:

$$\pi(t) = D \ln W(t) + \gamma J(t). \tag{3.59}$$

By substituting equation (3.59) into (3.58) it is possible to derive (3.60), which states that the change in the unemployment rate is negatively related to the Keynesian excess demand:

$$DU(t) = -\beta \gamma J(t). \tag{3.60}$$

Whenever aggregate demand (curve A in figure 2.2) is above the 45° line, output expands and the unemployment rate declines.

Unemployment rate equations (3.58) and (3.60) are equivalent, if the price change equation (3.59) (i.e. (2.7)) is accepted. Whereas Keynesians stress adjustments in the product market, they could focus instead on the labor market.

Keynesians emphasize that bond-financed fiscal policy has a stronger effect upon excess aggregate demand than is claimed by Monetarists. One disagreement between these groups concerns the value of $\partial J / \partial g$ described by equation (3.47). This is a disagreement concerning the magnitude of a parameter estimate and not a disagreement concerning the model. With the exception of this point, there is no reason why Keynesians cannot except the Monetarist model described by table 3.1 above and claim that the labor market and anticipations adjust very slowly. Then, a Keynesian could claim that expansionary monetary and/or fiscal policy can accelerate the return to U_e.

To emphasize the differences, rather than the similarities, consider the following Keynesian views concerning the rate of inflation. Modigliani and Papademos write: "It is shown that historical experience supports the proposition that there exists some *critical* rate of unemployment such that, as long as unemployment does not fall below it, inflation can be expected to decline ..." (1976: 4). James Tobin, who shares this point of view, divides the economy into three zones on the basis of the current unemployment rate. Zone I contains unemployment rates below 4.8 per cent, zone III consists of unemployment rates above 6 per cent, and zone II lies between zones I and III: "To a very close approximation, the path of inflation — accelerating, stable, decelerating — depends on the overall state of the economy, i.e., on which zone it is in, and not on the combination of policies and events that put it there" (1975).

The Keynesian position, reflected in the views of Modigliani and Papademos, Tobin and S. Weintraub, can be described as follows. The price level is a multiple of unit labor costs. In terms of growth rates, the rate of inflation of prices $\pi(t)$ is equal to the rate of inflation of unit labor costs $\omega(t)$, which they call the "underlying rate of inflation", plus exogenous disturbances $v(t)$ which depend upon the percentage change in the prices of raw materials (agricultural products and hydrocarbons). Disturbances $v(t)$ represent supply shocks.

$$\pi(t) = \omega(t) + v(t). \tag{3.61}$$

The Carter Council of Economic Advisers articulated this Keynesian view cogently in their Report dated January 1979.

The rate of price increase rose markedly in 1978. Some of the acceleration was the result of special factors discussed in the previous chapter [$v_1(t)$]: the sharp rise in food prices early in the year and in the fall in the value of the dollar that exceeded the depreciation warranted by underlying economic conditions. A minor offset to this was the stability of world oil prices after OPEC elected not to raise oil prices in face of the sluggish world economic recovery and the consequently weak demand for oil.

A large part of the 1978 acceleration, however, came from an unexpected increase in the underlying rate of inflation [$\omega(t)$]. The rise in consumer prices, excluding food and energy, quickened from 6.4 percent in 1977 to 8.6 percent in 1978 .... This is the development that has posed the most serious challenge to economic policy.

The behavior of the underlying rate of inflation is related to movements in costs. In 1978 the increase in unit labor costs in the private non-farm sector stepped up considerably $[\omega(t) - \omega(t-1)]$ from 6.3 percent in 1977 to 8.9 percent in 1978. Both of the determination factors of unit labor costs contributed to the acceleration. Compension per hour went up from a 7.6 percent rate increase in 1977 to a 9.8 percent rate during 1978. Productivity, which had risen only 1.3 percent for non-farm business in 1977, advanced even more slowly — at a 0.8 percent rate in 1978 . . . the rise in unit labor costs was . . . a major factor in the acceleration of inflation . . . . (1979: 56–7)

In terms of first differences, equation (3.61) implies that the change in the rate of inflation of prices is equal to the change in the rate of inflation of unit labor costs plus exogenous disturbances $v_1(t)$:

$$\pi(t) - \pi(t-1) = \omega(t) - \omega(t-1) + v_1(t). \tag{3.62}$$

Nominal unit labor costs are assumed to change slowly in response to unemployment or are relatively exogenous. One way of writing the wage change equation is

$$\omega(t) - \omega(t-1) = -c_1[U(t-1) - U_e] + \varepsilon_1(t), \tag{3.63}$$

where $\varepsilon_1(t)$ is an exogenous term, or could reflect slowly changing anticipations. By substituting (3.63) into (3.62) a Keynesian equation for the change in the rate of inflation can be derived:

$$\pi(t) - \pi(t-1) = -c_1[U(t-1) - U_e] + \varepsilon_2(t). \tag{3.64}$$

This equation is consistent with the Modigliani–Papademos and Tobin quotations, when U_e is between 4.8 and 6 per cent.

The Keynesian analysis adjoins to equation (3.64) the traditional IS–LM paradigm to obtain policy prescriptions. Nominal income $Y(t)$ is the product of the price level $p(t)$ and real output $y(t)$, as described by

$$Y(t) \equiv p(t)y(t). \tag{3.65}$$

Using the IS–LM framework, the level of nominal income $Y(t)$ is determined as a function of the money stock $M(t)$ and real disturbance $Z(t)$, which subsume fiscal policies and exogenous forces. The IS–LM solution is

$$Y(t) = F[M(t), Z(t)]. \tag{3.66}$$

By equating (3.65) to (3.66) and solving for the level of real output $y(t)$

$$y(t) = \frac{1}{p(t)} F[M(t), Z(t)]. \tag{3.67}$$

The Keynesian point of view can be understood from an inspection of equations (3.67) and (3.64). Monetary and fiscal policy affect nominal income directly. Prices, however, change quite slowly: the acceleration of inflation depends upon the Okun Gap reflected by the deviation of the unemployment rate from its equilibrium value. Therefore, the main effect of monetary and fiscal policy is upon the real output $y(t)$, and these policies have weak and indirect effects upon the rate of inflation.

Formally, by taking the logarithm of equation (3.67) and linearizing the logarithm of the $F(.)$ function:

$$\ln y(t) = h_1 \ln M(t) + h_2 \ln Z(t) - \ln p(t). \tag{3.68}$$

By taking first differences of (3.68), equation (3.69) can be obtained in terms of the growth of real output $\Delta \ln y(t)$, the rate of monetary expansion $\mu(t) \equiv \Delta \ln M(t)$, the rate of inflation $\pi(t) \equiv \Delta \ln p(t)$ and the growth rate of fiscal and real exogenous disturbances $z(t) \equiv \Delta \ln Z(t)$:

$$\Delta \ln y(t) = h_1 \mu(t) + h_2 z(t) - \pi(t). \tag{3.69}$$

Equation (3.64) can be used to obtain the rate of inflation and Okun's Law (equation (2.27)) used to relate the growth of real output to the change in the unemployment rate deviation $u(t) \equiv U(t) - U_e$:

$$\Delta u(t) = \frac{1}{a} \left[-h_1 \mu(t) + \pi(t-1) - h_2 z(t) + \alpha - c_1 u(t-1) + \varepsilon_2(t) \right]. \tag{3.70}$$

A deceleration of the rate of monetary expansion raises the unemployment rate quickly, because it has an indirect effect upon the rate of inflation. According to equation (3.64), the rate of inflation depends upon its previous value, the previous year's Okun Gap measured by $u(t-1)$ and exogenous forces.

A Keynesian policy to reduce inflation would simultaneously operate on the rate of monetary expansion to effect the growth of nominal income, and upon the wage bargaining process via an incomes policy. Then, an inflation could be reduced with a minimal iatrogenic effect upon the unemployment rate. For this reason, Tobin wrote the following:

Must we *either* hold the real performance of the economy hostage to disinflation *or* accommodate monetary demand to the inflation that history happens to have bequeathed us? . . . The way out, the only way out, is incomes policy . . . . The microeconomic distortions of incomes policy would be trivial compared to the economic costs of prolonged underemployment of labor and capital. It takes a heap of Harberger triangles to fill an Okun Gap. (1977: 467)

Each school of thought has a different conception of the dynamics of unemployment and inflation between-run equilibria. The scientific question is: what is the consistency of each school of thought with the existing data? This is the subject of the next chapter.

6 Appendix: mathematical solution of the Monetarist dynamical system and NCE as a special case

A mathematical analysis of the Monetarist dynamical system in table 3.1 is necessary in order to justify the trajectories drawn in the phase diagrams and to derive equation (3.55) for the time path of unanticipated inflation (i.e. the forecast error). Moreover, the approximations used in the empirical estimation and hypothesis testing are based upon the precise solution of the system.

The dynamical system (table 3.1) is written as the vector–matrix differential equation (A3.1). It is not necessary to assume that there is a Fisher effect $P_3 = 0$.

$$
\begin{bmatrix}
Du(t) \\
D[\pi(t) - \mu] \\
D[\pi^*(t) - \mu]
\end{bmatrix}
=
\begin{bmatrix}
-\beta h & -\beta & \beta \\
0 & -P_2 & -c(1+P_3) \\
0 & 0 & -c
\end{bmatrix}
\begin{bmatrix}
u(t) \\
\pi(t) - \mu \\
\pi^*(t) - \mu
\end{bmatrix}
\quad \text{(A3.1)}
$$

The three eigenvalues $(-\beta h, -P_2, -c)$ are real and negative, and hence the dynamical system is stable. By solving for the corresponding eigenvectors a general solution (A3.2)–(A3.4) can be derived. The constants are a_1, a_2 and a_3:

$$
u(t) = a_1 \exp(-\beta h t) + a_2 \exp(-P_2 t) + a_3 \exp(-ct). \quad \text{(A3.2)}
$$

$$
[\pi(t) - \mu] = \frac{a_2(P_2 - \beta h)\exp(-P_2 t)}{\beta} + \frac{a_3 c(1+P_3)(c - \beta h)\exp(-ct)}{\beta(P_2 + cP_3)}. \quad \text{(A3.3)}
$$

$$
[\pi^*(t) - \mu] = \frac{a_3(c - \beta h)(c - P_2)\exp(-ct)}{\beta(P_2 + cP_3)}. \quad \text{(A3.4)}
$$

Let the initial condition be $\pi(0) = \pi^*(0)$, that is, the economy initially lies along the 45° line in figure 3.7. There is no unanticipated inflation, but the rate of inflation need not equal the given rate of monetary expansion. Then equations (A3.3) and (A3.4) are equations (A3.5) and (A3.6) respectively:

$$
\pi(t) - \mu = \frac{[\pi(0) - \mu]}{(P_2 - c)}[(P_2 + cP_3)\exp(-P_2 t) - c(1+P_3)\exp(-ct)]. \quad \text{(A3.5)}
$$

$$\pi^*(t) - \mu = [\pi(0) - \mu] \exp(-ct). \tag{A3.6}$$

Unanticipated inflation, equation (A3.7), can be obtained by subtracting (A3.6) from (A3.5):

$$\pi(t) - \pi^*(t) = [\mu - \pi(0)] \frac{(P_2 + cP_3)[\exp(-ct) - \exp(-P_2 t)]}{(P_2 - c)}. \tag{A3.7}$$

This is precisely equation (3.55) in the text.

At time $t = 1$, the unanticipated inflation is (A3.8) or equation (3.56) in the text:

$$\pi(1) - \pi^*(1) = [\mu - \pi(0)](P_2 + cP_3). \tag{A3.8}$$

If the rate of monetary expansion exceeds the rate of inflation at time $t = 0$, then there will be unanticipated inflation at time $t = 1$. Recall that at $t = 0$ there is no unanticipated inflation.

It is easy to prove that the term $\exp(-ct) - \exp(-P_2 t)$ never changes sign from $t = 1$ to infinity when it becomes equal to zero. Therefore, the trajectories in figure 3.7 never cross the 45° line on their way to the origin.

The phase diagram of the unemployment rate, in figure 3.6, is derived by substituting the closed form solution for unanticipated inflation (A3.7) into the first equation from (A3.1). The time rate of change of the unemployment rate is then described by

$$Du(t) = -\beta h u(t) - \frac{\beta[\mu - \pi(0)]}{(P_2 - c)} (P_2 + cP_3)[\exp(-ct) - \exp(-P_2 t)]. \tag{A3.9}$$

It is obvious that the intercept term tends to zero and hence the unemployment rate deviation converges to zero along the line $\pi^* = \pi$ in figure 3.6. The solution of (A3.9) is precisely (A3.2) when the values of the constants are determined.

When there is a Fisher effect $P_3 = 0$. Then, the forecast error (A3.7) is

$$\pi(t) - \pi^*(t) = [\mu - \pi(0)] \frac{P_2}{(P_2 - c)} [\exp(-ct) - \exp(-P_2 t)]. \tag{A3.10}$$

A linear approximation of (A3.10) at $t = 1$ is equation (3.56) in the text, when $e^x \approx 1 + x$ is the first-order approximation.

Equation (A3.10) can be written as

$$\pi(t) - \pi^*(t) = [\mu - \pi(0)] \frac{(P_2/c)}{(P_2/c) - 1} [\exp(-ct) - \exp(-P_2 t)]. \tag{A3.11}$$

NCE results are obtained by letting the coefficient c of the ARE equation tend positively to infinity. Then (P_2/c) is zero, and there never is a forecast error:

$$\pi(t) - \pi^*(t) = 0. \tag{A3.12}$$

Graphically, the vectors from points A and F in figure 3.7 have slopes of unity, as is seen from equation (3.54) in the text when $c \to \infty$. Consequently, the differential equation for the unemployment rate (A3.9) becomes

$$Du(t) = -\beta h u(t). \tag{A3.13}$$

It has, therefore, been shown that NCE results are derived from the "Monetarist" model in table 3.1 in the *special case* where coefficient c of the ARE equation tends to unity. Monetarist results are derived when c is finite, as will occur when there is risk aversion and uncertainty.

Notes

1 A key to the symbols used can be found in table 2.1.
2 See the references in McCallum (1980). Equation (3.11) is from Sargent (1976a: 221). See Lucas (1972), Sargent (1973, 1976a) and Sargent and Wallace (1975).
3 In this chapter and the next, it is convenient to standardize capacity output *per capita* at unity. Then output *per capita* $y(t)$ is synonymous with the ratio of actual to capacity output. β is the same as β_1 in chapter 2.
4 The difference $[U(t) - U_e] - [U(t-1) - U_e] = \beta[\ln w(t) - \ln w(t-1)]$. Use equation (3.14) to derive (3.16).
5 The derivation is as follows:

$$E_{t-1}\pi(t) \equiv E_{t-1}\ln p(t) - \ln p(t-1) = E_{t-1}\ln M(t) - \ln p(t-1)$$

$$+ \frac{P_1}{P_2}(1 - \beta h)u(t-1) + \frac{1}{P_2}E_{t-1}z(t)$$

$$= [E_{t-1}\ln M(t) - \ln M(t-1)] + [\ln M(t-1) - \ln p(t-1)]$$

$$+ \frac{P_1}{P_2}(1 - \beta h)u(t-1) + \frac{1}{P_2}E_{t-1}z(t).$$

$E_{t-1}\mu(t) \equiv [E_{t-1}\ln M(t) - \ln M(t-1)]$ and $\ln m(t-1) \equiv [\ln M(t-1) - \ln p(t-1)]$, which implies equation (3.27).

6 Lucas (1973) and Hanson (1980) present evidence that the effects of unanticipated disturbances upon the unemployment rate or level of output are smaller in countries where variations in demand are less predictable. Specifically, the more difficult it is to predict money growth, the less

effective is unanticipated money growth in affecting output (see Hanson: Table 2).

7   See Friedman (1948) and McCallum and Whitaker (1979).

8   The effects of built-in stabilizers are well known in the Keynesian literature. Let output be $y(t)$, disposable income $y^d(t) = (1 - \tau)y(t)$, where τ is the tax rate, and "autonomous" sources of demand (including investment) are $v(t)$. Let consumption $c(t)$ be proportional to disposable income $c(t) = cy^d(t)$. Then output is

$$y(t) = c(1 - \tau)y(t) + v(t).$$

The level of output is

$$y(t) = \frac{v(t)}{1 - c(1 - \tau)}.$$

The variance of output, denoted by var $y(t)$, is

$$\text{var } y(t) = \frac{1}{[1 - c(1 - \tau)]^2} \text{ var } v(t).$$

The built-in stabilizer τ can decrease the variance of output, given the variance of the disturbances var $v(t)$. No forecasting ability or counter-cyclical policy is used.

9   The same argument applies if $\mu(t) = ax(t - 1)$, where a is a row vector of coefficients and $x(t - 1)$ is a column vector of variables whose values are known at $t - 1$. Then $\mu(t) - E_{t-1}\mu(t) = 0$.

10   Substitute (3.39) and (3.40) into (3.41). Call the resulting expression for $p(t)$ equation (3.41a). Take the expectation of (3.41a) and call it (3.41b). Subtract (3.41b) from (3.41a). Solve the resulting equation for $p(t) - E_{t-1}p(t)$ to derive equation (3.42).

11   See also Cyert and De Groot (1974) and Swamy et al. (1980).

12   Let n_M be the required number of monthly observations and n_Q be the required number of quarterly observations to obtain an estimate of $E\mu$ with the same degree of confidence and accuracy. Then, from equation (3.46b) above,

$$\frac{n_M}{n_Q} = \left(\frac{\sigma_M}{\sigma_Q}\right)^2.$$

The ratio of the number of observations is the square of the ratio of standard deviations of monthly σ_M to quarterly σ_Q rates of monetary expansion expressed as annual rates.

During the periods referred to in the text, $\sigma_M = 11.35$ per cent per annum and $\sigma_Q = 1.69$ per cent per annum. Therefore,

$$\frac{n_M}{n_Q} = 43.4.$$

It does not make sense to use monthly, rather than quarterly, observations to estimate $E\mu$.

13 This is fundamentally different from the NCE Ricardian doctrine. A lucid discussion of this issue can be found in Tobin (1980: 51–64).
14 This is the $P_5 < 0$ effect in Stein (1976).
15 See also Infante and Stein (1976) and Christ (1979).
16 Such a system can only be stable if θ tends to zero, in which case deficits are entirely money-financed.
17 This is consistent with the results of Andersen and Carlson (1970: Table 1).
18 See Cargill and Meyer (1977).
19 In this chapter and the next, the rate of monetary expansion is viewed as a control variable. Historically (see equation (2.49)), two-thirds of the rate of monetary expansion can be explained by the previous year's high employment deficit, and one-third must be explained by other factors.
20 Write $D\pi^* = d\pi^*/dt$ and $D\pi = d\pi/dt$. Divide equation (3.51) by equation (3.50), when $\pi(0) = \pi^*(0)$, and derive equation (3.54).
21 The rate of monetary expansion declined from 15.3 per cent per annum during 6/80–11/80 to 4 per cent per annum during 11/80–8/81. Nevertheless, William Nordhaus (who had been a member of the Carter Council) does not associate a decline in the rate of inflation with a decline in the growth of monetary aggregates. Nordhaus' views are unambiguous and commonly held:

> The United States has received very good, and quite surprising, news on the inflation front in the last three months. After rising at rates of around 13 percent annually since 1978, consumer price inflation has slowed to an annual rate of 7 percent over the last three months.
> ... the recent slowdown in inflation has not arisen from slower wage increases or more rapid productivity growth. Rather, it has arisen entirely from the more volatile, nonlabor components ....
> The central point for the prognosis on inflation, however, is that movements in oil or food prices lead to one shot, or transient, declines in inflation ....
> The last two years witnessed a bout of incredibly bad luck; the last few months have seen a string of unpredicted good luck. (*New York Times*, 1981: 12 July)

CHAPTER 4

Empirical Analysis
Hypothesis Testing and the Implications
for Stabilization Policy

1 Introduction and summary

Each one of the three gospels is logical. Their implications, concerning the etiology of unemployment and inflation and the efficacy of policies to cope with these problems, differ fundamentally. Generally, their proponents test whether their theories are inconsistent with the data at a high level of probability; and, if necessary, they introduce empirical modifications which are not part of the theory until they are able to state that their theory is not inconsistent with the evidence.

In this chapter each theory is reformulated as a set of statistical hypotheses; one set of hypotheses is then tested against a rival set of hypotheses. In section 2 below the NCE and Monetarist theories of the determination of the unemployment rate, and the ratio of actual to capacity output, are tested against each other. The variable to be explained by each hypothesis is $E_{t-1}U(t)$, which is the mathematical expectation (denoted by E) of the unemployment rate at time t conditional upon information known no later than at time $t - 1$, where the unit of time is one year. No contemporaneous variables are used as independent variables, because an explanation is logically equivalent to a prediction.[1] Keynesians can accept most of the Monetarist analysis of the unemployment rate, at this stage of the argument, so the attention is focused upon a comparison of the NCE and Monetarist points of view.

The NCE statistical hypothesis is that the unemployment rate at time t depends upon its lagged value and the *unanticipated* money growth from $t - 1$ to t plus unanticipated fiscal or real shocks. These unanticipated components have zero expectations and are not serially correlated. Therefore, the expected unemployment rate $E_{t-1}U(t)$ just depends upon its lagged values $U(t-i)$. In a regression of $U(t)$ upon its lagged values $U(t-i)$ and any set of past monetary, price or fiscal variables $V(t-i)$, the regression coefficients of $V(t-i)$ should not be significantly different from zero.

The Monetarist hypothesis starts from the same point as does that of NCE. Unemployment rate $U(t)$ depends upon its lagged value $U(t-1)$ and upon the non-observable unanticipated inflation. However, the unanticipated inflation is shown to be approximated by the percentage change in real balances from year $t-2$ to year $t-1$. Unlike NCE, the Monetarist model does not imply that the forecast error has an expectation of zero and is not serially correlated. Therefore, the Monetarist statistical hypothesis is that the expected unemployment rate E_{t-1} depends upon its lagged value $U(t-1)$ and upon $\mu(t-1) - \pi(t-1)$, the rate of monetary expansion $\mu(t-1)$ less the rate of inflation $\pi(t-1)$, from year $t-2$ to year $t-1$. The variable $\mu(t-1) - \pi(t-1)$ is one of the components of $V(t-1)$ that NCE claims has a regression coefficient which is not significantly different from zero.

There are two parts to the statistical tests to determine which of the two hypotheses is inconsistent with the data. First, it is asked whether past unanticipated money growth $\mu(t-i) - E_{t-i-1}\mu(t-i)$, as claimed by NCE, or the previous year's change in real balances $\mu(t-1) - \pi(t-1)$ as claimed by the Monetarist hypothesis, significantly contributes to the explanation of the current unemployment rate. The answer is that the Monetarist hypothesis is accepted, and the NCE hypothesis is rejected. This test is not amenable to the "observational equivalence" ambiguity.

Secondly, it is tested whether the addition of the previous year's percentage change in real balances $\mu(t-1) - \pi(t-1)$, to a regression of $U(t)$ on its lagged values $U(t-i)$, has a regression coefficient significantly different from zero. It is found that the regression coefficient is very significantly negative, as is claimed by the Monetarists. The same results are obtained when the tests are performed on the ratio of actual to capacity output. Therefore, the NCE hypothesis is rejected and the Monetarist hypothesis is accepted.

Then the predictive power of the statistical Monetarist equation (4.25) for $E_{t-1}U(t)$ is examined,

$$E_{t-1}U(t) = 3.48 + 0.401\,U(t-1) - 0.39\,[\mu(t-1) - \pi(t-1)]\,, \quad (4.25)$$

and shown graphically against the actual $U(t)$ in figure 4.1. It explains 80 per cent of the variance of the US unemployment rate from 1958 through 1979.

A Monetarist unemployment rate equation is estimated for the period 1958–72 and used to predict the unemployment rate from 1973 to 1980. The prediction, outside of the sample period, is done directly and also with a dynamic ex-ante simulation with no correction for past errors. The values of R^2 between the actual and predicted unemployment rates are approximately 80 per cent.

In section 3, the Keynesian and Monetarist theories of inflation are tested against each other. The variable to be explained is $E_{t-1}\pi(t)$, which is the mathematical expectation of the percentage change in the price level (generally the GNP deflator) between year $t-1$ and year t, conditional upon information known no later than at year $t-1$. NCE implies a special case of the Monetarist equation. Most of the discussion is devoted to a comparison of the Keynesian and Monetarist hypotheses.

It is shown that a statistical implication of the Monetarist model (table 3.1) is that the mathematical expectation of the rate of inflation from year $t-1$ to year t, conditional upon information known no later than at year $t-1$, denoted by $E_{t-1}\pi(t)$, is a weighted average of the rate of inflation $\pi(t-1)$ and the rate of monetary expansion $\mu(t-1)$ from year $t-2$ to year $t-1$. The Keynesian hypothesis is that $\pi(t)$ depends upon $\pi(t-1)$, the difference between the unemployment rate in period $t-1$ and the "non-inflationary rate of unemployment" (NIRU) and unpredictable exogenous disturbances in year t. Keynesians claim that the rate of monetary expansion can only affect the rate of inflation by first affecting the unemployment rate.

First, the Keynesian critique of the Monetarist hypothesis is examined. It is shown that it consists of correlating the inflation of one price index against the inflation of other price indices, the contemporaneous value of the unemployment rate and the past rates of monetary expansion $\mu(t-i)$. Since the regression coefficients of $\mu(t-i)$ are not significant, the Keynesians reject the Monetarist hypothesis. The Keynesian regression is not a test of a theory to explain $E_{t-1}\pi(t)$. As it requires a knowledge of the values of contemporaneous variables, it is not a prediction of the inflation rate in year t conditional upon information known no later than at $t-1$. Hence, it is not an explanation of inflation, but just a correlation of various price indices and other contemporaneous variables, and it is devoid of any predictive power.

Secondly, there is a direct test of the Keynesian hypothesis that monetary policy can only affect the rate of inflation by first lowering the unemployment rate below the NIRU. A regression of the *change* in the rate of inflation $\pi(t) - \pi(t-1)$ upon the initial unemployment rate $U(t-1)$ and the percentage change in real balances $\mu(t-1) - \pi(t-1)$

from year $t-2$ to year $t-1$ is performed on the period 1958 through 1979 in the US. The Monetarist hypothesis is that the previous year's percentage change in real balances $\mu(t-1) - \pi(t-1)$ is very significant, whereas the Keynesians claim that only the initial unemployment rate $U(t-1)$ is significant. The results are that $U(t-1)$ is not significant and $\mu(t-1) - \pi(t-1)$ is highly significant. The Keynesian hypothesis is rejected and the Monetarist hypothesis is accepted.

Thirdly, the predictive power and robustness of the Monetarist statistical hypothesis is examined. For the US the hypothesis is that the mathematical expectation of the rate of inflation of the GNP deflator from year $t-1$ to year t is a simple average of the rate of inflation in the previous year $\pi(t-1)$ and the rate of M1B monetary expansion $\mu(t-1)$ from year $t-2$ to year $t-1$:

$$E_{t-1}\pi(t) = 0.5\pi(t-1) + 0.5\mu(t-1). \tag{4.41}$$

The predictive power of the Monetarist explanation is examined as follows. An arbitrary year $t = 0$ is selected and the rate of monetary expansion is specified in each of the subsequent years $t = 0, 1, 2, \ldots, T$. No information is provided concerning the actual rate of inflation or any other developments from $t = 1, \ldots, T$. This means that the prediction for one year $E_{t-2}\pi(t-1)$ is used to predict $E_{t-1}\pi(t)$ in the next year, as described by

$$E_{t-1}\pi(t) = 0.5E_{t-2}\pi(t-1) + 0.5\mu(t-1). \tag{4.43}$$

Whereas Keynesians cannot predict inflation, but simply attribute its variation to *ad hoc* unpredictable factors, equations (4.41) and (4.43) are predictions. For the US, predictive equation (4.43) explains over 80 per cent of the variance in the actual rate of inflation, and is described in figure 4.2. It implies that over a period of five years, the rate of inflation will be approximately (97 per cent) equal to the constant rate of monetary expansion. Let $\pi(t)$ be the rate of inflation in year t and let μ be a constant rate of monetary expansion. Then equation (4.41) implies equation (4.46e):

$$\pi(5)/\mu = 0.97 + 0.03\pi(0)/\mu. \tag{4.46e}$$

It is found that the rate of inflation of the *world consumer price index* (CPI) is just like equation (4.41) except for a constant, and it is described in figure 4.3. A major conclusion is that long-range (10–25 years) predictions of the rate of US or world inflation, based upon forecasts of developments in the energy or any non-monetary sector, are devoid of scientific content. Over a period of five or more years, only monetary policy systematically affects the rate of inflation.

Equation (4.41) is a very specific equation which (modulus a constant) is valid for the US, Canada or the world. Such an equation does not explain the annual rates of inflation of the other major countries. However, equation (4.46e) does explain the rates of inflation among a cross-section of twelve countries over a period of five years. Over 85 per cent of the international differences in the compound annual rates of inflation from 1975 to 1980, in the set of countries contained in table 4.12, are explained by the differences in the compound annual rates of monetary expansion during that same period.

Section 4 consists of a quantitative analysis of the efficacy of demand management policies, within the context of the statistical equations of the Monetarist model. Two issues are discussed.

First, what causes the paradox of *stagflation*, where inflation and unemployment both rise, or where "high" inflation coexists with an unemployment rate above its equilibrium value? It is shown that stagflation is produced if the following monetary policy is pursued. Whenever the rate of unemployment is too high, raise the rate of monetary expansion. When the rate of inflation is too high, reduce the rate of monetary expansion. Figure 4.4 describes the resulting stagflation.

Secondly, suppose that the monetary authority decides to reduce the rate of inflation significantly. Compare the effects of a *gradualist* policy, that reduces the rate of monetary expansion gradually to its target level, with a *bang-bang* policy that reduces it immediately to its target level. An implication of the Monetarist model is that, after the second year, there is less inflation and less unemployment with a bang-bang policy than with a gradualist policy. If the "misery index," that is, the sum of the unemployment and inflation rates, is used to define social loss, then the social loss in every year is less with a bang-bang policy than with a gradualist policy. This result is then explained on the basis of the theoretical model.

2   The unemployment rate, the ratio of actual to capacity output and the growth of real output

2.1   *The statistical hypotheses implied by NCE and the Monetarists*

The NCE view implies that the mathematical expectation, taken at time $t - 1$, of the unemployment rate or ratio of actual to capacity output at time t, is just a function of its own lagged values. Equations (3.19a) and (3.19b) describe this point of view.

In the extract below, Sargent is most explicit. (He denotes the unemployment rate deviation by Un.)

Using the method of least squares, estimate the linear regression of $Un(t)$ on lagged Un's and lagged Y's as

$$\hat{U}n(t) = \sum_{j=1}^{m} \alpha_j Un(t-j) + \sum_{j=1}^{n} \beta_j Y(t-j), \tag{2.5}$$

where the α_j's and β_j's are least square centimetres. As the null hypothesis that Y does *not* cause Un, the parent parameters $\beta_j, j = 1, \ldots, n$ equal zero. The natural rate hypothesis can then be tested by testing the null hypothesis $\beta = 0$ (when $j = 1, \ldots, n$) for various choices of Y. Alternatively, lagged values of several variables can be added to the right side of (2.5). On the natural rate hypothesis, all such variables bear zero coefficients. (1976a: 217)

The logic of this hypothesis is seen from equation (3.31), repeated here as equation (4.1a) and abbreviated as equation (4.1b) when the fiscal and real disturbances are subsumed under noise term $\varepsilon(t)$. The unemployment rate deviation $u(t)$ depends upon its lagged value $u(t-1)$, "unanticipated" money growth $\mu(t) - E_{t-1}\mu(t)$ and "unanticipated" fiscal and real shocks $z(t) - E_{t-1}z(t)$:

$$u(t) = (1-\beta h)u(t-1) - \frac{\beta}{(1+P_2+P_1\beta)}\{P_2[\mu(t) - E_{t-1}\mu(t)]$$
$$+ [z(t) - E_{t-1}z(t)]\}. \tag{4.1a}$$

$$u(t) = a_{11}u(t-1) - a_{12}[\mu(t) - E_{t-1}\mu(t)] + \varepsilon(t). \tag{4.1b}$$

Since NCE, relying upon the MRE hypothesis, claims that the "unanticipated" money growth, fiscal shocks and real disturbances have zero expectations and are not serially correlated, the expectation of the unemployment rate deviation $E_{t-1}u(t)$ just depends upon its lagged value $u(t-1)$. This is equation (3.19a). The same is true for the ratio of actual to capacity output, as described by (3.19b).

A very general NCE statistical hypothesis is described by equation (4.2). The mathematical expectation, taken at $t-1$, of the deviation of the unemployment rate from its equilibrium value $E_{t-1}u(t) \equiv E_{t-1}[U(t) - U_e]$ just depends upon lagged values of this deviation:

$$E_{t-1}u(t) = \sum_{i=1} a(i)u(t-i). \tag{4.2}$$

The Monetarist equation for the mathematical expectation of the unemployment rate deviation is quite different, because the mathematical expectation of the price forecast error is not necessarily zero, and is serially correlated when inflation accelerates or decelerates.

The unemployment rate equation (3.49) can be written as equation (4.3) in discrete time:

$$u(t) = (1 - \beta h)u(t - 1) - \beta [\pi(t) - \pi_{t-1}^*(t)].$$ (4.3)

The closed form solution for the forecast error, that is, unanticipated inflation, is described by equations (3.55) and (3.56), repeated here as equation (4.4a):

$$\pi(t) - \pi^*(t) = \frac{[\mu(0) - \pi(0)]}{(P_2 - c)} P_2 [\exp(-ct) - \exp(-P_2 t)].$$ (4.4a)

When $t = 1$, and e^x is linearized as $1 + x$, equation (4.4b) is obtained from equation (4.4a). It is a first-order approximation around the origin:

$$\pi(1) - \pi^*(1) = [\mu(0) - \pi(0)]P_2.$$ (4.4b)

It was illustrated in figure 3.7 that the forecast error, that is, unanticipated inflation, never changes sign and goes monotonically to zero, given the rate of monetary expansion $\mu(t) = \mu(0)$. If ARE coefficient c is infinite, then equation (4.4a) implies that $\pi^*(t)$ and $\pi(t)$ are always equal.

At time $t = 1$, the unobserved unanticipated rate of inflation $\pi(1) - \pi_0^*(1)$ is a multiple of the growth of the money supply less the rate of inflation in the previous period $\mu(0) - \pi(0)$. By using equation (4.4b) it is possible to *approximate* the unobserved unanticipated inflation at time t as

$$\pi(t) - \pi_{t-1}^*(t) = P_2 [\mu(t - 1) - \pi(t - 1)].$$ (4.5)

When the rate of monetary expansion $\mu(t - 1)$ exceeds (is less than) the rate of inflation $\pi(t - 1)$, then the actual rate of inflation $\pi(t)$ exceeds (is below) the anticipated rate $\pi_{t-1}^*(t)$. When the rate of inflation is constant, there is no forecast error.

The scenario, described in chapter 3, is as follows. A rise in the rate of monetary expansion initially raises real balances, since prices change differentially. The Keynesian excess demand for goods is raised, because the rise in real balances shifts the aggregate demand curve upwards. This is one force raising the rate of inflation. In addition, the asymptotically rational anticipated rate of inflation is raised slowly in the direction of the higher rate of monetary expansion because: (i) there is uncertainty whether the monetary change is transitory or permanent; and (ii) there is a friction between the expected rate of inflation $E\pi$ and the risk-adjusted anticipated rate of inflation π^* which determines the demand for productive services. *Therefore, the actual rate of inflation, which is the sum of the two effects, rises by more than the anticipated rate.* As the rate of inflation converges to the steady state, the unanticipated component goes to zero.

The approximation is seen in figure 3.7. Along trajectory AB or FG, the forecast error $\pi(t) - \pi^*_{-1}(t)$ has the same sign as the change in real balances $\mu(t-1) - \pi(t-1)$. As the economy approaches the origin along trajectory $BC0$ or $GH0$, this approximation loses its validity. This is the price paid for converting a system which contains an unobserved π^* into one which contains observable variables and which is amenable to statistical hypothesis testing. It is shown below that the approximation seems to be worth the cost.

The approximation of unanticipated inflation, equation (4.5), is substituted into unemployment rate equation (4.3) to derive a testable Monetarist unemployment rate equation (4.6a) or (abbreviated) (4.6b):

$$u(t) = (1 - \beta h)u(t-1) - \beta P_2[\mu(t-1) - \pi(t-1)] + \varepsilon(t). \quad (4.6a)$$

$$U(t) = a_0 + a_{11}U(t-1) + a_{12}[\mu(t-1) - \pi(t-1)] + \varepsilon(t). \quad (4.6b)$$

The variable $\varepsilon(t)$ is a random term.

Monetarist equation (4.6a) or (4.6b) implies that the mathematical expectation, taken at $t-1$, of the unemployment rate deviation at time t depends upon its lagged value $u(t-1)$ and the percentage change in real balances from $t-2$ to $t-1$ denoted by $\mu(t-1) - \pi(t-1)$. Monetarist equation (4.7) can then be derived:[2]

$$E_{t-1}u(t) = a_{11}u(t-1) + a_{12}[\mu(t-1) - \pi(t-1)]; \quad a_{12} < 0. \quad (4.7)$$

The difference between the NCE and the Monetarist hypothesis is that the NCE hypothesis implies that the regression coefficient of $\mu(t-1) - \pi(t-1)$ in equation (4.7) is not significantly different from zero, whereas the Monetarist hypothesis implies that coefficient a_{12} is negative.

Keynesians can accept the Monetarist hypothesis, equation (4.7), and most certainly reject the NCE hypothesis equation (4.2). However, Keynesians would also add a bond-financed fiscal policy variable to Monetarist equation (4.7). Insofar as $E_{t-1}U(t)$ is concerned, I shall only test the Monetarist against the NCE point of view.

The ex-post disturbance in NCE equation (4.1a) is a function of the current period's "unanticipated" money growth and "unanticipated" fiscal and exogenous shocks. These disturbances are unknown at time $t-1$ and their expectations are zero. For this reason, they do not feature in the tests considered here, which are exclusively based upon information known no later than at $t-1$.

2.2   The observational equivalence problem

There is an observational equivalence problem (Sargent, 1976b;

McCallum, 1979) that must be resolved if the NCE hypothesis is to be tested against the alternative Monetarist hypothesis. It is *theoretically* possible that the NCE hypothesis equation (4.1a) could imply a variant of Monetarist equation (4.6a). Therefore, the goodness of fit *per se* of Monetarist equation (4.7) does not necessarily reject the NCE hypothesis, for the following reason.

Suppose that the *anticipated* rate of monetary expansion $E_{t-1}\mu(t)$ in equation (4.1a) were a linear combination of the previous period's rates of monetary expansion and rates of inflation as described by

$$E_{t-1}\mu(t) = \alpha\pi(t-1) + (1-\alpha)\mu(t-1). \tag{4.8a}$$

Presumably, equation (4.8a) is the control law used by the monetary authority. "Unanticipated" money growth is equation (4.8b) when control law (4.8a) is used:

$$\mu(t) - E_{t-1}\mu(t) = \mu(t) - \mu(t-1) + \alpha[\mu(t-1) - \pi(t-1)]. \tag{4.8b}$$

Equation (4.9) is derived from the substitution of (4.8b) into (4.1b):

$$u(t) = a_{11}u(t-1) - a_{12}[\mu(t) - \mu(t-1)] - \alpha a_{12}[\mu(t-1) - \pi(t-1)] + \varepsilon(t). \tag{4.9}$$

This equation looks very much like Monetarist equation (4.6a) or (4.6b), except for the term $\mu(t) - \mu(t-1)$, although it is derived from an assumption that the NCE hypothesis is true. In fact, equation (4.9) looks like the antithesis of the NCE hypothesis, even though it is an implication of NCE equation (4.1a) and hypothetical monetary policy equation (4.8a). This difficulty in distinguishing between the NCE Policy Ineffectiveness Proposition (see equations (3.19a) and (3.19b)) and the Keynesian–Monetarist viewpoint must be surmounted if there is to be a meaningful statistical testing of alternative hypothesis.

It is obvious that as monetary policy, described by coefficient α in equation (4.8a), changes the coefficient of $\mu(t-1) - \pi(t-1)$ in reduced form equation (4.9) will also change. This result is known as the Policy Evaluation Proposition (Lucas, 1976). The problem is that there may be a *confounding* between the effect of unanticipated money growth stressed by the NCE hypothesis, for example, equation (4.8b), and the effect of the change in real balances $\mu(t-1) - \pi(t-1)$ stressed by the Monetarist hypothesis.

The way to resolve this problem of confounding is to use *direct estimates* of unanticipated money growth $\mu(\tau) - E_{\tau-1}\mu(\tau)$ supplied by NCE, as well as changes in real balances $\mu(t-1) - \pi(t-1)$ in unemployment rate equation (4.10):

$$E_{t-1}U(t) = a_0 + a_1 U(t-1) + \sum_{i=1} a_2(i)[\mu(t-i) - E_{t-i-1}\mu(t-i)]$$
$$+ a_3[\mu(t-1) - \pi(t-1)]. \qquad (4.10)$$

Since *direct* estimates of unanticipated money growth are used, there is no confounding between the two effects.

This general equation (4.10) can be used to test the NCE against the Monetarist hypothesis. *The NCE hypothesis* is that $E_{t-1}U(t)$, the mathematical expectation taken at $t-1$ of the unemployment rate at time t, depends upon: (i) the lagged value of the unemployment rate $U(t-1)$; and (ii) past values of unanticipated money growth[3] $\mu(\tau) - E_{\tau-1}\mu(\tau)$. (iii) The previous year's change in real balances $\mu(t-1) - \pi(t-1)$ is not statistically significant in explaining $E_{t-1}U(t)$. *The Monetarist hypothesis* is that the previous year's change in real balances $\mu(t-1) - \pi(t-1)$ is statistically significant, but past rates of unanticipated money growth are not statistically significant.

Many NCE statistical tests ignore the fact that each school of thought claims that the equilibrium unemployment rate is independent of monetary variables. Therefore, each school of thought's unemployment equation, or equation for the ratio of actual to capacity output, must imply that the effect of the monetary variables must converge to zero. In the Monetarist model, the change in real balances goes to zero (see table 3.1). In the NCE model, unanticipated money growth is zero on average. Hence, monetary neutrality always occurs in equilibrium. Keynesians believe that the convergence to equilibrium is very slow. In their empirical work they are generally not as scrupulous as they are in their theoretical work in using equations where the equilibrium values of the real variables are independent of monetary variables.

2.3   Statistical testing of the NCE against the Monetarist hypothesis

Unanticipated money growth or the previous year's change in real balances

By using equation (4.10) the NCE hypothesis can be tested against the Monetarist hypothesis. There is no observational equivalence ambiguity in this test.

With annual data for the unemployment rate for the period 1958 through 1977, $U(t)$ is regressed upon the lagged unemployment rate $U(t-1)$, Barro's measure of "unanticipated" money growth[4] $X(t-1)$, $X(t-2)$ in the past two years and upon $\mu(t-1) - \pi(t-1)$, the percentage change in the money stock less the percentage change in the price level from year $t-2$ to year $t-1$. *The NCE hypothesis is that the* *coefficient of $\mu(t-1) - \pi(t-1)$ is not significant when past "unanticipated" money growth is taken into account. The Monetarist hypothesis is that past rates of "unanticipated" money growth are not significant when the previous year's growth of real balances is taken into account.*

The results of this test[5] are described by regression equation (4.11), and even more clearly by the analysis of variance tables 4.1 and 4.2:

$$U(t): \quad [1958, \ 1977]$$

$$U(t) = 3.23 + 0.44U(t-1) - 0.397[\mu(t-1) - \pi(t-1)]$$
$$(t=) \quad (3.86) \quad (2.92) \quad (-4.25)$$

$$+ \ 0.0279X(t-1) + 0.0958X(t-2) \qquad (4.11)$$
$$(0.186) \qquad (0.731)$$

$$R^2 = 0.806; \quad DW^6 = 2.01; \quad SE = 0.669.$$

It is clear that the coefficients of lagged "unanticipated" money growth $X(t-1)$ and $X(t-2)$ are not significantly different from zero, whereas the change in real balances $\mu(t-1) - \pi(t-1)$ from year $t-2$ to year $t-1$, emphasized by the Monetarist hypothesis, is significantly different from zero at the one per cent level.

Analysis of variance tables 4.1 and 4.2 are clearer ways of presenting the results of regression equation (4.11). In table 4.1, the addition of Monetarist variable $\mu(t-1) - \pi(t-1)$ to the variables stressed by NCE significantly increases the explained sum of squares. The value of $F(1,15) = 18.01$ is significant at the one per cent level. This result is inconsistent with the NCE hypothesis in any form.

In table 4.2, the addition of past rates of "unanticipated" money growth $X(t-1)$ and $X(t-2)$ to the variables stressed by the Monetarists does not significantly increase the explained sum of squares. The value of $F(2,15) = 0.31$ is not significantly different from zero.

To summarize, regression equation (4.11) and tables 4.1 and 4.2 test the NCE against the Monetarist hypothesis in a way that is not amenable to the observational equivalence problem. The results are unambiguous. The NCE hypothesis is inconsistent with the data, whereas the Monetarist hypothesis is consistent with the data over the sample period.

Of course, it is possible that the NCE hypothesis is correct but that Barro's measure of "unanticipated" money growth is incorrect. Since there is no objective measure of "unanticipated" money growth, Barro's series has elicited controversy. Makin (1980) devised a measure of "anticipated" money growth based upon an autoregressive model,

TABLE 4.1 *Analysis of variance of the unemployment rate: addition of the previous year's growth in real balances $U(t)$: [1958, 1977].*

Source of variation	Sum of squares	Degrees of freedom	Mean square	F
(1) $U(t-1), X(t-1), X(t-2)$	21.2	3	7.067	
(2) Addition of $\mu(t-1) - \pi(t-1)$	8.62	1	8.62	18.01†
(3) $U(t-1), X(t-1), X(t-2), \mu(t-1) - \pi(t-1)$	29.82	4		
(4) Residual	7.18	15	0.48	
(5) Total	37	19		

Symbols: $U(t)$ is unemployment; $X(t)$ is Barro's (1978) $DMR(t)$ multiplied by 100; $\mu(t-1)$ is the growth of M1B from year $t-2$ to year $t-1$; $\pi(t-1)$ is the growth of the GNP deflator from year $t-2$ to year $t-1$; † significantly different from zero at the one per cent level.

TABLE 4.2 *Analysis of variance of the unemployment rate: addition of unanticipated money growth in the years $t-1$ and $t-2$.*

Source of variation	Sum of squares	Degrees of freedom	Mean square	F
(1) $U(t-1), \mu(t-1) - \pi(t-1)$	29.53	2	14.77	
(2) Addition of $X(t-1), X(t-2)$	0.29	2	0.15	0.31
(3) $U(t-1), \mu(t-1) - \pi(t-1), X(t-1), X(t-2)$	29.82	4		
(4) Residual	7.18	15	0.48	
(5) Total	37	19		

and Sheffrin (1979) also provided a series for "unanticipated" money growth. Moreover, a series for "anticipated" money growth could be obtained using equation (2.49a) which relates $\mu(t)$ to the ratio of the high employment deficit to the money stock in $t-1$, denoted by $F^H(t-1)/M(t-1)$.

There is reason to believe that the trouble lies with the NCE hypothesis rather than with the particular series of "unanticipated" money growth that is used. Makin reports that his ARIMA model for quarterly data produced a series whose correlation coefficients with the comparable series of Barro–Rush and Sheffrin were, respectively, 0.87 and 0.91. The Barro series is also significantly related to the series derived from my equation (2.49a); the correlation coefficient is 0.727. I therefore conclude that the flaw is with the NCE hypothesis and not with Barro's series on "unanticipated" money growth.

A test of Sargent's NCE hypothesis against the Monetarist hypothesis

Now that it has been shown that there is no observational equivalence problem, the NCE hypothesis described by Sargent's equation (2.5) quoted above, or equation (4.2), can be compared to Monetarist equation (4.7). The NCE hypothesis is that no equation for the mathematical expectation $E_{t-1}U(t)$ of the unemployment rate can outperform autoregressive equation (4.2), and the addition of other variables will not be statistically significant.

For the 22-year sample period for $U(t)$: [1958, 1979] an analysis of variance in table 4.3 shows net effects upon the explained sum of squares of: (i) adding $U(t-1)$; (ii) adding both $U(t-2)$ and $U(t-3)$; and (iii) then adding $\mu(t-1) - \pi(t-1)$. The NCE hypothesis is that (ii) significantly increases the explained sum of squares, whereas (iii) is not statistically significant. The Monetarist hypothesis is that (iii) significantly increases the explained sum of squares.

The addition of lagged unemployment rates $U(t-2)$ and $U(t-3)$ does not significantly increase the explained sum of squares. The value

TABLE 4.3 *Analysis of variance of the unemployment rate $U(t)$, annual data $1958 \leqslant t \leqslant 1979$.*

Source of variation	Sum of squares	Degrees of freedom	Mean square, F (degrees of freedom)
(1) $U(t-1)$	13.5062	1	
addition of:			
(2) $U(t-2)$, $U(t-3)$	0.5168	2	0.2584; $F(2,17) = 0.9196$
subtotal:			
(3) $U(t-1)$, $U(t-2)$, $U(t-3)$	14.0230	3	
addition of:			
(4) $\mu(t-1) - \pi(t-1)$	15.707	1	15.707; $F(1,17) = 55.9$†
subtotal:			
(5) $U(t-1)$, $U(t-2)$, $U(t-3)$, $\mu(t-1) - \pi(t-1)$	29.73	4	
(6) Residual	4.78	17	0.281
(7) Total sum of squares	34.4545	21	

†Significant at the one per cent level.

of $F(2,17) = 0.9196$ is not statistically significant. However, the addition of the percentage change in real balances from $t-2$ to $t-1$ significantly increases the explained sum of squares. The value of $F(1,17) = 55.9$ is significant at the one per cent level. It is concluded that the NCE hypothesis, advanced by Sargent concerning the unemployment rate, is inconsistent with the data during the period $1958 \leqslant t \leqslant 1979$, whereas the Monetarist hypothesis is consistent with the data.

Alternatively, consider regression equations $(4.12)-(4.16)$ which reject the NCE and are consistent with the Monetarist hypothesis. In regressions (4.12) and (4.13), the dependent variable is the annual observation of the unemployment rate $U(t)$: $[1958, 1979]$. Equation (4.12) is an autoregressive equation conforming to NCE equation (4.2). Equation (4.13) is the Monetarist equation (4.7) which states that since prices change differentially and expectations are asymptotically rational, the mathematical expectation of the unemployment rate at year t, given the information available at $t-1$, depends upon the unemployment rate in year $t-1$ and the growth of real balances from year $t-2$ to $t-1$.

$$1958 \leqslant t \leqslant 1979$$

$$U(t) = 2.24 + 0.71U(t-1) - 0.192U(t-2) + 0.0855U(t-3)$$
$$(t=) \quad (1.87) \quad (3.04) \quad\quad (-0.673) \quad\quad (0.358) \quad (4.12)$$

$$R^2 = 0.407; \quad SE = 1.07; \quad DW = 1.72; \quad \bar{R}^2 = 0.308.$$

$$U(t) = 3.48 + 0.401U(t-1) - 0.39[\mu(t-1) - \pi(t-1)] \quad (4.13)$$
$$(t=) \quad (5.68) \quad (3.72) \quad\quad (-6.09)$$

$$R^2 = 0.794; \quad SE = 0.615; \quad DW' = 1.88; \quad \bar{R}^2 = 0.772.$$

The Monetarist hypothesis demonstrably outperforms the NCE hypothesis, on the basis of information known at $t-1$. The value of R^2 is raised from 0.4 to 0.8 and the standard error is reduced from 1.1 to 0.6. Each coefficient in the Monetarist equation is significant at the one per cent level.

Results similar to those obtained with the unemployment rate are obtained for the Okun Gap in equations $(4.14)-(4.16)$. The Okun Gap $y_1(t)$ is the percentage difference between capacity output and actual output.[8] Equations (4.14) and (4.15) are the NCE autoregressive equations corresponding to equation (4.2) or equation $(3.19b)$ and equation (4.16) corresponds to Monetarist equation (4.7), when Okun's Law is used:

Okun Gap $y_1(t)$: [1958, 1978]

$$y_1(t) = 0.849 + 0.652y_1(t-1); \quad R^2 = 0.424. \tag{4.14}$$
$$(t=) \qquad\qquad\qquad (3.74)$$

$$y_1(t) = 0.956 + 0.914y_1(t-1) - 0.456y_1(t-2) \tag{4.15}$$
$$(t=) \quad (1.435) \quad (3.824) \qquad\qquad (-1.5)$$
$$+ 0.149y_1(t-3); \quad R^2 = 0.498.$$
$$(0.623)$$

$$y_1(t) = 1.819 + 0.336y_1(t-1) - 0.668[\mu(t-1) \tag{4.16}$$
$$(t=) \quad (3.052) \quad (1.931) \qquad\qquad (-3.243)$$
$$- \pi(t-1)]; \quad R^2 = 0.633.$$

The results of the statistical tests are unambiguous and consistent. The coefficient of $\mu(t-1) - \pi(t-1)$ is significantly different from zero at the one per cent level. The NCE hypothesis is rejected and the Monetarist hypothesis is accepted.

2.4 The robustness and generality of the Monetarist hypothesis

Within sample explanation

This section examines the robustness and generality of the Monetarist equations for the unemployment rate and level of real GNP from three points of view. First, since there is a direct link between the unemployment rate and ratio of actual to capacity output (via Okun's Law), there should be a consistency between the Monetarist equation for the unemployment rate and the Monetarist equation for the level of real GNP. Secondly, the Monetarist equation for the unemployment rate should be relatively invariant for various subperiods; it should not change drastically from one subperiod to the next. Thirdly, approximately the same results should be obtained whether the rate of growth of the money supply or the rate of growth of the monetary base is used as the control variable in the unemployment rate equation. Consider each criterion in turn.

First, equation (4.17) is Okun's Law, which states that the ratio of actual to capacity output is related to the deviation of the unemployment rate from its equilibrium value. Let $y(t)$ be real GNP in billions of 1972 dollars and $f(t) = f(0)\exp(\tau t)$ be potential (capacity) GNP. Variable $u(t)$ is the unemployment rate deviation $U(t) - U_e$. Then Okun's Law is

$$\ln y(t) - \ln f(t) = -au(t). \tag{4.17}$$

The unemployment rate deviation is described by equation (4.18) (see equation (3.16)), which can be accepted by all three schools of thought:[9]

$$u(t) = (1 - \beta h)u(t-1) - \beta[\pi(t) - \pi^*_{t-1}(t)].\qquad(4.18)$$

The Monetarist hypothesis implies approximation equation (4.19) (see equations (4.4b) and (4.5) above) that unanticipated inflation $\pi(t) - \pi^*_{t-1}(t)$ is positively related to the growth of real balances from year $t-2$ to year $t-1$:

$$\pi(t) - \pi^*_{t-1}(t) = c_1[\mu(t-1) - \pi(t-1)].\qquad(4.19)$$

Equations (4.18) and (4.19) imply unemployment rate deviation equation (4.7) above. These three equations imply equation (4.20) for the logarithm of real GNP:

$$\ln y(t) = a_0 + a_1 \ln y(t-1) + a_2[\mu(t-1) - \pi(t-1)] + a_3t,\qquad(4.20)$$

where $a_1 = 1 - \beta h$, $a_2 = a\beta c_1$, $a_3 = \beta h\gamma$, and $a_0 = \beta h \ln f(0) + \gamma(1 - \beta h)$.

During the period 1958 through 1977, regression equation (4.21) is the statistical counterpart of Monetarist equation (4.20) and regression equation (4.22) is the statistical counterpart of Monetarist equation (2.7) where the dependent variable is the *change* in the unemployment rate from year $t-1$ to year t:

$$\ln y(t) = \underset{(3.59)}{4} + \underset{(2.25)}{0.387 \ln y(t-1)} + \underset{(3.3)}{0.00843[\mu(t-1) - \pi(t-1)]}$$
$$(t=)$$
$$+ \underset{(3.5)}{0.0218t}\qquad(4.21)$$

$$R^2 = 0.993;\quad SE = 0.0195;\quad DW = 1.76.$$

$$U(t) - U(t-1) = \underset{(5.34)}{3.8} - \underset{(-5.19)}{0.663U(t-1)} - \underset{(-5.47)}{0.403[\mu(t-1)}$$
$$(t=)$$
$$- \pi(t-1)];\quad U_e = 5.73\%\qquad(4.22)$$

$$R^2 = 0.701;\quad SE = 1.8;\quad DW = 1.8.$$

These two equations are perfectly consistent with each other and confirm the Monetarist hypothesis. Each coefficient is significantly different from zero at a very high level of significance, and *the explanatory power of these extremely simple equations is very high.* No contemporaneous information is used to predict contemporaneous variables. I know of no Keynesian or NCE equations which can match this performance. We can explain growth of real GNP and the change in the measured unemployment rate equally well with the same model.

Secondly, the unemployment rate equation is relatively invariant by

TABLE 4.4   *The Monetarist unemployment rate equation by subperiod*
1953−79, $U(t) = a_0 + a_1 U(t-1) + a_2 [\mu(t-1) - \pi(t-1)]$.

Span for U(t) inclusive	a_0, (t_0)	a_1, (t_1)	a_2, (t_2)	R^2	SE	DW	U_e
1953−79	3.67 (5.37)	0.37 (3.08)	−0.39 (−5.57)	0.78	0.67		5.83
1958−79	3.48 (5.68)	0.401 (3.72)	−0.39 (−6.09)	0.79	0.615	1.88	5.81
1958−72	3.15 (4.55)	0.453 (3.39)	−0.47 (−5.31)	0.78	0.533	2.18	5.76
1965−79	2.95 (3.81)	0.491 (3.59)	−0.35 (−4.19)	0.824	0.681	1.81	5.8

Note: The t statistic is in parentheses. The h statistic, implied by DW, is not significant.

subperiods. Table 4.4 reports the regressions of Monetarist unemployment rate equation (4.7) above by subperiods, along with the implied equilibrium rate of unemployment. It is clear that the Monetarist results are not very sensitive to the particular subperiod chosen. Each coefficient is significantly different from zero at the one per cent level.

There may have been differences in monetary policies during the various subperiods. Nevertheless, there are no fundamental differences in the values of the parameters obtained for the different subperiods.

Thirdly, it is important to examine the unemployment rate equation when the control variable is the growth of the monetary base $\beta(t)$ instead of the growth of the money supply $\mu(t)$. The growth of the money supply is the sum of the growth of the monetary base and the growth of the money multiplier. In the theoretical sections it was assumed that the money multiplier is unity, but, in fact, it is not constant. The change in the money multiplier depends upon changes in the ratio of reserves to deposits and the ratio of currency to deposits, which are determined by the public rather than by monetary authority. Therefore, for the purposes of stabilization policy it is important to determine whether changes in the monetary base from $t-2$ to $t-1$ affect the unemployment rate $U(t)$ in the manner described by the Monetarist theoretical model.

Denote the rate of growth of the money multiplier as $\delta(t)$. Then the rate of monetary expansion $\mu(t)$ is defined as

$$\mu(t) \equiv \beta(t) + \delta(t). \tag{4.23a}$$

When the above definition is substituted into Monetarist unemployment rate equation (4.23b)

$$U(t) = a_0 + a_1 U(t-1) - a_2[\mu(t-1) - \pi(t-1)], \qquad (4.23b)$$

it is possible to derive

$$U(t) = [a_0 - a_2\delta(t-1)] + a_1 U(t-1) - a_2\beta(t-1) + a_2\pi(t-1). \qquad (4.23c)$$

Equation (4.23c) states that the unemployment rate $U(t)$ is negatively related to the growth of the monetary base and positively related to the rate of inflation from period $t-2$ to $t-1$. If the growth of the monetary base $\beta(t-1)$ is the same as the rate of inflation $\pi(t-1)$, then there is no impact from the monetary sector upon the real sector.

A regression of the unemployment rate $U(t):[1958, 1979]$ on $U(t-1)$, $\pi(t-1)$ and the rate of growth of the adjusted monetary base $\beta(t-1)$ from year $t-2$ to year $t-1$ is described by equation (4.24). Each coefficient is significantly different from zero at the one per cent level, and this equation explains about 80 per cent of the variation in the unemployment rate.

$$U(t) = 2.66 + 0.494U(t-1) + 0.487\pi(t-1) - 0.326\beta(t-1)$$
$$(t=) \quad (4.1) \quad (4.36) \qquad\qquad (5.66) \qquad\qquad (-4.24) \quad (4.24)$$

$$R^2 = 0.79; \quad SE = 0.657; \quad DW = 2.16.$$

Therefore, the Monetarist hypothesis is consistent with the data: (i) whether we use real GNP or the unemployment rate as the dependent variable; (ii) whether we use the rate of monetary expansion or the growth of the adjusted monetary base as an independent variable. It is relatively invariant by subperiod.

Table 4.5 and figure 4.1 describe the accuracy of the Monetarist unemployment rate equation (4.25) for $U(t):$ [1958, 1979] (it was contained in table 4.4 above):

$$E_{t-1}U(t) = 3.48 + 0.401U(t-1) - 0.39[\mu(t-1) - \pi(t-1)]$$
$$(t=) \qquad (5.68) \quad (3.72) \qquad\qquad (-6.09) \qquad\qquad (4.25)$$

$$R^2 = 0.79; \quad DW = 1.88; \quad SE = 0.615.$$

The first column in table 4.5 is the actual unemployment rate $U(t)$. The second column is the mathematical expectation of the unemployment rate $E_{t-1}U(t)$ conditional upon information known no later than at year $t-1$, and the third column is the forecast error $U(t) - E_{t-1}U(t)$. This simple Monetarist equation explains about 80 per cent of the variance of $U(t)$, without using any contemporaneous information.

TABLE 4.5 *Actual and expected unemployment rates and forecast error 1958–79.*

t	Actual $U(t)$ (%)	$E_{t-1}U(t)$† (%)	$U(t) - E_{t-1}U(t)$ (%)
1958	6.8	6.3	0.5
1959	5.5	6.4	−0.9
1960	5.5	5.1	0.4
1961	6.7	6.4	0.3
1962	5.5	5.7	−0.2
1963	5.7	5.5	0.2
1964	5.2	5.14	0.06
1965	4.5	4.7	−0.2
1966	3.8	4.5	−0.7
1967	3.8	4.5	−0.7
1968	3.6	4.6	−1.0
1969	3.5	3.9	−0.4
1970	4.9	4.5	0.4
1971	5.9	6.1	−0.2
1972	5.6	5.2	0.4
1973	4.9	4.6	0.3
1974	5.6	4.9	0.7
1975	8.5	7.6	0.9
1976	7.7	8.8	−1.1
1977	7.0	6.5	0.5
1978	6.0	5.7	0.3
1979	5.8	5.5	0.3

†Equation (4.25).

Prediction outside the sample period

A fundamental objection raised by NCE against econometric models is that the estimated coefficients are functions of the monetary and fiscal policies pursued. For example, in NCE equation (4.9) above, the coefficient αa_{12} of the change in real balances $\mu(t-1) - \pi(t-1)$ from year $t-2$ to year $t-1$ is a function of policy parameter α in equation (4.8a). As policy parameter α changes, the coefficient of $\mu(t-1) - \pi(t-1)$ is also expected to change. Is my Monetarist unemployment rate equation (4.7) or (4.23b) amenable to this NCE criticism?

A simple test of the validity of this NCE criticism is to examine the ability of the Monetarist unemployment rate equation to predict *outside* of the sample period.

The third equation in table 4.4 is an estimated Monetarist unemploy-

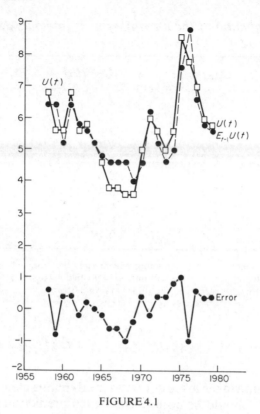

FIGURE 4.1

ment rate equation over the sample period 1958–72. It is denoted as equation (4.26):

$$E_{t-1}^{a}U(t) = 3.15 + 0.453\,U(t-1) - 0.47\,[\mu(t-1) - \pi(t-1)]\,. (4.26)$$

This equation can be used to predict the unemployment rate $U(t)$ from 1973 through 1980. This prediction, denoted by $E_{t-1}^{a}U(t)$, is shown in the second column of table 4.6. The actual unemployment rate is in the first column.

Moreover, a dynamic ex-ante prediction can be performed outside the sample period. Instead of using the previously realized unemployment rate $U(t-1)$ to predict $U(t)$, the previously predicted values $E_{t-2}U(t-1)$ can be used to predict the current period's unemployment rate $U(t)$. The dynamic ex-ante prediction is denoted by $E_{t-1}^{b}U(t)$ as described by equation (4.27). It is used to predict the unemployment rate from 1973 through 1980:

TABLE 4.6 *Prediction of the unemployment rate outside the sample period.*

	$U(t)$ (%)	$E^{a}_{t-1}U(t)$ (%)	$E^{b}_{t-2}U(t)$ (%)
1973	4.9	4.3	4.3
1974	5.6	4.7	4.4
1975	8.5	7.9	7.4
1976	7.7	9.35	8.85
1977	7	6.5	7.02
1978	6	5.6	5.63
1979	5.8	5.4	5.3
1980	7.1	6.1	5.9
RMSE		0.85	0.89
R^2		0.79	0.75

Notes: The first column is the actual unemployment rate; the second column is the prediction from equation (4.26); the third column is the prediction from equation (4.27). The root mean square error is *RMSE*. The values of R^2 are between the predicted and the actual rates.

$$E^{b}_{t-1}U(t) = 3.15 + 0.453 E^{b}_{t-2}U(t-1) - 0.47 [\mu(t-1) - \pi(t-1)].$$
$$(4.27)$$

The third column in table 4.6 contains the dynamic ex-ante prediction.

Three points should be noted. First, each prediction states that the unemployment rate will (i) rise from 1973 to 1976, (ii) decline from 1976 to 1979, and (iii) rise from 1979 to 1980. (The predicted unemployment rate for 1981, $E^{a}_{80}U(81) = 7.6$ per cent.) Actually, the predictions missed the peak by one year. The peak unemployment rate occurred in 1975 not in 1976, and it was less severe than predicted. Secondly, the root mean square errors of prediction are 0.85 and 0.89 for the two methods of prediction. These exceed the standard error of estimate for the third equation in table 4.4 and are due to the large error made in 1976. Thirdly, the values of R^2 between the actual and predicted unemployment rates are 79 per cent for $E^{a}_{t-1}U(t)$ and 75 per cent for $E^{b}_{t-1}U(t)$. These are extraordinary high degrees of accuracy outside the sample period, particularly with a dynamic ex-ante simulation.

The conclusion is that the NCE objection is without foundation. Despite the significant shocks and policy changes in 1973–80, relative to 1958–72, there was no significant change in structure.

3   The rate of inflation

3.1   *The Keynesian criticisms of the Monetarist hypothesis*

The Keynesian view of inflation was described in equation (3.64), repeated here as equation (4.28). It is summarized by the quotation from Modigliani and Papademos (1976: 4): "It is shown that historical experience supports the proposition that there exists some *critical* rate of unemployment such that, as long as unemployment does not fall below it, inflation can be expected to decline":

$$\pi(t) - \pi(t-1) = -c_1[U(t-1) - U_e] + \varepsilon_2(t), \tag{4.28}$$

where $\varepsilon_2(t)$ represents exogenous shocks and U_e is the critical rate of unemployment.

Neo-Keynesians[10] draw far-reaching conclusions from this hypothesis. A high rate of monetary expansion is perfectly consistent with decelerating inflation as long as $U(t-1)$ exceeds U_e, which they refer to as the non-inflationary rate of unemployment (NIRU) and estimate it at 5.5 per cent.

Modigliani and Papademos have advocated a rate of monetary expansion from 9–16 per cent per annum during 1976 to reduce the unemployment rate to the NIRU. As long as the unemployment rate exceeds 6 per cent:

There is no danger that such a growth rate for the next two or three quarters would lead to increasing inflation contemporaneously or even at some later date (1976: 17). [The Neo-Keynesian] ... analysis confronts a widely held concern, encouraged by at least some monetarists, that such a rapid growth and sudden acceleration of the money supply, implying a two- to three-fold increase over recent rates, would unfavorably influence prices and inevitably set off a new round of inflation .... Another concern of the monetarists is that an increase in the money supply somehow has a direct effect on inflation, whatever the slack in the economy. (1975: 159–60)

Modigliani and Papademos adduce the following as evidence in favor of the Neo-Keynesian hypothesis. They regress $\pi_1(t)$, the rate of inflation of the CPI excluding food, during the period 1953–71, upon the following variables: (i) $UA^{-1}(t)$, the reciprocal of the unemployment rate standardized for the composition of the labor force; (ii) $\pi_1(t-1)$, the lagged value of the dependent variable; (iii) $\alpha(t)$, the rate of change of productivity in the private non-farm business sector; (iv) $\pi_2(t)$, the

rate of change of a price index of imports excluding crude and manu-
factured goods; (v) $\pi_3(t-1)$, the rate of change of a price index of farm
products lagged one year; (vi) $\mu(t)$, $\mu(t-1)$, the current and lagged
rates of monetary expansion of the M_1 money supply.

Their results are summarized in table 4.7, with the appropriate t
statistics. On the basis of this regression, they reject the Monetarist
view and accept the Keynesian analysis. They state that, if the rate of
monetary expansion has an independent effect on inflation then the
coefficients of $\mu(t)$ and $\mu(t-1)$ in table 4.7 should be significantly
positive. They claim that the

... result of this test ... [shown in my table 4.7] is striking and unequivocal:
when [$\mu(t)$ or $\mu(t-1)$] is added to ... [$\pi_1(t-1)$, $UA^{-1}(t)$, $\alpha(t)$, $\pi_2(t)$, $\pi_3(t-1)$]
singly or in combination, the estimated coefficients turn out to be actually
negative, although not very significant. The safe conclusion is that absolutely
no evidence supports any systematic effect of the rate of growth of the money
supply on inflation except insofar as it helps determine aggregate demand in
relation to the available labor force ....

Put somewhat differently, the evidence supports the view that the rate of
inflation depends on aggregate demand through its impact on unemployment,
but does not depend on the mix of fiscal policy and growth of monetary
aggregates that determines the aggregate demand for labor. (1975: 161–2)

There are several reasons why their rejection of the Monetarist
hypothesis is unconvincing. First, a Monetarist believes that a rise in
the rate of monetary expansion raises the rate of inflation, which is
defined as a pervasive rise in prices. Some prices respond faster, and to
a larger extent, than do others. Table 2.5 shows that prices of intermediate materials respond to a larger extent than do prices of finished
goods, in both expansions and contractions. Moreover, insofar as the
US is a large source of world demand, import prices in foreign currency
will rise as a result of the US inflation. If the exchange rate is free, then
a rise in imports relative to exports, or the anticipation of future inflation, will raise the dollar price of foreign exchange. The net result
would be that a rise in the rate of monetary expansion induces rises in
a wide variety of price indices at different rates. Therefore, Modigliani
and Papademos are correlating the rate of inflation of one subset of
prices $\pi_1(t)$ with its own lagged value $\pi_1(t-1)$ and with rates of inflation
of other subsets of prices $\pi_2(t)$, $\pi_3(t-1)$. That is what builds up the
value $\bar{R}^2$ and reduces the standard error of estimate. They are just
correlating different components of the rate of inflation and are not
testing any significant economic hypothesis.

The intercorrelation matrix between variable X_1, the rate of inflation

TABLE 4.7 *Modigliani–Papademos regression equation for the rate of inflation of the CPI, excluding food, $\pi_1(t)$, 1953–71.*

Variable	Symbol	Regression coefficient	t-value
Constant		-0.78	-0.89
Reciprocal of adjusted unemployment rate	$UA^{-1}(t)$	12.2	2.98
Lagged dependent variable	$\pi_1(t-1)$	0.77	5.5
Rate of change of productivity in private non-farm business sector	$\alpha(t)$	-0.29	-2.07
Rate of inflation of imports, excluding crude and manufactured foods	$\pi_2(t)$	0.11	2.04
Lagged rate of change of price index of farm products	$\pi_3(t-1)$	0.0555	1.67
Rate of monetary expansion	$\mu(t)$	-0.004	-0.03
Lagged rate of monetary expansion	$\mu(t-1)$	-0.21	-1.4
Standard error		0.58	
Adjusted $\bar{R}^2$		0.88	
DW		1.84	

Source: Modigliani and Papademos (1975: table 1, equation (3), 150).

of the CPI excluding food, the rate of inflation of food or farm products X_2 and the lagged rate of monetary expansion X_3 is given in table 4.8 for 1953–71 and, in parentheses, 1958–77. The reason why the coefficient of the rate of monetary expansion is not significant is quite apparent from the intercorrelation matrix. The zero-order correlation between the rate of inflation of the CPI excluding food X_1 and the lagged rate of monetary expansion X_3 is r_{13} equals 0.53 for 1953–71 and 0.62 for 1958–77, which coefficients are significant at the 5 per cent and 1 per cent levels respectively. But the partial correlation coefficient between X_1 and X_3, given X_2, denoted by $r_{13.2}$ equals 0.39 for 1953–71 and 0.246 for 1958–77, which coefficients are not significant at the 5 per cent level. The high degree of correlation between the two price indices X_1 and X_2, $r_{12} = 0.71$ for 1953–71 and 0.719 for 1958–77, dominates the effect of the rate of monetary expansion upon the rate of inflation of either price index. Hence, the partial correlation coefficient $r_{13.2}$ is not significant. In no way can the results in table 4.7 justify their conclusion that the Monetarist hypothesis is inconsistent with the data.

TABLE 4.8 *Intercorrelation matrix r_{ij} for 1953−71 (1958−77).*

	X_1	X_2	X_3
X_1 rate of inflation of CPI excluding food	1	0.71 (0.719)	0.53 (0.62)
X_2 rate of inflation of food component of CPI		1	0.39 (0.69)
X_3 lagged rate of monetary expansion			1

Source: Economic Report of the President (1979: Table B-54, 244) for price data.

Secondly, contemporaneous variables appear on both sides of the inflation equation. The rates of inflation $\pi_1(t)$, $\pi_2(t)$ and the rate of unemployment $UA^{-1}(t)$ all refer to the same period. It is not possible to predict the rate of inflation $\pi_1(t)$ unless the values of $\pi_2(t)$ and $UA^{-1}(t)$ are known. As all rates will be known at the same time, the regression is not the same as $E_{t-1}\pi_1(t)$, which is the mathematical expectation of $\pi_1(t)$ given information available at prior time $t-1$. Modigliani and Papademos do not have an explanation or a prediction of inflation.

Thirdly, the Monetarist model (chapter 3) claims that a rise in the rate of monetary expansion $\mu(t)$ lowers $U(t+1)$ and raises $\pi(t+1)$. The negative correlation between the current inflation rate and the current unemployment rate does not represent a causation running from the current unemployment rate to the current inflation rate. Both are affected by the same control variable in the manner described in chapter 3.

For these reasons, the Modigliani−Papademos *ad hoc* equation described in table 4.7 cannot be considered as evidence rejecting the Monetarist and supporting the Keynesian view. A different approach must be taken to test which alternative hypothesis is consistent with the data.

3.2 *A direct test of the competing hypotheses*

There are fundamental differences among the three schools of thought concerning the rate of inflation. *Keynesians* believe that the change in the rate of inflation is determined to some extent by the Okun Gap and primarily by exogenous forces $\varepsilon_2(t)$ as described by equation (4.28) above. Monetary and fiscal policy affect the rate of inflation by first changing the Okun Gap. Since the Okun Gap can be varied either by fiscal or by monetary policy, there need be no systematic relation between monetary policy and the rate of inflation. Moreover, as the quotations from the Carter Council (cited in chapter 3) indicate, Keynesians believe that the main source of variation in the inflation rate is $\varepsilon_2(t)$ exogenous prices of food, imports and nominal unit labor costs.

NCE believes (equation (3.27)) that a one per cent change in the expected money stock changes the expected price level by one per cent. According to the Policy Ineffectiveness Proposition, the expected unemployment rate is only affected by unanticipated policy (equation (3.31)). Inflation can therefore be reduced quickly without adverse effects upon the unemployment rate by an appropriate reduction in the rate of monetary expansion.

The *Monetarist* view lies between these positions. The change in the rate of inflation depends upon the rate at which the Keynesian excess demand is changing and upon the asymptotically rational anticipated rate of inflation. This is described by equation (3.50), repeated here as equation (4.29a), when the rate of monetary expansion is constant:

$$D\pi(t) = -P_2[\pi(t) - \mu] - c[\pi^*(t) - \mu]. \tag{4.29a}$$

At time $t = 0$, let the actual and anticipated rates of inflation be equal. Then the change in the rate of inflation equation (4.29a) is

$$D\pi(0) = [P_2 + c][\mu - \pi(0)]. \tag{4.29b}$$

Approximating (4.29a) for $t \geqslant 0$:

$$\pi(t+1) - \pi(t) = [P_2 + c][\mu(t) - \pi(t)] = a_{22}[\mu(t) - \pi(t)]. \tag{4.30}$$

The approximation corresponds to trajectories AB or FG in figure 3.7, but it loses its validity close to the origin along trajectories BC or GH. This approximation is the price paid for converting a system with an unobserved π^* to one with observable variables. It is shown below that this is a low price to pay for the predictive accuracy obtained.

In discrete time, equation (4.30) states that the rate of inflation from year $t-1$ to t is a weighted average of the rate of monetary expansion and rate of inflation from year $t-2$ to year $t-1$. No distinction is made between "anticipated" and "unanticipated" money growth, and the rate of inflation can increase if $\mu > \pi$, regardless of the slack in the economy:

$$\pi(t) = (1 - a_{22})\pi(t-1) + a_{22}\mu(t-1). \tag{4.31}$$

Monetary policy changes the inflation rate differentially according to this Monetarist formulation, but, in the NCE formulation, anticipated monetary policy changes the inflation rate algebraically. The

Keynesian version claims that there is no direct link between monetary policy and the rate of inflation.

A direct test of the competing Keynesian and Monetarist hypotheses is described by regression equation (4.32). The dependent variable is the *change in the rate of inflation* of the GNP deflator $p(t)$, that is,

$$\pi(t) - \pi(t-1) = \left[\left(\frac{p(t)}{p(t-1)} - 1\right) - \left(\frac{p(t-1)}{p(t-2)} - 1\right)\right] \times 100$$

between year $t-1$ and year t. The independent variables are the unemployment rate $U(t-1)$ in year $t-1$ and the rate of M1B monetary expansion $\mu(t-1)$, less the rate of inflation, from year $t-2$ to year $t-1$:

$$\pi(t) - \pi(t-1) = a_0 + a_1 U(t-1) + a_2[\mu(t-1) - \pi(t-1)]. \quad (4.32)$$

The Monetarist hypothesis is that the significant variable is the change in real balances, whereas the Keynesian hypothesis is that it is the unemployment rate.

Equations (4.33)–(4.35) are strictly concerned with testing the Keynesian against the Monetarist hypothesis. Equations (4.33) and (4.34) refer to the United States, where the dependent variable is the change in the rate of inflation of the GNP deflator $\pi(t) - \pi(t-1)$. Equation (4.33) refers to $\pi(t)$: [1958, 1979], and equation (4.34) refers to $\pi(t)$: [1920, 1939]. Equation (4.35) refers to Canada, where the dependent variable is $\pi(t)$, and the period for $\pi(t)$ is [1962, 1979]. The independent variables here are $U(t-1)$, $\pi(t-1)$ and $\mu(t-1)$.

US [1958, 1979]

$$\pi(t) - \pi(t-1) = \underset{(0.251)}{0.314} - \underset{(-0.182)}{0.04\,U(t-1)} + \underset{(3.59)}{0.468\,[\mu(t-1)}$$
$$(t=) \qquad\qquad\qquad\qquad\qquad\qquad\qquad\qquad - \pi(t-1)] \quad (4.33)$$

$R^2 = 0.451; \quad SE = 1.23; \quad DW = 1.93.$

US [1920, 1939]

$$\pi(t) - \pi(t-1) = \underset{}{-4.51} + \underset{(0.908)}{0.211\,U(t-1)} + \underset{(1.8)}{0.599\,[\mu(t-1)}$$
$$(t=) \qquad (-1.35) \qquad\qquad\qquad\qquad\qquad\qquad - \pi(t-1)] \quad (4.34)$$

$R^2 = 0.189; \quad SE = 8.34; \quad DW = 2.24.$

Canada [1962, 1979]

$$\pi(t) = \underset{(-0.989)}{-1.85} + \underset{(0.554)}{0.174\,U(t-1)} + \underset{(3.77)}{0.512\,\pi(t-1)} + \underset{(3.54)}{0.468\,\mu(t-1)}$$
$$(t=) \qquad\qquad\qquad\qquad\qquad\qquad\qquad\qquad\qquad\qquad\qquad (4.35)$$

$R^2 = 0.806; \quad SE = 1.8; \quad DW = 2.03.$

The results are unambiguous in rejecting the Keynesian hypothesis. In no case is $U(t-1)$, the initial period's unemployment rate, statistically significant; and, in equations (4.34) and (4.35), it has the wrong sign.

In equation (4.33), which refers to the period 1958 through 1979, the change in real balances $\mu(t-1) - \pi(t-1)$ is significantly different from zero at the one per cent level. In equation (4.34), which refers to the interwar period[11], the coefficient is close to that found in equation (4.33), but it is significantly different from zero only at the ten per cent level. Alternatively, the coefficient of $\mu(t-1) - \pi(t-1)$ in the interwar period of 0.599 is not significantly different from unity. In equation (4.35), where the dependent variable is the Canadian rate of inflation $\pi(t)$, the coefficients of $\pi(t-1)$ and $\mu(t-1)$ have the correct signs and are significantly different from zero at the one per cent level. It is obvious from the Durbin–Watson statistics that the implied h statistics indicate that there is no serial correlation of residuals.

The *conclusion* is that, in a direct test of the Keynesian against the Monetarist hypothesis, *the Keynesian hypothesis is decisively rejected, and the Monetarist hypothesis is accepted.*

There has been an extensive controversy (Stein, 1976) whether bond-financed fiscal policy can significantly affect the rate of inflation. Keynesians argue that the excess demand for goods can be raised by any combination of monetary or fiscal policy; and the change in the rate of inflation responds slowly to the excess demand for goods. Since the driving force behind the rate of inflation could be bond-financed fiscal policy, there need be no relation between the rate of inflation and the rate of monetary expansion.

The Monetarist assumption [A3] (chapter 3, section 4.1) is that a bond-financed rise in government expenditures raises the ratio θ of federal debt to money. As ratio θ of bonds to money rises, the real rate of interest increases to induce the public to hold a greater fraction of its wealth in the form of bonds. Moreover, the ratio θ rises steadily as a result of cumulative government budget deficits. Consequently, the real rate of interest also tends to rise steadily. Real private investment is crowded out by the steady rise in the real rate of interest, and excess aggregate demand is increased by substantially less than the initial rise in real government expenditure. In fact, as equation (3.47) indicates, there will eventually be a decline in real excess aggregate demand when θ is sufficiently high. Therefore, the Monetarists do not believe that a bond-financed rise in government expenditure is inflationary after three quarters.

Studies by Maital (1979: Table 2), Stephens (1980: Table 1) and Butkiewicz (1981: Table 2) are all consistent with this Monetarist specification. An increase in the growth of real government expenditures, unaccompanied by a rise in the rate of monetary expansion, does not produce a rise in the rate of inflation when the span of time is at least three quarters. Therefore, the only systematic force determining the rate of inflation is the rate of monetary expansion in the manner described by Monetarist equation (4.31) above.

3.3   The predictive accuracy and generality of the Monetarist inflation equation

In this section, I consider the predictive accuracy of Monetarist equation (4.31) for the rate of inflation in the United States, Canada, the World and a sample of 12 countries. Five issues are discussed.

First, the stability of the US inflation equation is examined by subperiods. Secondly, it is asked whether similar results are obtained whether the control variable is the rate of monetary expansion $\mu(t)$ or whether it is the rate of expansion of the monetary base $\beta(t)$. Thirdly, the predictive accuracy of the inflation equation is examined by using a dynamic ex-ante simulation with no correction for earlier prediction errors. Fourthly, I compare the inflation equations for the US, Canada and the World as an aggregate. Fifthly, the Monetarist view is applied to explain differences in the rates of inflation among a cross-section of countries.

Similar inflation equations are obtained for the US, Canada and the World
Table 4.9 contains regression equations (4.36)−(4.40) which correspond to Monetarist equation (4.31), where the dependent variable $\pi(t)$, the rate of inflation in year t, is a linear combination of the previous year's rates of inflation $\pi(t-1)$ and monetary expansion $\mu(t-1)$. All variables are measured in per cent per annum. Equation (4.36) refers to the rate of inflation of the GNP deflator in the US during 1958−79; equation (4.37) is based upon subperiod 1958−72; and equation (4.38) is based upon (overlapping) subperiod 1965−79. Equation (4.39) refers to the rate of inflation of the GNP deflator in Canada during the period 1962−79; and equation (4.40) refers to the rate of inflation of the CPI of the World as a whole for 1953−79. The t statistics are in parentheses.

Equations (4.36) for the US, (4.39) for Canada and (4.40) for the World as a whole are remarkably similar and strongly support the Monetarist hypothesis. The coefficients of $\pi(t-1)$ and $\mu(t-1)$ are all close to 0.5, and the values of R^2 are generally approximately 80 per cent. The only notable difference is that the constant in the world CPI

TABLE 4.9 *The Monetarist rate of inflation equation $\pi(t)$ for the US by subperiods, and Canada and the World as a whole:*
$\pi(t) = a_0 + a_1\pi(t-1) + a_2\mu(t-1)$.

Series	a_0, (t_0)	a_1, (t_1)	a_2, (t_2)	R^2	SE	DW
US 1958−78	−0.436	0.569	0.545	0.802	1.21	2.28 (4.36)
	$t = (-0.717)$	(4.38)	(3.81)			
US 1958−72	0.214	0.574	0.298	0.78	0.722	2.45 (4.37)
	$t =$ (0.465)	(3.2)	(2.32)			
US 1965−79	−0.901	0.588	0.619	0.659	1.45	2.36 (4.38)
	$t = (-0.575)$	(3.43)	(2.36)			
Canada 1962−79	−1	0.523	0.495	0.802	1.76	2 (4.39)
	$t = (-0.961)$	(3.98)	(3.72)			
World 1953−79	−1.96	0.538	0.548	0.89	1.34	1.49 (4.40)
	$t =$ (2.45)	(4.52)	(4.12)			

Notes: US data are taken from the Federal Reserve Bank of St Louis, *Annual US Economic Data*, appendix to this chapter. Canadian data are from Federal Reserve Bank of St Louis, *International Economic Conditions, Annual Data*. The International Monetary Fund 1979: *Survey*, November 12, p. 352 contains data for the World CPI rate of inflation and rate of monetary expansion. The money growth figure for 1958 was missing, so that year was excluded.

inflation is significant, whereas the constant is not significant in the US and Canadian inflation equations for the GNP deflator.

The US equation (4.36) for the inflation of the GNP deflator can be rounded[12] and written as

$$\pi(t) = 0.5\pi(t-1) + 0.5\mu(t-1). \tag{4.41}$$

If the rate of M1B monetary expansion is constant, then the US rate of inflation of the GNP deflator converges to the constant rate of monetary expansion. The reason why the constant is not significant in the equation for the US is that it is due to the trend in the velocity of M1B, but there is no trend in the velocity of M2. Consider the proportionate rates of growth in the US, between 1961 and 1980, of M1B (denoted by μ_{1B}), M2 (denoted by μ_2), the GNP deflator (π), real GNP (denoted by $G(y)$) and nominal GNP (denoted by $G(y_N)$).

There are three points to note: (i) The rate of growth of nominal GNP is equal to the rate of M2 monetary expansion: $G(y_N) = 8.8 = \mu_2$. (ii) The rate of inflation $\pi = 5.1$ per cent per annum is approximately equal to the rate of M2 monetary expansion less the growth of real GNP:

$\mu_2 - G(y) = 8.8 - 3.6 = 5.2$ per cent per annum is approximately equal to $\pi = 5.1$ per cent per annum. (iii) The rate of inflation $\pi = 5.1$ per cent per annum is approximately equal to the rate of M1B monetary expansion $\mu_{1B} = 5.5$ per cent per annum.

During a 20-year subperiod, the Monetarist results are extremely clear cut: inflation and the rate of growth of nominal GNP are equal to the rate of monetary expansion, modulus a constant, which depends upon the definition of money that is used.

During the subperiods 1958–72 and 1965–79 in the US, there was a difference in the regression coefficient of the rate of monetary expansion. The question then arises: how valid is Monetarist equation (4.41) for the US or (4.40) for the World as a whole as a short-run predictor of inflation? This is the subject of the next section.

The Monetarist equation as a short-run predictor of inflation

A prediction or an explanation of inflation is an equation where the dependent variable is $E_{t-1}\pi(t)$, which is the mathematical expectation of the percentage change in the price level from year $t-1$ to year t, *given information available at earlier date $t-1$*. Keynesians attribute inflation at time t to *ad hoc* factors which occur at time t but which are not known at earlier date $t-1$. Therefore, there is no Keynesian theory which can explain and predict inflation. Monetarist equations (4.41) and those in table 4.9 simply require information concerning this year's rates of inflation and monetary expansion to predict the rate of inflation which will prevail next year.

An extremely rigorous test of the Monetarist explanation of inflation is reported in table 4.11 and figure 4.2. Consider equation (4.41) and start in 1957 where $\pi(57) = 3.4$ per cent per annum and $\mu(57) = 0.6$ per cent per annum. Then the prediction of the 1958 inflation is described by

$$E_{57}(58) = 0.5\pi(57) + 0.5\mu(57) = 0.5(3.4) + 0.5(0.6) = 2\% \text{ p.a.}$$
$$(4.42)$$

For the 21 years 1959 through 1979, the *previously predicted* rate of inflation $E_{t-2}\pi(t-1)$ and the actual rate of monetary expansion $\mu(t-1)$ are used to obtain the predicted rate of inflation in year t as described by

$$E_{t-1}\pi(t) = 0.5E_{t-2}\pi(t-1) + 0.5\mu(t-1); \quad t: [1959, 1979]. \quad (4.43)$$

This approach only requires a knowledge of the rates of monetary expansion, and the rate of inflation in some initial period, to predict the rate of inflation in the subsequent period. There is no built-in

TABLE 4.10 *Growth rates (% p.a.) for 1961–80 of nominal GNP,*
money and real GNP.

μ_{1B}	5.5	π	5.1	$G(y_N)$	8.8
μ_2	8.8	$G(y)$	3.6		

correction for previous forecasting errors and only monetary factors
are considered. To be sure, exogenous forces and fiscal policy affect
the price level, but they do not affect its rate of change over a sustained
period of time (see table 4.10).

The first column in table 4.11 contains the actual rate of inflation $\pi(t)$
in the United States between year $t-1$ and year t; the second column
contains the prediction $E_{t-1}\pi(t)$ based upon forecasting equation (4.43).
The third column is the policy input $\mu(t)$. Figure 4.2 compares $\pi(t)$
with $E_{t-1}\pi(t)$ in a vivid manner. The value at R^2 between the actual rate

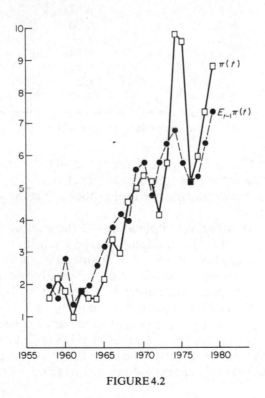

FIGURE 4.2

TABLE 4.11 *Actual and expected inflation rates 1958–79.*

t	Actual $\pi(t)$ (% p.a.)	$E_{t-1}\pi(t)$ (% p.a.)†	$\mu(t)$ (% p.a.)
1958	1.6	2.0	1.2
1959	2.2	1.6	3.8
1960	1.7	2.7	−0.1
1961	0.9	1.3	2.1
1962	1.8	1.7	2.4
1963	1.5	2.05	3.1
1964	1.6	2.58	3.9
1965	2.2	3.24	4.2
1966	3.3	3.72	4.6
1967	2.9	4.16	3.9
1968	4.5	4.03	7.1
1969	5.0	5.57	6.0
1970	5.4	5.78	3.7
1971	5.1	4.74	6.7
1972	4.1	5.72	7.1
1973	5.8	6.41	7.3
1974	9.7	6.86	4.9
1975	9.6	5.88	4.6
1976	5.2	5.24	5.5
1977	6.0	5.37	7.5
1978	7.3	6.44	8.2
1979	8.8	7.32	7.9

†This column is a dynamic ex-ante simulation of equation (4.43).

of inflation in the first column of the table and the dynamic ex-ante prediction in the second column is over 80 per cent. The large errors in 1974 and 1975 reflect transitory supply shocks, but the system adjusts to its normal level.

There are four important implications of the analysis of the US rate of inflation. First, the US and Canadian rates of inflation are amenable to a simple explanation in terms of Monetarist equation (4.41) or (4.43). There is no need to consider the innumerable exogenous *ad hoc* disturbances to the price level; they are ephemeral and do not account for more than 20 per cent of the variation in the rate of inflation. The only systematic influence is the rate of monetary expansion.

Secondly, the driving force behind the US inflation, the rate of monetary expansion, is directly related to the rate of expansion of the monetary base which is indeed a control variable. A clear way to see this is to substitute the rate of expansion of the adjusted monetary base, denoted by $\beta(t)$, for the rate of monetary expansion $\mu(t)$, in Monetarist rate of inflation equation (4.31). For the period of $\pi(t)$: [1958, 1979], the regression results are described by

$$\pi(t) = -0.247 + 0.465\pi(t-1) + 0.478\beta(t-1) \qquad (4.44)$$
$$(t=) \quad (-0.38) \quad (2.77) \qquad\qquad (3.13)$$

$$R^2 = 0.768; \quad SE = 1.31; \quad DW = 1.77.$$

Equation (4.44), involving the rates of expansion of the adjusted monetary base, yields the same results as do the equations using the rate of monetary expansion. The rate of inflation in year t is an average of the rate of inflation in year $t-1$ and the rate of growth of the monetary base from year $t-2$ to year $t-1$. Therefore, *the United States can control more than 75 per cent of the variation in its rate of inflation by controlling the growth of its monetary base.*

Thirdly, the United States determines its own rate of inflation because it can pursue a relatively independent monetary policy. It has been able to do so, in the period of stabilized exchange rates, because the dollar has been the reserve currency. Foreign central banks have held their dollar assets in the form of Treasury securities. When the US had a balance of payments deficit, the foreign central banks, which acquired the dollars from its nationals, reinvested those dollars in US Treasury securities. Similarly, when the US had a balance of payments surplus, the foreign central bank sold some of its Treasury securities to provide the dollars demanded by its nationals. Consequently, foreign official capital flows designed to stabilize exchange rates have offset US payments imbalances. For this reason, the US balance of payments has had little effect upon the US monetary base during the period of stabilized exchange rates.

Fourthly, after four years the rate of inflation has converged very closely to the rate of monetary expansion. Therefore, long-range predictions of the rate of inflation after 10 or 25 years based upon predictions of developments in energy or any other non-monetary sector are considered by Monetarists to be devoid of scientific content. Only monetary policy systematically affects the rate of inflation.

The speed of response of the rate of inflation is derived by solving inflation equation (4.41) in closed form, when the initial rate of inflation is $\pi(0)$ and the rate of monetary expansion is constant at μ:

$$\pi(t) = (0.5)^t\pi(0) + \mu[1 - (0.5)^t]. \qquad (4.45)$$

Equations (4.46a)–(4.46e) are the ratios of the rate of inflation $\pi(t)$ to the rate of monetary expansion μ for $t = 1, 2, 3, 4, 5$ years from the initial condition:

$$\pi(1)/\mu = 0.5 + 0.5\pi(0)/\mu. \tag{4.46a}$$

$$\pi(2)/\mu = 0.75 + 0.25\pi(0)/\mu. \tag{4.46b}$$

$$\pi(3)/\mu = 0.88 + 0.13\pi(0)/\mu. \tag{4.46c}$$

$$\pi(4)/\mu = 0.94 + 0.06\pi(0)/\mu. \tag{4.46d}$$

$$\pi(5)/\mu = 0.97 + 0.03\pi(0)/\mu. \tag{4.46e}$$

After four or five years, the adjustment of the rate of inflation to the rate of monetary expansion is almost complete, and the initial condition at time $t = 0$, that is, $\pi(0)$, has a negligible effect.

International tests of the Monetarist inflation hypothesis

The United States is less subject to outside disturbances than are smaller and more open economies. Although every country is affected by the world rate of inflation, the degree of sensitivity varies by country. In the last decade, much attention has been devoted to the effects of supply shocks upon the world rate of inflation and, from the latter, to the rates of inflation of particular countries. Quotations from the Carter Council and the Keynesians indicate the importance that Keynesians place upon unpredictable supply shocks as determinants of the world rate of inflation.

It is shown here that the world rate of inflation is primarily a monetary phenomenon and that the volatility of food and fuel prices simply reflects the phenomenon described in chapter 2: that these prices have always been more sensitive than prices of finished goods in both expansions and contractions. Therefore, the role of supply shocks in world inflation has been exaggerated. World inflation is primarily due to the world monetary policies that have been followed. Those who account for world inflation in terms of exogenous supply shocks cannot specify the mathematical expectation of inflation $E_{t-1}\pi(t)$ at time t, conditional upon information known no later than at $t-1$. They can neither explain when it will rise nor when it will decline.

The world (subscript w) inflation of the consumer price index described by equation (4.40) in table 4.9 above can be written as equation (4.47), where the regression coefficients have been rounded:

$$\pi_w(t) = 0.5\pi_w(t-1) + 0.5[\mu_w(t-1) - 3.92]. \tag{4.47}$$

If the world rate of monetary expansion is constant, then the world rate of inflation of the CPI converges to the rate of monetary expansion less 3.92 per cent per annum, which is a measure of the long-term growth rate of the economy.

Figure 4.3 and table 4.12 (first and second columns) compare the actual world rate of inflation with that predicted by regression equation (4.40) or (4.47), where no contemporaneous information is used. This simple equation explains almost 90 per cent of the variance of the world inflation from 1953 through 1979. To be sure, there was a large error in 1974 which can be attributed to supply shocks; but it was a disturbance to the 1974 price level, and had no further effects upon the rate of inflation.

A rigorous test of the Monetarist hypothesis (equation (4.47)) concerning the world rate of inflation is done by a dynamic ex-ante simulation, as was done for the US in equation (4.43). This rigorous test is designed to determine the significance of strictly monetary factors in determining the world rate of inflation. It states that all that is needed to predict the rate of inflation is a knowledge of the monetary policies which will be followed, quantified by variable $\mu'_w(t) \equiv \mu_w(t) - 3.92$ per cent per annum. Other disturbances, which feature prominently in Keynesian discussions and which Keynesians cannot predict, are not significant on average. Recall that Keynesians do not supply an $E_{t-1}\pi_w(t)$

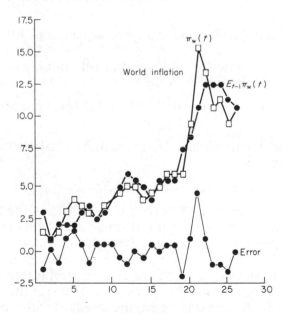

FIGURE 4.3

TABLE 4.12 *World rate of inflation $\pi_w(t)$ of the CPI, 1953–79, and predicted rates.*

Date t	$\pi_w(t)$ (% p.a.)	$E_{t-1}\pi_w(t)$	$E_{t-1}\pi_w(t)$	Date t	$\pi_w(t)$ (% p.a.)	$E_{t-1}\pi_w(t)$	$E_{t-1}\pi_w(t)$
1953	1.5	3.04	2.64	1967	4.2	4.95	4.2
1954	1.1	1.2	1.51	1968	4.4	4.13	3.64
1955	1.3	2.19	2.05	1969	5.2	5.39	4.41
1956	3.0	1.86	1.91	1970	6.0	5.6	4.59
1957	3.9	2.23	1.35	1971	5.9	5.43	4.14
1959	3.3	2.87	1.06	1972	5.8	7.74	6.06
1960	2.9	3.65	2.07	1973	9.6	8.5	7.77
1961	2.6	2.34	1.58	1974	15.3	10.8	8.87
1962	3.6	3.16	2.33	1975	13.4	12.6	8.28
1963	4.1	3.81	2.65	1976	11.1	12.3	8.58
1964	4.6	5.23	3.92	1977	11.4	12.3	9.88
1965	4.9	5.83	4.85	1978	9.7	11.4	9.53
1966	5.1	5.33	4.71	1979	11.0	11.0	9.90

Notes: The source for the first column is noted in table 4.9, where 1958 is missing. The second column is the prediction from regression equation (4.40). The third column is the prediction from dynamic ex-ante simulation equation (4.48b).

whereas equation (4.47) (as is regression equation (4.40)) is a prediction.

We start with $\pi_w(1952) = 3.9$ per cent per annum and $\mu_w'(1952) = 1.38$ per cent per annum. Then the predicted 1953 world inflation is

$$E_{52}\pi_w(53) = 0.5(3.9) + 0.5(1.38) = 2.64 \text{ per cent per annum}$$
$$(4.48a)$$

From 1953 on, the previously predicted rate of inflation $E_{t-2}\pi_w(t-1)$ can be used in

$$E_{t-1}\pi_w(t) = 0.5E_{t-2}\pi_w(t-1) + 0.5\mu_w'(t-1). \qquad (4.48b)$$

The third column in table 4.12 presents the results of the dynamic ex-ante prediction of the world rate of inflation. The dynamic ex-ante prediction explains 85 per cent of the variance of the actual world rate of inflation. Therefore, world inflation is the result of the world rate of monetary expansion. Since the regression coefficients of the world rate of inflation equation (4.40) are about the same as the US equation (4.36), except for the constant term, the speeds of convergence are the same. *Within four to five years, the world rate of inflation converges* *closely to the world rate of monetary expansion less the long-term growth rate μ_w − 3.92 per cent per annum.*

The Monetarist model of a closed economy described in chapter 3 and the implied inflation equation (4.31) above describe the US, Canadian and World inflation process. Since the Canadian economy is most responsive to the US economy, the model successfully explains the US and World rates of inflation.

Equation (4.31) does not explain the variations in the *annual* rates of inflation in the major European countries and Japan, which are more subject to worldwide disturbances and have different institutional arrangements than exist in the US. There is a less direct relation between the annual rate of inflation and the annual rate of monetary expansion in the European countries than in the US, Canada and the World. Nevertheless, within a period of four to five years, their rates of inflation converge very closely to their rates of monetary expansion, as described in equations (4.46c) and (4.46e).

Table 4.12 considers a cross-section of 12 major economies over the period 1975−80. The first column is the compound rate of inflation of the GNP deflator measured in per cent per annum from 1975 to 1980, denoted by π. The second column is the compound rate of monetary expansion from 1975 to 1980, measured in per cent per annum, denoted by μ. A regression of π (first column) on μ (second column) yields

$$\pi = -1.91 + 1.05\mu \qquad R^2 = 0.86. \qquad (4.49a)$$
$$(t=) \qquad\quad (7.7)$$
$$(s=) \qquad\quad (0.137)$$

The regression coefficient of the compound rate of monetary expansion is equal to 1.05. It is significantly different from zero, not significantly different from unity, and very close to the value predicted by equations (4.46e). A unit increase in the sustained rate of monetary expansion raises the sustained rate of inflation by the same amount.

The conclusion drawn from this sample of 12 major countries is as follows. *Over a period of five years, the Monetarist result holds: the change in the compound annual rate of inflation is very close to the change in the compound rate of monetary expansion.* This equation explains more than 85 per cent of the variation of rates of inflation among major countries, just on the basis of the monetary policies followed. No recourse is made to the *ad hoc* factors, which cannot be predicted in advance, used by the Carter Council and Keynesians. The main reason why some countries had high rates of inflation and others had low rates of inflation, during this five-year period, is that there were differences in their rates of monetary expansion. Although they

TABLE 4.13 *International rates of inflation of the GNP deflator and*
rates of monetary expansion, compound annual rates,
1975–1980.

Country	Rate of inflation (% p.a.)	Rate of monetary expansion (% p.a.)	Rate of monetary expansion less long-term growth rate (% p.a.)
Spain†	18.4	18.2†	11.7
Italy†	16.8	19.1†	14.9
UK	14.4‡	13.1	10.6
France†	10.4†	11.4†	6.4
Sweden†	10.3†	12.3†	8.7
Canada	8.7	8.0	2.7
US	7.2	7.1	3.5
Netherlands	6.0	7.6	3.1
Belgium	5.8	5.4	0.9
Japan	4.4	8.5	−0.1
Germany	4.0	8.3	4.6
Switzerland†	3.3†	6.9	3.9

Source: Federal Reserve Bank of St Louis, International Economic Conditions, Annual Data
1961–1980, June 1981; †1974–79; ‡inflation of the CPI; the long-term growth rate is
the compound rate of growth of real GNP from 1961–75.

were all subjected to the same worldwide influences, the "supply
shocks", etc., they had different monetary policies.[13]

4 Quantitative analysis of demand management policies

It has been shown in sections 2 and 3 that only the Monetarist model is
consistent with the data concerning the unemployment and inflation
rates. Therefore, the effects of demand management policies to control
unemployment and inflation are examined *quantitatively* only within
the context of the Monetarist model.

A theoretical analysis of demand management, within the context
of this model, was developed in chapter 3, section 4.3, and was illustrated in figures 3.6 and 3.7. A quantitative analysis of how demand
management policy can produce stagflation is the subject of this section.
Stagflation is a term used to describe the following phenomenon: (i)
inflation and unemployment both rise; or (ii) "high" inflation coexists
with an unemployment rate above the equilibrium rate. It is shown

that if the rate of monetary expansion is raised when the unemployment rate is too high, and the rate of monetary expansion is reduced when the rate of inflation is too high,[14] then: (i) a cycle is produced in the unemployment rate; (ii) the paradoxical situation of stagflation is generated; and (iii) the resulting time series of the unemployment and inflation rates display both positive and negative relations between these variables.

The empirical unemployment rate equation (4.50) is based upon equation (4.22), and the empirical inflation rate is equation (4.41) repeated here as (4.51):

$$U(t+1) = 3.8 + 0.34U(t) + 0.4\pi(t) - 0.4\mu(t). \tag{4.50}$$
$$\pi(t+1) = \qquad\qquad 0.5\pi(t) + 0.5\mu(t). \tag{4.51}$$

These equations are *approximations* of the Monetarist theoretical equations (table 3.1). The unit of time is one year.

4.1 Stagflation is produced by a demand management policy which focuses upon the immediate problem exclusively

It is now shown that if the rate of monetary expansion is raised when the unemployment rate is too high, and it is lowered when the inflation rate is too high, stagflation results.

Suppose that at time $t = 0$, the unemployment rate is 7.7 per cent, the inflation rate is 5.2 per cent per annum and the rate of monetary expansion is 5.5 per cent per annum (the 1976 situation). To respond to political pressures, the monetary authority attempts to reduce the unemployment rate to its equilibrium value $U_e = 5.73$ per cent. It raises the rate of monetary expansion to 8.2 per cent per annum in $t = 1$ (this was the 1978 value). Figure 4.4 or table 4.14 describes the course of the economy implied by equations (4.50) and (4.51). This approximates the theoretical analysis in figures 3.6 and 3.7.

Trajectory $ABC0$ in figure 3.7 corresponds to period $t = 1, 2, \ldots, 5$. The rise in the rate of monetary expansion above the current rate of inflation raises the rate of inflation regardless of the initial unemployment rate. The rate of inflation converges monotonically to 8.2 per cent per annum for the reasons cited in chapter 3, section 4.3. When the rate of inflation rises, unanticipated inflation occurs, real unit labor costs decrease and the unemployment rate declines even below the equilibrium rate.

Anticipated inflation rises towards the rate of monetary expansion and unanticipated inflation converges to zero. As a result of the low

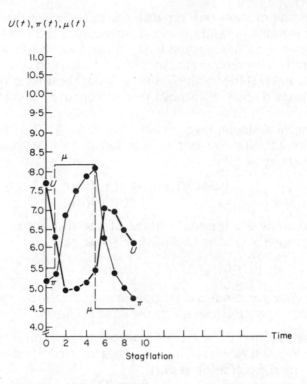

FIGURE 4.4

TABLE 4.14 *Effects of demand management policy: stagflation results.*

Time (year)	Unemployment rate (%)	Inflation rate (% p.a.)	Rate of monetary expansion (% p.a.)
0	7.7	5.2	5.5
1	6.3	5.35	8.2
2	4.8	6.78	8.2
3	4.86	7.49	8.2
4	5.17	7.84	8.2
5	5.41	8.02	4.5
6	7.05	6.26	4.5
7	6.9	5.38	4.5
8	6.5	4.94	4.5
9	6.19	4.72	4.5

unemployment rate, nominal unit labor costs rise relative to prices. Consequently, the unemployment rate rises towards the equilibrium rate.

In year $t = 4$, the unemployment rate is 5.17 per cent (and below the equilibrium rate) and the inflation rate is 7.84 per cent per annum. Suppose that the monetary authority responds to the current inflation rate and decides to reduce the rate of monetary expansion, since it has succeeded in its previous task of reducing the unemployment rate. The rate of monetary expansion is reduced to 4.5 per cent per annum.

The theoretical system is described by trajectory $FGH0$ in figure 3.7 and $ef0$ in figure 3.6. The entries in table 4.14, and figure 4.4, from $t = 5$ to $t = 9$ approximate the path of the economy. The inflation rate declines asymptotically to 4.5 per cent per annum. Initially, the actual rate of inflation declines by more than the anticipated rate (see figure 3.6 vector FF'). Nominal unit labor costs rise relative to prices and the unemployment rate rises to over 7 per cent. As the anticipated rate of inflation declines towards the rate of monetary expansion of 4.5 per cent per annum, the high unemployment rate reduces the growth of nominal unit labor costs relative to prices. With the decline in real unit labor costs, the unemployment rate starts to decline (in $t = 7$) towards the equilibrium rate of unemployment.

Figure 4.4 vividly portrays the effects of this demand management policy which tries to cope with the immediate problem: unemployment or inflation in turn. *Stagflation* has been produced during years $t = 2$ to $t = 7$. Inflation and unemployment rise together for a period of time, and high inflation coexists with unemployment in excess of the equilibrium rate. Stagflation does not necessarily result from external events (the sun, the moon and the stars) — it results from a "stop–go" monetary policy which is commonly practiced.

4.2   Policies to reduce inflation: gradualism or "bang-bang"

A prominent policy issue in recent years has been the effects upon unemployment and output of alternative policies to reduce the rate of inflation. Chapter 3 described in detail the answers implied by the Keynesian, New Classical Economics and Monetarist *theories* to this issue. Meyer and Rasche (1980) compared quantitative estimates of the social costs, in terms of lost output, of reducing the rate of inflation to zero in several models: the Keynesian model of Perry (1978), the Monetarist model of Stein (1978) (see also Carlson, 1978), the Monetarist model of the Federal Reserve Bank of St Louis (Andersen and Carlson, 1970) and NCE.

Since NCE claims that there is no social cost, in terms of lost output or of excessive unemployment, from an anticipated decline in the rate of monetary expansion (see equation (3.31)), the question becomes: how long does it take for the public to anticipate correctly the current rate of monetary growth?

Barro's measure of anticipated money growth (1978: equation (1)) abounds with logical difficulties. His equation for anticipated money growth DM_t, denoted here by $E_{t-1}\mu(t)$, is a function of rates of money growth in the previous two years $\mu(t-1)$, $\mu(t-2)$, a measure of federal government expenditures relative to trend $FEDV(t)$ and a lagged measure of the unemployment rate $UN(t-1) \equiv \log U(t-1)/[1 - U(t-1)]$. His "anticipated" money growth is described by equation (4.52a) below and is based upon annual observations:

$$E_{t-1}\mu(t) = 0.083 + 0.41\mu(t-1) + 0.21\mu(t-2) + 0.072\,FEDV(t)$$
$$+ 0.026\,UN(t-1). \qquad (4.52a)$$

If the unemployment rate U is equal to the equilibrium rate of 5.8 per cent (my estimate) and if federal government expenditures do not deviate from trend $FEDV(t) = 0$, then (4.52a) implies

$$E_{t-1}\mu(t) = 0.051 + 0.41\mu(t-1) + 0.21\mu(t-2). \qquad (4.52b)$$

Anticipated money growth $E_{t-1}\mu(t)$ depends upon the rates of monetary expansion in years $t-2$ and $t-1$. It must take two years for a "permanent" change in the rate of monetary expansion to be fully reflected in the anticipated rate of money growth. There must be serial correlation of errors when the rate of monetary expansion is changing, contrary to the MRE hypothesis. Until the anticipations catch up to the actual rate of monetary expansion, equations (3.31) and (4.25b) imply the Keynesian and Monetarist results that there will be social costs of decelerating an inflation. Barro's equation for anticipated money growth is inconsistent with the theory advanced by NCE.

A more fundamental difficulty with this equation is that there are inconsistent anticipations in the steady state. Suppose that the rate of monetary expansion is constant at μ. Then the anticipated rate of monetary expansion is described by

$$E\mu = 0.051 + 0.62\mu. \qquad (4.52c)$$

Only if $\mu = 13.4$ per cent per annum is the steady-state rate of monetary expansion correctly anticipated. Otherwise, there are permanent forecast errors of the rate of monetary expansion in the steady state. This occurs because the slope of the straight line describing $E\mu$ is less than unity and there is a strictly positive intercept. Therefore, Barro's measure of anticipated money growth is inconsistent with rationality on the part of economic agents. If μ does not equal 13.4 per cent per annum, then there is a permanent forecast error. For this reason, there seems to be an inconsistency between the theory of NCE as summarized in the Policy Ineffectiveness Proposition (see equation (3.11)) and Barro's empirical estimates of "anticipated" money growth.

Perry's Keynesian equation for the rate of inflation is similar to the Keynesian equation (3.63). Any unemployment rate in excess of 5.5 per cent, if maintained long enough, would eradicate inflation. Quantitatively, the cumulative loss of output required to eradicate an initial rate of inflation of 7.5 per cent per annum exceeds 1.6×10^{12} in 1972 prices, according to the Keynesian model.

In the approximation of the Monetarist model described by equations (4.50) and (4.51), the inflation rate converges to the rate of monetary expansion. The change in the unemployment rate from t to $t+1$ depends upon the initial deviation $u(t)$ of the unemployment rate from its equilibrium value of 5.73 per cent and the change in real balances $\mu(t-1) - \pi(t-1)$ from year $t-2$ to $t-1$. The value of $\mu(t-1) - \pi(t-1)$ is an approximation of the forecast error $\pi(t) - \pi_{t-1}^*(t)$ between the actual and anticipated rate of inflation. Therefore, a decline in $\mu(t)$ below $\pi(t)$, which is necessary to reduce the rate of inflation, raises the unemployment rate $U(t+1)$ relative to $U(t)$.

Two policies are described in table 4.15 to reduce the rate of inflation from 8 to 4 per cent per annum: a "gradualist" policy and a "bang-bang" policy. The trajectories of $U(t)$ and $\pi(t)$ are also shown in figures 4.5 and 4.6.

The bang-bang policy reduces the rate of monetary expansion immediately to the desired rate; the gradualist policy does it by steps. At the end of the third year, the inflation rate has been reduced to 4.5 per cent per annum with a bang-bang policy, whereas it is 5.88 per cent per annum with a gradualist policy.

Our interest is in the trajectory of the unemployment rate under the two policies. Only in the first two years is the unemployment rate higher with a bang-bang policy; after the second year, there is less unemployment and less inflation with a bang-bang policy.

This paradoxical result is explained as follows. The decline in real balances, which is associated with a rise in the anticipated less the actual rate of inflation, tends to raise the unemployment rate. A gradualist policy keeps dropping the rate of monetary expansion below the rate of inflation, and it is a force tending to raise the unemployment rate. The deviation of the unemployment rate from the equilibrium rate restrains the growth of nominal unit labor costs and tends to bring the

TABLE 4.15 *Policies to reduce inflation: gradualist or bang-bang.*

	Gradualist				Bang-bang			
Time	U (%)	π (% p.a.)	μ (% p.a.)	Z	U (%)	π (% p.a.)	μ (% p.a.)	Z
0	5.5	8.0	7.0	13.5	5.5	8.0	4.0	13.5
1	6.07	7.5	6.0	13.57	7.27	6.0	4.0	13.27
2	6.46	6.75	5.0	13.21	7.07	5.0	4.0	12.07
3	6.7	5.88	4.0	12.58	6.6	4.5	4.0	11.0
4	6.83	4.94	4.0	11.77	6.25	4.25	4.0	10.5
5	6.5	4.47	4.0	10.97	6.02	4.13	4.0	10.15
6	6.2	4.23	4.0	10.43	5.90	4.06	4.0	9.96
7	6.0	4.12	4.0	10.12	5.83	4.03	4.0	9.86
8	5.89	4.06	4.0	9.95	5.79	4.02	4.0	9.81
Mean	6.24	5.55		12.02	6.25	4.89		11.12
Standard deviation	0.42	1.54		1.40	0.61	1.33		1.47

Note: Z is the "misery index" $U + \pi$. Entries are derived from equations (4.50) and (4.51).

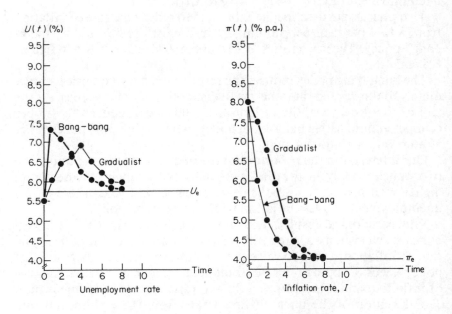

FIGURE 4.5   FIGURE 4.6

unemployment rate back to its equilibrium value. Only after $t = 4$ does the unemployment rate decline towards U_e with a gradualist policy.

A bang-bang policy produces a severe decline in real balances in the first years. As a consequence, there is a drastic rise in the anticipated less the actual price level, and this produces a drastic rise in the unemployment rate. However, the rate of inflation converges closely to the rate of monetary expansion after two years. Therefore, there is only a small gap between the anticipated and actual price levels after $t = 2$. The $p^*_{t-1}(t) - p(t)$ force no longer raises the unemployment rate. Unemployment rate deviation $u(2) = 7.07 - 5.73$ decreases the growth of nominal unit labor costs relative to prices. The decline in real unit labor costs lowers the unemployment rate steadily to the equilibrium value. A bang-bang policy produces a large but ephemeral price level forecast error, whereas a gradualist policy produces a smaller initial error which rises and then decays gradually. That is why a bang-bang policy produces a lower unemployment rate after the second year.

The only way to evaluate which policy is better is to assign weights to the unemployment rate deviation $u(t)$ and the inflation rate $\pi(t)$ in a social loss function $f(u(t), \pi(t))$, and to calculate the discounted (at rate δ) value L of the cumulative losses. Equation (4.53) is such a cumulative loss function:

$$L(t) = \int_{s=t}^{\infty} f(u(s), \pi(s))\exp(-\delta s)\mathrm{d}s. \qquad (4.53)$$

A politically popular version of the loss function f is the misery index Z, which is the sum of the unemployment and inflation rates:

$$f(u(t), \pi(t)) = Z(t) = U(t) + \pi(t). \qquad (4.54)$$

The fourth column in table 4.15 calculates the misery index associated with each policy. *The bang-bang policy produces a lower misery index in each year than does the gradualist policy.* By this criterion, the bang-bang policy is to be preferred to the gradualist policy.[15]

This chapter tested the empirical hypotheses implied by the Keynesian, NCE and Monetarist hypotheses concerning the unemployment and inflation rates. It has been shown that only the Monetarist hypothesis is consistent with the data. Then the implications of the Monetarist equations have been examined for stabilization policy. Stagflation is seen to be produced by a stop—go monetary policy, which attempts to cope with the unemployment and inflation rates in turn. Finally, it is demonstrated that a bang-bang monetary policy to reduce the rate of inflation produces a lower misery index each year than does a gradualist policy.

5   Appendix: basic US data

Year	Unemployment $U(t)$ (%)	Inflation $\pi(t)$ (% p.a.)	Rate of monetary expansion $\mu(t)$ (% p.a.)
1957	4.3	3.4	0.6
1958	6.8	1.6	1.2
1959	5.5	2.2	3.8
1960	5.5	1.7	−0.1
1961	6.7	0.9	2.1
1962	5.5	1.8	2.4
1963	5.7	1.5	3.1
1964	5.2	1.6	3.9
1965	4.5	2.2	4.2
1966	3.8	3.3	4.6
1967	3.8	2.9	3.9
1968	3.6	4.5	7.1
1969	3.5	5.0	6.0
1970	4.9	5.4	3.7
1971	5.9	5.1	6.7
1972	5.6	4.1	7.1
1973	4.9	5.8	7.3
1974	5.6	9.7	4.9
1975	8.5	9.6	4.6
1976	7.7	5.2	5.5
1977	7.0	6.0	7.5
1978	6.0	7.3	8.2
1979	5.8	8.5	7.8
1980	7.1	9.0	6.4

Sources: Federal Reserve Bank of St Louis, *Annual US Economic Data* for the rate of inflation
of the GNP deflator and the rate of M1B monetary expansion: *Economic Report of
the President* for the unemployment rate.

Notes

1   The reader is urged to read Hempel and Oppenheim (1948).
2   In equilibrium $U_e = a_0 + a_{11} U_e$. Subtract this equation from (4.6b), take
the expectation and derive (4.7).
3   Barro's (1978) equations for the unemployment rate use contemporaneous
as well as lagged "unanticipated" money growth as independent variables.
Since I am focusing upon condition expectations $E_{t-1} X(t)$ or predictions,
I cannot use contemporaneous variables in my tests of alternative
hypotheses.

4   Barro (1978: Table 1, column 3). My $X(t)$ is his $DMR(t)$ multiplied by 100.
5   The period for $U(t)$, 1958 through 1977, is dictated by the fact that
    Barro's "unanticipated" money growth is reported through 1977, and
    my standard data source, Federal Reserve Bank of St Louis, *Annual US
    Economic Data* was available from 1957 to 1980. My $\mu(t)$ is the percentage
    change in M1B from year $t - 1$ to year t, and $\pi(t)$ is the percentage change
    in the GNP deflator from year $t - 1$ to t. See section 5.
6   The h statistic is consistent with the hypothesis that there is no auto-
    correlation of residuals.
7   The h statistic is consistent with the hypothesis that there is no auto-
    correlation of residuals.
8   The Okun Gap is from Carlson (1980).
9   See chapter 3, section 3.5 for the reasons why a Keynesian can accept this
    equation.
10 See also the quotations from Tobin in chapter 3, section 5.
11 The data are from US Department of Commerce (1973).
12 The coefficients a_1 and a_2 in equation (4.36) are not significantly different
    from each other, and the Monetarist model implies that they sum to
    unity. Hence, they are rounded at 0.5.
13 In models of money and growth (see chapter 5) the steady-state rate of
    inflation π_e is equal to the constant rate of monetary expansion μ less the
    long-run rate of growth of output, which is equal to n, the long-run
    growth of effective labor. Steady-state velocity is constant. The third
    column in table 4.13 is the rate of monetary expansion μ from 1975–80
    less an estimate of n, the compound rate of growth of real GNP from
    1961–75.
       There are two interesting results. First, the mean of the first column,
    the rate of inflation π, is significantly different from the mean of the
    third column, the rate of monetary expansion less the long-term growth
    rate $\mu - n$. The pairwise t statistic is 4.83 with 11 degrees of freedom.
       Secondly, a regression of π on $\mu - n$ is described by

$$\pi \quad = 3.38 + \ 0.976(\mu - n) \qquad R^2 = 0.792. \tag{4.49b}$$
$$(t=) \qquad\qquad (6.171)$$
$$(s=) \qquad\qquad (0.158)$$

    The regression coefficient of $\mu - n$ is not significantly different from unity.
However, this equation does not explain as much as does (4.49a), which uses
the rate of monetary expansion as the independent variable.
    It is not edifying to use the rate of inflation π, the rate of monetary expan-
sion μ and the rate of growth of output $G(y)$, *all over the same period*, in an
equation which regresses the rate of inflation π on $\mu - G(y)$. The reason is
that they are linked by the identity $\pi \equiv \mu - G(y) + v$, where v is the actual
growth of velocity. In the US and the UK, velocity has been rising at about
3 per cent per annum from 1960–79.
14 The Federal Reserve operating policy has not been in terms of the growth

of monetary aggregates (see Kane, 1980: 202, table 2). However, according to the Monetarist model, the crucial monetary input is the resulting rate of monetary expansion resulting from whatever policy is followed.

15 For a discussion of optimal stabilization policies, see Stein and Infante (1973).

CHAPTER 5

Monetary and Fiscal Policy in a Growing Economy

*A Synthesis of Macroeconomics with
Keynes – Wicksell Models of Money
and Economic Growth*

1 Introduction and summary

No clear line of demarcation exists between the short, medium and
long run. As the stock of money changes so does the stock of capital.
From 1950 to 1970, the stock of capital has grown at a faster rate than
either the stock of money or the stock of total government debt.
Policies which affect the unemployment rate, inflation rate and
interest rate also affect the trajectory of the capital stock. In turn, the
stock of capital affects capacity output and the rate of investment.
There is a feedback to the level of aggregate demand and the
unemployment rate. A hiatus exists between macroeconomics and
growth theory. The macroeconomic models discussed in chapter 3 are
medium-run models where the stock of capital is a parameter and the
money stock is a control variable. Variables to be explained are the
unemployment and inflation rates. The closest growth models to
macroeconomics have been the Keynes – Wicksell models of money
and growth.[1] In this set of models, the capital stock and inflation rate
are endogenous variables, there are independent saving and investment equations, but the unemployment rate is always at its
equilibrium value. Moreover, in both the macroeconomic models and
the Keynes – Wicksell models, the rate of monetary expansion is a
control variable.

The general model described in chapter 2 synthesizes the
macrodynamics analyzed in chapters 3 and 4 with the
Keynes – Wicksell models of economic growth. A continuous
interdependence exists between the current level of the Okun Gap (i.e.

163

the unemployment rate), the level of capacity output, the rate of inflation, the rate of investment and the capital intensity. Productivity as well as the employment rate are endogenous variables. Moreover, this synthesis, referred to as the IS growth model, combines what seems to be the valid elements of Keynesian, Monetarist and New Classical Economics. The IS growth model is derived in section 2 below as a special case of the general model in table 2.1.

The government budget constraint states that the government budget deficit must be financed by some combination of high-powered money and government bonds. If the growth of the money stock is constant, then deficits and surpluses are financed by bonds. At present, many Monetarists and almost all New Classical Economists accept Friedman's later view that the monetary authority should produce a constant rate of monetary expansion. Keynesians do not accept a constant money growth rule. However, they have argued that bond-financed fiscal policy is more efficacious than money-financed fiscal policy in affecting aggregate demand.

Section 3 is concerned with the stability implications of two different methods of financing government deficits. It is shown that if the rate of monetary expansion is constant, so that deficits and surpluses are financed by bonds, then the dynamic system tends to be unstable. Contrary to the Keynesian point of view, bond-financed fiscal policy is not an effective tool of stabilization policy. It is an element of instability in many models. Similarly, Friedman's rule for a constant rate of money growth implies that realized deficits and surpluses are financed by bonds; and such a system tends to destabilize the economy in many models.

In 1948, Friedman proposed that the change in the money stock be an endogenous variable, which is the sole means of financing budget deficits or surpluses. Unlike the constant money growth rule, this control law is a strong element of stability. It accelerates the return of the economy to the equilibrium rate of unemployment. Consequently, the IS growth model is based upon a control law whereby the rate of monetary expansion is directly linked to the budget deficit or surplus.

Section 4 analyzes the dynamic structure and steady-state properties of the IS growth model. Suppose that there is a rise in real government purchases of goods *per capita* (denoted by g) to reduce an Okun Gap. There is a positive impact effect upon aggregate demand, described by the Keynesian multiplier. Price flexibility and the endogenous money growth rule are sufficient to return the economy to capacity output, but the demand management policy, in the form of a higher g, accelerates the return. When output returns to the current capacity output, there is a higher real rate of interest than would have occurred had there been no rise in g. In effect, the rise in g lowers real balances *per capita* and raises the real rate of interest. Some real consumption and some real investment are crowded out by the rise in real government purchases. This is exactly Keynes' description of the effects of government expenditures quoted in chapter 2. Consequently, there is a lower rate of capital formation associated with every level of real output and capital intensity.

The economy converges to a lower capital intensity and a lower level of capacity output *per capita* than would have been reached if g were not increased. There is also a lower level of real balances *per capita* associated with the lower levels of capacity output *per capita* and the capital intensity. A real price is paid for the demand management rise in real government purchases *per capita*.

At the new steady state, there is a larger budget deficit. Not only are there larger real government expenditures but there are lower tax revenues. Budget balance is most definitely not a condition for equilibrium in the IS growth model.

The rate of monetary expansion is the ratio of the real government deficit to real balances. Since the numerator rises and the denominator declines, the steady-state rate of monetary expansion rises as a result of the rise in g. The equilibrium rate of inflation is equal to the rate of monetary expansion *per capita*. Consequently, the larger g raises the steady-state rate of inflation.

Demand management policy, which is implemented by a rise in real government purchases *per capita*, accelerates the return of current output to the *current* level of capacity output. However, it lowers the steady-state capacity output and raises the steady-state rate of inflation.

2 The IS growth model[2]

No clear line of demarcation exists between the medium run and the long run. In the analysis of the medium run, it is assumed that the stock of capital is relatively constant, and attention is focused upon the rate of monetary expansion or growth of the government debt as the variable stocks. Such an assumption is not necessarily valid, as is shown below in table 5.1. During the period 1950 – 70, for example, the stock of capital grew more rapidly than either the stock of money (M1) or the stock of federal, state or local debt.

Policies which affect the ratio of actual to capacity output also affect capacity output. The stocks of financial assets (money and

TABLE 5.1　*Growth rates of stocks (% p.a.): capital, money and debt 1950 – 70.*

		1950 – 60	1950 – 70
(i)	Stock of fixed business capital, 1958 dollars, net of straight line depreciation	3.5	3.81
(ii)	Money stock (M1)	2.15	3.05
(iii)	Federal, state and local government debt	2.5	3.5

Source: US Department of Commerce, *Long-Term Economic Growth, 1860–1970*, Tables A153, B101, B109 – 110.

government bonds) are not exogenous variables, but are affected by the government budget constraint (see equation (2.43)). For this reason, the following issues are analyzed within the context of the IS growth model, which is a special case of the general growth model described in chapter 2 and summarized in table 2.1. Suppose that there is a rise in real government purchases *per capita g*, designed to reduce the current Okun Gap. Will the positive impact effects upon output and employment be amplified, reversed or moderated as a result of endogenous changes in the stocks of capital and of financial assets? What will be the trajectories of output *per capita* $y(t)$, the ratio of actual to capacity output $y(t)/f(k(t))$, the capital intensity $k(t)$ and the price level $p(t)$, when the stocks of capital and money are endogenous? What determines the rate of inflation, when the money stock is an endogenous variable determined by the government budget constraint? What are the stability implications of financing government deficits with bonds rather than with money?

Four changes are made in the general growth model summarized in table 2.1 to derive the IS growth model summarized in table 5.2. For notational simplicity, time subscripts are omitted.

First, the goods market is always assumed to be in equilibrium, where planned consumption plus planned investment plus government expenditures equal the level of output. Nevertheless, the resulting level of output *per capita* $y(t)$ is not necessarily equal to capacity output *per capita* $f(k(t))$. This change is introduced to simplify the analysis. Equation (5.1) states that aggregate demand *per capita* equals output *per capita* produced. Aggregate demand *per capita* consists of consumption demand $C(.)$ plus investment demand

TABLE 5.2   *The IS growth model.*

$$y = C(y, k, m; \tau, v_c) + (Dk + nk) + g \tag{5.1}$$

$$\pi = \pi^* + \lambda(y - f(k)) \tag{5.2}$$

$$\rho = \pi^* + i(y, m, k) \tag{5.3}$$

$$Dk = \zeta[r(k, y; v_I, \tau) - (\rho - \pi^*)] \tag{5.4}$$

$$Dm/m = \mu - n - \pi \tag{5.5}$$

$$\mu = (g - \tau y)/m \tag{5.6}$$

$$\pi^* = \frac{g - \tau f(k)}{m} - n. \tag{5.7a}$$

Symbols: y is output *per capita*; k is the capital intensity (capital *per capita*); m is real balances *per capita*; τ is the proportional tax rate; v_c and v_I are exogenous consumption and investment parameters respectively; $D \equiv d/dt$; n is the growth of population; g is real government purchases of goods *per capita*; π is the rate of inflation; π^* is the anticipated rate of inflation; ρ is the nominal rate of interest on private bonds; μ is the rate of monetary expansion; $f(k)$ is capacity output *per capita*. Each endogenous variable is to be understood with a time subscript. Endogenous variables are $y, k, m, \pi, p^*, \rho, \mu$; control variables are g, τ; exogenous variables are v_c, v_I, n.

$Dk(t) + nk(t)$ plus real government purchases g. Consumption demands depend upon: disposable income $(1 - \tau)y(t)$, where τ is the proportional tax rate τ; wealth, in the form of the capital intensity $k(t)$ and real balances *per capita* $m(t)$; and exogenous parameters v_c. Real taxes *per capita* are proportional to real income *per capita*. Equation (5.1) determines the level of output.

Secondly, the inflation equation is simplified as equation (5.2). The actual rate of inflation $\pi(t)$ is the sum of the effective (or risk-adjusted) anticipated rate of inflation π^* plus a constant λ times the difference between output *per capita* and capacity output *per capita* $(y(t) - f(k(t)))$. Capacity output *per capita* is output *per capita*, when the unemployment rate is equal to its equilibrium value U_e. Coefficient λ reflects the degree of price flexibility resulting from an Okun Gap of one unit. This inflation equation simplifies the growth analysis considerably, but its empirical validity is questionable (see chapter 4).

Equation (5.3) is interest rate equation (2.6) when (i) there are private bonds but no government bonds, and (ii) there is a Fisher effect. The Fisher effect states that: a unit change in the risk-adjusted anticipated rate of inflation changes the nominal rate of interest, which equilibrates the private bond market, by one unit $\partial\rho/\partial\pi^* = 1$. It does not state that a unit change in the actual rate of inflation changes the nominal rate of interest by one unit.[3] Alternatively, the real rate of interest $i(t) = \rho(t) - \pi^*(t)$, which equilibrates the private bond market, depends upon output *per capita* $y(t)$, real balances *per capita* $m(t)$ and the capital intensity $k(t)$, for the reasons discussed in chapter 2.

Equation (5.4) is equation (2.5) describing the change in the capital intensity, when equation (2.2) is used to describe the determinants of the rent per uit of capital. For simplicity, the depreciation rate is ignored. A rise in output per unit of capital y/k raises the rent per unit of capital and stimulates the rate of capital formation. A rise in the real rate of interest $i(t) = \rho(t) - \pi^*(t)$ inhibits the rate of capital formation. Parameter v_1 describes shifts in the investment demand schedule and τ is the tax rate parameter.

Equation (5.5) defines the growth of real balances *per capita*. It is the endogenous growth of the money stock $\mu(t)$ less the endogenous rate of inflation $\pi(t)$ less the exogenous growth of population.

Thirdly, government surpluses and deficits are the sole determinants of the endogenous rate of monetary expansion. There are no government bonds, although there are private bonds, and the government debt is entirely in the form of non-interest-bearing money. The reason for this assumption is the subject of the next part of this chapter. It is shown in section 3 below that a regime where deficits and surpluses are financed by bonds tends to be dynamically unstable in many models.

Equation (5.6) describes the endogenous growth of the money supply. The rate of monetary expansion $\mu(t)$ is equal to the real *per capita* government budget deficit $g - \tau y(t)$ divided by the real *per capita* money stock $m(t)$. Nominal tax revenues are assumed to be derived from a proportional income tax at rate τ levied upon nominal income. Real tax revenues *per capita* are $\tau y(t)$.

Fourthly, the price anticipations equation is based upon an endogenous rate of monetary expansion. It combines elements of the MRE and ARE hypotheses discussed in chapter 2. Two assumptions underlie the derivation of the anticipated rate of inflation described by equation (5.7a). Equation (5.7b) states the first assumption: the anticipated rate of inflation π^* is equal to the anticipated growth of the money supply *per capita*, when equation (5.6) is used to describe the endogenous rate of monetary expansion over the planning period.

The current values of g and $m(t)$ are assumed to be known, but real income $y(s)$ and real revenues $\tau y(s)$, over the planning period are unknown:

$$\pi^*(t) = E_t\left(\frac{g - \tau y(s)}{m(t)}\right) - n = \frac{g - \tau E_t y(s)}{m(t)} - n. \tag{5.7b}$$

Equation (5.7c) states the second assumption that, on average, over the planning period, anticipations are correct:

$$\pi^* = E\pi. \tag{5.7c}$$

Insofar as anticipations are correct on average, then equation (5.2) implies that on average, output is equal to capacity output. The derivation is as follows. Equation (5.7c) is substituted into (5.2) to derive

$$\pi - E\pi = \lambda(y - f(k)). \tag{5.7d}$$

The expectation of both sides is taken and (5.7c) is used to derive (5.7e) and (5.7f):

$$E(\pi - E\pi) = E\lambda[y - f(k)] = 0. \tag{5.7e}$$

Since capacity output $f(k(t))$ changes slowly, and is known at the time expectations are taken, the uncertainty is associated just with the level of output:

$$Ey = f(k). \tag{5.7f}$$

With the substitution of (5.7f) into (5.7b) the price anticipations equation (5.7a) in table 5.2 can be derived. The effective anticipated rate of inflation is equal to the expected growth of the money supply *per capita*. The latter is equal to the *high employment deficit* as a fraction of the money stock $[g - \tau f(k(t))]/m(t)$ less the growth of population n.

The seven equations in the IS growth model in table 5.2 contain seven *endogenous* variables: output *per capita* $y(t)$, the capital intensity $k(t)$, real balances *per capita* $m(t)$, the nominal rate of interest $\rho(t)$, the actual $\pi(t)$ and anticipated $\pi^*(t)$ rates of inflation, and the rate of monetary expansion $\mu(t)$. *Control* variables are real government purchases of goods *per capita* g and the tax rate τ. *Exogenous* variables are parameters v_c and v_1 of the consumption and investment equations respectively, and the growth of population n.

3   Stability implications of endogenous changes in the stocks of financial assets

Many Monetarists favor a policy whereby the money stock grows at a constant rate. NCE overwhelmingly favors such a policy, but it is argued that the real variables are independent of the money supply rule that is followed. NCE therefore selects a money supply rule solely on the basis of its implications for the path of the inflation rate.

   The aim of this section is to explain why control law equation (5.6) in the IS growth model is used to determine the rate of monetary expansion. It is proved that the choice of a money supply rule is of fundamental importance in determining the stability of the system, as well as the paths of the real and nominal variables.

3.1   *The two fundamentally different Friedman proposals for economic stability*

Equations (2.9) and (2.11) describe how the stocks of (high-powered) money and bonds change endogenously. These equations are control laws which profoundly affect the stability and growth of the economy. Several different control laws, concerning the financing of budget deficits, have been proposed to stabilize the economy.

   Milton Friedman has advocated two fundamentally different control laws designed to increase economic stability. Originally (1948), he advocated a control law where the rate of monetary expansion is an endogenous variable which depends upon the budget deficit or surplus. Let us refer to this as an "*M Regime*." It is shown in sections 3.5 and 4 below that an "M Regime" is a (direct control) built-in stabilizer. The 1948 Friedman proposal is an excellent stabilizer of the economy against external demand disturbances. In recent years, he has favored a rule whereby the money stock grows at a constant rate of μ per cent per annum. As a result, the rate of monetary expansion is independent of both the state of the government budget and the state of the economy. This proposal, referred to as a "B Regime," implies that (modulus a constant), budget deficits and surpluses are associated with changes in the stock of government bonds held by the public.

   Recently Keynesians Alan Blinder and Robert Solow (1974), and James Tobin and Willem Buiter (1976) have argued that, in a "B Regime," where government deficits and surpluses are financed by bonds, fiscal policy is most effective in affecting the level of real income.

   In this section, the implications of bond-financed fiscal policy are examined. It is shown that a "B Regime" can be expected to be dynamically unstable. *Whereas an "M Regime" is a built-in stabilizer, a "B Regime" provides a positive feedback and produces economic instability* in many models. That is why control equation (5.6), based upon an "M Regime," is used in the IS growth model.

Friedman suggested two possible values for the constant rate of monetary expansion μ. (i) His "optimal" rate of monetary expansion is $\mu = 2$ per cent per annum such that the steady-state rate of deflation is equal to his estimate of society's rate of discount.[4] (ii) If constant rate $\mu = 5$ per cent per annum were chosen, then there would be price stability in the steady state of an growing economy.

The government budget constraint is equation (5.8a) in nominal terms. Variable $M(t)$ is the stock of money, and the money multiplier is assumed to be unity. Variable $B(t)$ is the nominal value of the interest payments on the government debt. Each of the $B(t)$ bonds promises to pay \$1 per annum in perpetuity. Nominal interest rate $\rho(t)$ is the reciprocal of the bond price. Government expenditures in nominal terms are $G(t)$. Tax receipts net of transfer payments are proportional, at tax rate τ, to personal income $Y(t) + B(t)$, the sum of nominal income produced $Y(t)$ and interest payments $B(t)$ on the government debt. The right-hand side of the equation is the budget deficit, and the left-hand side represents the changes in the stocks of financial assets:

$$DM(t) + \frac{1}{\rho(t)} DB(t) = G(t) + B(t)$$
$$- \tau[Y(t) + B(t)]; \quad D \equiv d/dt. \tag{5.8a}$$

Suppose that the constant rate of monetary expansion μ is equal to the rate of growth n of "effective" population $N(t)$ as described by

$$M(t) = M(0)\exp(nt), \tag{5.8b}$$
$$N(t) = N(0)\exp(nt). \tag{5.8c}$$

Then, the government budget constraint is described by equation (5.9a). All surpluses or deficits are financed by changes in the stock of government bonds, modulus a constant term $nM(0)/N(0)$. *Define a "B Regime" as a situation where equation (5.9a) is valid. The stock of government bonds is an endogenous variable determined by the government budget constraint.*[5]

$$\frac{DB(t)/N(t)}{\rho(t)} = \frac{G(t)}{N(t)} + \frac{B(t)}{N(t)} - \tau\left(\frac{Y(t)}{N(t)} + \frac{B(t)}{N(t)}\right) - \frac{nM(0)}{N(0)}.$$

$$\tag{5.9a}$$

To simplify the exposition in this section, assume that $n = 0$, the population and money stock are constant, and normalize the initial population $N(0)$ at unity. Equation (5.9a) represents the government budget constraint in a "B Regime," when the money stock *per capita* is constant, and (5.9b) assumes that population is constant:

$$DB(t)/\rho(t) = G(t) + (1 - \tau)B(t) - \tau Y(t). \tag{5.9b}$$

Friedman's "B Regime" proposal (i.e. constant rate of monetary expansion) most certainly does not advocate that G and τ be varied with the Okun Gap. Keynesians, however, advocate variations in G *and* τ to stabilize the economy.

Some implications of a "B Regime," where deficits and surpluses are associated with changes in the stock of bonds, as well as some implications of a constant rate of monetary expansion, have been drawn by Keynesians Blinder and Solow from their "Rock Bottom" model. This is the same Keynesian model referred to in equations (1.1) $-(1.4)$. I use their model to show that "B Regimes" tend to be unstable; and hence their equilibrium properties cannot be used as guides to policy. Since the same results are obtained from richer but more complex models,[6] the analysis in this section[7] focuses upon the widely used, extremely simple, Keynesian "Rock Bottom" model.[8]

3.2   *Equilibrium and stability of a "B Regime" within the context of the Keynesian "Rock Bottom" model*

At any time, the parameters of the IS – LM curves are: nominal government expenditures $G(t)$, interest payments on the government debt or number of bonds outstanding $B(t)$, the stock of money $M(t)$ and exogenous disturbances $v(t)$. The IS – LM solutions for the level of nominal income $Y(t)$ and the nominal rate of interest $\rho(t)$ are therefore described by equations (5.10) and (5.11) respectively:

$$Y(t) = F(G(t), M(t), B(t); \tau, v(t)). \tag{5.10}$$

$$\rho(t) = R(G(t), M(t), B(t); \tau, v(t)). \tag{5.11}$$

Price level $p(t)$ is a fixed multiple of nominal unit labor cost.[9] Since the money stock *per capita* is assumed to be constant (equations (5.8b), (5.8c)), Keynesians assume that nominal unit labor cost is also constant as long as output is below capacity output. Then the price level is also constant, and it can be standardized at unity:

$$p(t) = 1. \tag{5.12}$$

No distinction need be made between nominal income $Y(t)$ and real income $y(t) \equiv Y(t)$ in this Keynesian model.

Budget balance is indeed a condition for equilibrium in the Keynesian "Rock Bottom" model. If the level of income $Y(t)$ in equation (5.10) is to be constant, given the stock of money, the value of government expenditures and tax rate, then the stock of bonds must also be constant $DB(t) = 0$. Government budget balance equation (5.13) must therefore be satisfied as an *equilibrium* condition: (Time subscripts are not needed in equilibrium.)

$$G + (1 - \tau)B = \tau Y. \tag{5.13}$$

The left-hand side represents government expenditures G plus net of taxes interest payments on the government debt $(1 - \tau)B$. The right-hand side represents tax revenues from income produced $\tau F(G, M, B; \tau, v)$.

Keynesians Blinder and Solow use equation (5.13) to demonstrate the potency of fiscal policy for changing the level of income. Their argument is as follows. Let there be a parametric rise in government expenditures. Then the equilibrium multiplier can be derived from equation (5.13) by solving for dY/dG:

$$\frac{dY}{dG} = \frac{1}{\tau} + \frac{(1 - \tau)}{\tau} \frac{dB}{dG}. \tag{5.14}$$

Blinder and Solow argue that: (i) A rise in government expenditures generates a government deficit. (ii) The stock of bonds rises, which (iii) raises the level of income and also (iv) raises the interest payments on the government debt. (v) Consumption increases and the level of income rises further. Since the level of government expenditures plus the interest on the debt increases, budget balance can only occur if the equilibrium level of income is even higher than would have occurred if deficits were financed by money instead of by interest-bearing bonds. They explicitly state that:

... contrary to the usual supposition, the long-run multiplier for bond-financed deficit spending [equation (5.14)] exceeds that for money-financed deficit spending [$1/\tau$]. (1973: 327; 1974: 50)

A prior and important question is whether a "B Regime" (i.e. a constant money growth rule) is dynamically stable. Stability of a "B Regime" is examined by considering differential equation (5.15), which is based upon equations (5.9b) and (5.10):

$$\frac{DB(t)}{\rho(t)} = G + (1 - \tau)B(t) - \tau F(G, M(0), B(t); \tau, v). \tag{5.15}$$

In the neighborhood of an equilibrium (equation (5.13)), the stability condition is either equation (5.16a) or (5.16b). The equilibrium rate of interest is ρ_e:

$$\frac{1}{\rho_e} \frac{dDB(t)}{dB} = (1 - \tau) - \tau F_B < 0 \tag{5.16a}$$

or

$$\tau F_B > (1 - \tau). \tag{5.16b}$$

Stability condition (5.16b) has a simple interpretation. Let the stock of bonds exceed its equilibrium value by one unit. The net interest cost to the government of the extra bond is $(1 - \tau)$ since interest income is taxable. A unit deviation in the stock of bonds from its equilibrium value has an income multiplier of F_B. Induced tax revenues on income produced rise by τF_B. If τF_B exceeds $(1 - \tau)$, a budget surplus is generated, and the stock of bonds returns to its equilibrium value.

Figure 5.1 describes the stable process. Curve YY' describes equation (5.10), the IS – LM solution for the level of income. A rise in B raises the level of income Y. The slope of this curve is the multiplier F_B which must be positive (see equation (5.16b)). Curve BB' describes the government budget balance equation (5.13). If the stock of bonds rises by one unit, the level of income must rise by $(1 - \tau)/\tau$ units if the government budget is to be in balance. Stability conditions (5.16a) and (5.16b) require that the YY' curve be steeper than the BB' curve, for the following reason.

At any time, the level of income is described by the YY' curve (equation (5.10)). If the stock of bonds were B_1, the level of income produced by the IS – LM curves will be Y_1. At this income, there is a budget surplus. The stock of bonds declines, and, via the multiplier F_B, the level of income declines. Arrows along the YY' curve describe the direction of movement. Similarly, if the stock of bonds were B_2, the level of income produced by the IS – LM curve would be Y_2. There is a budget deficit, and the stock of bonds rises. Arrows indicate how $Y(t)$ converges to its equilibrium value Y_e, where the government budget is in balance. Figure 5.1 describes a stable system.

It is generally believed that the following conditions describe the macroeconomy. (i) The sume of the marginal propensity to consume and the marginal propensity to invest is a fraction between zero and unity. (ii) A parametric rise in the stock of money, or an exogenous

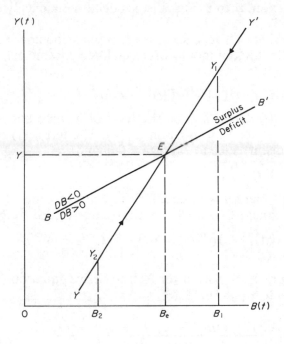

FIGURE 5.1

rise in aggregate demand, is associated with a higher equilibrium level of nominal income. I now show that if conditions (i) and (ii) are valid, then the "Rock Bottom" model of a "B Regime" is unstable, that is, equation (5.16b) is not satisfied. Consequently, if conditions (i) and (ii) are valid:

(a)   A fixed money growth rule leads to a dynamically unstable economy.

(b)   The Keynesian proposition, concerning the potency of bond-financed fiscal policy in increasing the level of income, is invalid.

These propositions are proved in sections 3.3 and 3.4 below.

3.3   The Keynesian fiscalist model is dynamically unstable

The commonly used Keynesian fiscalist model, which is a special case of equation (5.10), contains a vertical IS curve. This model has been used to demonstrate the efficacy of fiscal policy in affecting the level of income. I prove that: "If the marginal propensity to spend is a positive fraction, then the fiscalist model is dynamically unstable in a 'B Regime.'"

Consumption $C(t)$ depends upon disposable income $(1 - \tau)[Y(t) + B(t)]$ and the stock of money M_0 (which is a parameter), as described by

$$C(t) = c_1(1 - \tau)[Y(t) + B(t)] + c_2 M_0. \tag{5.17}$$

Investment $I(t)$ depends upon the level of income but is interest inelastic, as described by equation (5.18). The term $v(t)$ represents an exogenous disturbance to aggregate demand:

$$I(t) = aY(t) + v(t). \tag{5.18}$$

The goods market is in equilibrium when income $Y(t)$ is equal to aggregate demand $C(t) + I(t) + G(t)$, as described by

$$Y(t) = c_1(1 - \tau)[Y(t) + B(t)] + c_2 M_0 + aY(t) \\ + v(t) + G. \tag{5.19}$$

Equation (5.19) is solved for $Y(t)$ to derive equation (5.20), which corresponds to equation (5.10):

$$Y(t) = \frac{c_1(1 - \tau)B(t) + c_2 M_0 + v(t) + G}{1 - c_1(1 - \tau) - a}$$
$$= F[G, B(t); M_0, \tau, v(t)]. \tag{5.20}$$

The coefficients of $B(t)$, M_0 and G are the conventional multipliers. It is generally assumed that the sum of the marginal propensity to consume c_1 and the marginal propensity to invest a is a positive fraction:

$$1 > c_1 + a > 0. \tag{5.21}$$

Equation (5.20) can be written as (5.22) in terms of the well-known multiplier for government expenditures F_G as described by (5.22b):

$$Y(t) = c_1(1 - \tau)F_G B(t) + c_2 F_G M_0 + F_G v(t) + F_G G. \tag{5.22a}$$

$$F_G = [1 - c_1(1 - \tau) - a]^{-1} > 0. \tag{5.22b}$$

Condition (5.21) implies that the impact multipliers are positive.

Equation (5.22a) is probably the most widely used Keynesian equation describing the determination of the level of nominal income $Y(t)$. As it is one equation with two unknowns, the level of nominal income $Y(t)$ and the number of bonds outstanding $B(t)$, the equilibrium levels of Y and B must be jointly determined by equation (5.22a) (the YY' line) and the government budget balance equation (5.13) (the BB' line).

Stability condition (5.16b), in the context of equation (5.20), is

$$\tau F_B = \frac{\tau c_1(1 - \tau)}{1 - c_1(1 - \tau) - a} > (1 - \tau). \tag{5.23}$$

This inequality implies

$$c_1 + a > 1, \tag{5.24}$$

which states that the sum of the marginal propensity to consume and invest exceeds unity. Equation (5.24) then contradicts equation (5.21). It has, therefore, been proved that the widely used Keynesian fiscalist model is unstable in a "B Regime," if the marginal propensity to spend is a positive fraction.

3.4 *Effects of parametric changes in the money stock on exogenous sources of aggregate demand*

Another implication of a "B Regime" is that, if stability condition (5.16b) is satisfied, then a parametric *rise* in the stock of money M_0, or in aggregate demand v, must *lower* the equilibrium level of nominal income. Consequently, if it is believed that a parametric rise in the stock of money or in aggregate demand raises the level of nominal income, a "B Regime" must be dynamically unstable.

The proof is given for the general "Rock Bottom" model rather than for the special fiscalist case described in section 3.3. A parametric rise in the stock of money shifts the IS and LM curves to the right and raises the level of nominal income by $F_M \Delta M$ (equation (5.10)). Graphically, the YY' curve rises from $Y_0 Y_0'$ to $Y_1 Y_1'$ in figure 5.2 (based upon figure 5.1). Given the initial stock of bonds B_0, the level of income rises by $F_M \Delta M = E_0 H$. This is the impact effect of a parametric rise in the money stock.

At point H, where the level of nominal income has risen to $Y_0 + F_M \Delta M$, there is now a budget surplus. A decline occurs in the stock of bonds and the flow of interest payments to the public. Personal income $Y(t) + B(t)$ declines, aggregate demand is reduced, and the level of income $Y(t)$ declines in the direction of the arrows along the curve $Y_1 Y_1'$. When the level of income declines to its original level Y_0, the economy is at point L. At this point, $L = (B_2, Y_0)$, there is a smaller flow of interest payments than existed initially ($B_2 < B_0$). A budget surplus exists at point L, whereas the budget was in balance at point E_0. More bonds are retired, as a result of the budget surplus, and personal income continues to decline. Equilibrium occurs at point E_1. There is a lower level of income $Y_1 < Y_0$ and a smaller stock of bonds

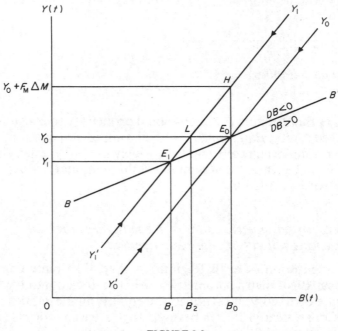

FIGURE 5.2

$B_1 < B_0$. Consequently, in a dynamically stable system, a parametric rise in the stock of money, or an exogenous rise in aggregate demand, reduces the level of income.

Algebraically, the proof of the graphic result described in figure 5.2 is as follows. From equations (5.10) and (5.13), equations (5.25) and (5.26) are derived. Equation (5.25) is the IS – LM solution for the level of income; impact multiplier F_M is positive:

$$\frac{dY}{dM} - F_B \frac{dB}{dM} = F_M. \tag{5.25}$$

Equation (5.26) is derived from the government budget balance condition:

$$\tau \frac{dY}{dM} - (1 - \tau)\frac{dB}{dM} = 0. \tag{5.26}$$

By solving for dY/dM,

$$\frac{dY}{dM} = \frac{-(1 - \tau)F_M}{\tau F_B - (1 - \tau)} < 0. \tag{5.27}$$

In a dynamically stable system, the denominator is positive as described by equation (5.16b). Consequently, dY/dM is negative; the level of income declines from Y_0 to Y_1. This section is summarized in Theorem I.

Theorem I
If a parametric rise in the stock of money, or in aggregate demand, raises the equilibrium level of nominal income, then a "B Regime" is dynamically unstable.

Two interesting implications of Theorem I are as follows. First, the Keynesian argument (Blinder – Solow, Tobin – Buiter) that the long-run multiplier for bond-financed government expenditure is positive and greater than for money-financed government expenditure is invalid; the dynamic system underlying this argument is expected to be unstable. Secondly, the Friedman proposal for a constant rate of monetary expansion implies that the economy is in a "B Regime," where the money stock *per capita* is a predetermined variable, and deficits and surpluses are financed by bonds; this regime is likely to be unstable. Instead of stabilizing such a system, Friedman's proposal for a constant rate of monetary expansion destabilizes an economy described by the "Rock Bottom" model.

3.5 Endogenous changes in the stock of money in the "Rock Bottom" model

A fundamentally different control law from the constant money growth rule is Friedman's 1948 proposal, which is described as follows. (See Friedman, 1953: 133 – 56.) (i) Government expenditures are financed entirely by tax revenues or by the creation of money. (ii) The government does not issue interest-bearing securities to the public; and the Federal Reserve System does not operate in the open market. (iii) The quantity of money is increased only when the government has a deficit, and then by the amount of the deficit; and it is decreased only when the government has a surplus, and then by the amount of the surplus.

This proposal is described by differential equation (5.28), which is based upon equation (5.8a) and conditions (i) – (iii) above, when $B(t)$ = 0. This equation defines an "M Regime":

$$DM(t) = G - \tau Y(t); \quad D \equiv \mathrm{d}/\mathrm{d}t. \tag{5.28}$$

Within the framework of the "Rock Bottom" model , the "M Regime" is described by figure 5.3. The YY' curve is the IS − LM solution or the level of income as a function of the stock of money; it is based upon equation (5.10). The slope of this curve is the impact multiplier F_M which is positive. The MM curve, equation (5.29), describes the budget balance condition. It is derived from (5.28) when $DM(t) = 0$:

$$G = \tau Y(t). \tag{5.29}$$

Whenever the level of nominal income is above the MM' line (i.e. when $Y(t) > G/\tau$), there is a budget surplus. The quantity of money is reduced, and the IS − LM solution for the level of income declines. Arrows along the YY' curves indicate the direction of movement. It is obvious from figure 5.3 that an "M Regime" is dynamically stable.

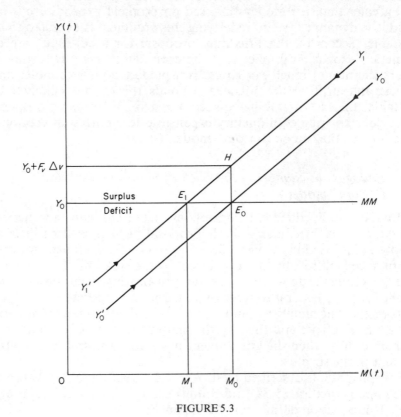

FIGURE 5.3

Formally, from equation (5.28) and (5.10), stability condition (5.30) is satisfied:

$$\frac{dDM(t)}{dM(t)} = -\tau F_M < 0. \tag{5.30}$$

External disturbances to nominal income are offset by endogenous variations in the money stock. Let there be a shock Δv to aggregate demand which shifts the YY' curve from $Y_0 Y_0'$ to $Y_1 Y_1'$. Distance $E_0 H$ is $F_v \Delta v$ based upon equation (5.10), the IS – LM solution for the level of nominal income.

Nominal income rises from $Y_0 = G/\tau = M_0 E_0$ to $Y_0 + F_v \Delta v = M_0 H$, as a result of the demand shock which shifts the IS curve to the right. At point H, there is now a budget surplus, and the money stock is reduced. As a result of the smaller money stock, the IS and LM curves shift to the left, and the level of nominal income declines in the direction of the arrows to point E_1.

The net effect of the shock is to shift the equilibrium from E_0 to E_1. No change occurs in the level of *nominal* income.[10] The endogenous reduction in the money stock offsets the external disturbances $F_M \Delta M + F_v \Delta v = 0$. The "M Regime" is a (direct control or) built-in stabilizer which effectively offsets external demand disturbances.

3.6   *Endogenous Money and Bonds: An M – B Regime*

Intermediate between the "B Regime" and the "M Regime" is an "M – B Regime" where both money and bonds are endogenous. Deficits and surpluses are financed in such a manner as to keep the bond – money ratio $\theta \equiv B/M$ constant. In a "B Regime," the marginal bond – money ratio $dB/dM = \theta$ is infinite; and in an "M Regime" the marginal bond – money ratio $dB/dM = \theta$ is zero. If a "B Regime" is stable, then a mixed regime (with $\infty > \theta > 0$) will also be stable. Theorem II is proved in this section for an "M – B Regime."

Theorem II
(i) If a ''B Regime'' is unstable, then a sufficiently small θ is required for economic stability. (ii) In the fiscalist model described in section 3.3, where the sum of the marginal propensity to consume and to invest is less than unity, an "M – B Regime" can be stabilized by selecting a "sufficiently small" ratio θ of bonds to money.

Again, the Keynesian "Rock Bottom" model is used to prove these propositions. The policy is described by equations (5.31a) and (5.31b). The debt – money ratio is kept constant at θ, which is finite and positive.

$$B = \theta DM; \qquad \infty > \theta > 0 \tag{5.31a}$$

$$DB = \theta DM; \qquad D = \mathrm{d}/\mathrm{d}t. \tag{5.31b}$$

The IS – LM solution for nominal income, based upon equations (5.10) and (5.31a), is

$$Y(t) = F(G, M(t), \theta M(t); \tau, v). \tag{5.32}$$

Budget constraint equation (5.8a) becomes equation (5.33), when equations (5.32), (5.31a) and (5.31b) are used:

$$\left(1 + \frac{\theta}{\rho(t)}\right) DM(t) = G + (1 - \tau)\theta M(t)$$

$$- \tau F(G, M(t), \theta M(t); \tau, v). \tag{5.33}$$

In the neighborhood of the equilibrium, the system will be stable if inequality (5.34a) or (5.34b) is satisfied:

$$\theta[\tau F_B - (1 - \tau)] + \tau F_M > 0 \tag{5.34a}$$

or

$$F_M + \theta F_B > \theta(1 - \tau)/\tau. \tag{5.34b}$$

The impact multiplier F_M is positive. If a "B Regime" is stable, then the term $[\tau F_B - (1 - \tau)]$ is positive. Consequently, a combined "M – B Regime" is stable. If a "B Regime" is unstable, that is, $(1 - \tau) > \tau F_B$, then the combined system will be stable if θ satisfies inequality (5.35):

$$\theta < \frac{\tau F_M}{(1 - \tau) - \tau F_B} \tag{5.35}$$

Inequality (5.35) proves the first part of Theorem II, namely: if a "B Regime" is unstable, then a sufficiently small θ can stabilize a combined "M – B Regime."

In the fiscalist model, where the IS – LM solution for nominal income $Y(t)$ is described by equation (5.20), stability condition (5.35) becomes (5.36). The latter is derived by substituting the values of F_M and F_B from equation (5.20):

$$\theta < \frac{\tau c_2}{(1 - \tau)(1 - c_1 - a)} \tag{5.36}$$

Here, the sum of the marginal propensity to consume c_1 and the marginal propensity to invest a are less than unity, and the system can be stable if θ satisfies inequality (5.36). This proves the second part of Theorem II.

In conclusion, an endogenous money stock that varies with government budget deficits and surpluses is a built-in stabilizer. If the rate of growth of the money supply is predetermined, a "B Regime" is produced; and a "B Regime" is likely to be unstable. Therefore, Friedman's (1948) proposal is an excellent built-in stabilizer (direct control), whereas his constant money growth rule may tend to destabilize an economy. For this reason, an endogenous money supply equation (5.6) is used in the IS growth model (table 5.2).

4 The dynamic structure and steady-state properties of the IS growth model: the synthesis

The IS growth model in table 5.2 is solved for the trajectories of output *per capita* $y(t)$, capacity output *per capita* $f(k(t))$, the capital intensity $k(t)$, real balances *per capita* $m(t)$, the real rate of interest $i(t)$, the rate of monetary expansion $\mu(t)$ and the rate of inflation $\pi(t)$. Section 4.1 describes the dynamics and section 4.2 describes the steady-state solutions. Section 4.2 and the appendix to this chapter discuss the stability conditions. Section 4.3 explains the short- and long-run effects of changes in government expenditures designed to reduce the current Okun Gap $f(k(t)) - y(t)$.

4.1 *Derivation of the dynamic process*

Output *per capita* is determined by solving simultaneously an IS and an LM equation. The IS curve is derived by substituting investment equation (5.4) into the goods market balance equation (5.1) to derive IS equation (5.37):

$$y = C(y, k, m; \tau, v_c) + \zeta[r(k, y; v_1, \tau) - (\rho - \pi^*)]$$
$$+ nk + g. \tag{5.37}$$

The LM curve embodying the Fisher effect is equation (5.3) repeated here:

$$i = \rho - \pi^* = i(y, m, k). \tag{5.3}$$

The IS and LM curves are shown in figure 5.4(a). They can be solved simultaneously for the level of output (equation (5.38)) and the real rate of interest (equation (5.39)):

$$y = F(k, m; g, \tau, v_c, v_1, n). \tag{5.38}$$

$$i = \rho - \pi^* = j(k, m; g, \tau, v_c, v_1, n). \tag{5.39}$$

Equation (5.38) states that, given the values of $(k, g, \tau, v_c, v_1, n)$, a parametric rise in real balances *per capita* shifts the IS and LM curves to the right. As a result, the level of output *per capita* is increased. Relation $\partial y / \partial m = F_m > 0$ is shown in figure 5.4(b), which relates y to m, for two values of real government purchases *per capita* $g_1 > g_0$. It is useful to view this relation through its inverse, $\partial m / \partial y = 1/F_m > 0$, which relates m to y, given the values of the exogenous variables and control parameters. Equation (5.38) can be solved for m in terms of y to derive

$$m = M(y, k; g, \tau, v_c, v_1, n). \tag{5.40}$$

Here $My = 1/F_m > 0$ and $Mg = -Fg/F_m < 0$. Equations (5.38) and (5.40) are the same equation, as is obvious from an inspection of figure 5.4(b).

There are two essential differential equations in the system: both real balances *per capita* $m(t)$ and the capital intensity $k(t)$ change differentially, and constitute the dynamics of the system.

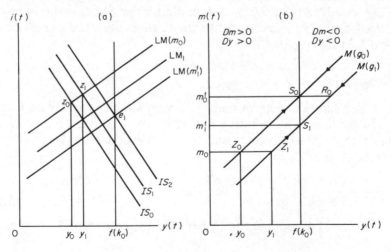

FIGURE 5.4

The rate of change of the capital intensity (growth equation (5.41a)) is derived by substituting equations (5.3) and (5.40) into equation (5.4). The equation is abbreviated as equation (5.41b), where the function I is the difference between the rent per unit of capital and the real rate of interest functions ($r - i$):

$$Dk = \xi[r(k,y;v_1, \tau) - i(y,k,M(y,k;g,\tau,v_c, v_1, n))] \qquad (5.41a)$$

$$Dk(t) = I(k(t), y(t); g, \tau, v_c, v_1, n). \qquad (5.41b)$$

The locus of points (y, k), where the rent per unit of capital r is equal to the real rate of interest i, is described by the II' curve in figure 5.5, which is the graph of

$$I(k, y; g, \tau, v_c, v_1, n) = 0 \qquad (5.42a)$$

Along this curve, there is no tendency for the capital intensity to change. In the stable case which concerns us, this curve is upward sloping. Given the level of output, a rise in the capital intensity diminishes the rent per unit of capital relative to the real rate of interest, and the rate of capital formation tends to decline. Formally I_k is negative. Given the capital intensity, a rise in output *per capita* tends to raise the rate of capital formation since the marginal propensity to invest is positive. Formally I_y *is positive. If the capital intensity is to remain at its new level, then a rise in the capital intensity must be accompanied by a rise in output per capita* produced and demanded. The slope of the II' curve is positive:

$$\left.\frac{dy}{dk}\right|_{Dk\,=\,0} = -\frac{I_k}{I_y} > 0, \qquad (5.42b)$$

as drawn in figure 5.5.

Along the II' curve, the marginal product of capital is equal to the real rate of interest. Above the curve, the marginal product of capital exceeds the real rate of interest, and the capital intensity rises. A decline in output y, or a rise in the capital intensity k, below the II' curve lowers the marginal product of capital below the real rate of interest, and the capital intensity declines. The horizontal vectors (figure 5.5) describe the movement of the capital intensity.

The proportionate rate of change of real balances *per capita* is derived by substituting equations (5.6), (5.2) and (5.7a) into (5.5). The first term in parenthesis in equation (5.43a) is the growth of the money supply *per capita* (from equation (5.6)). The second term is the rate of inflation (from equations (5.2) and (5.7a)):

$$\frac{Dm}{m} = \left(\frac{g - \tau y}{m} - n \right) - \left(\frac{g - \tau f(k)}{m} - n + \lambda [y - f(k)] \right).$$

$$\text{(5.43a)}$$

By grouping and cancelling terms, equation (5.43a) is written simply as

$$\frac{Dm}{m} = - \left(\frac{\tau}{m} + \lambda \right) [y - f(k)]. \tag{5.43b}$$

An important result is derived: *The proportionate rate of change of real balances per capita is a multiple of the Okun Gap f(k(t)) − y(t).* As the level of output $y(t)$ rises by Δy, tax revenues rise, and the rate of monetary expansion, which finances the deficit, is reduced by $(\tau/m)\Delta y$. The Okun Gap is reduced, and the rate of inflation (the second term in parenthesis in (5.43a)) is raised by $\lambda \Delta y$. Real balances *per capita* decline, as a result of the two effects, by $(\tau/m + \lambda)\Delta y$. Real government purchases *per capita* do not affect the proportionate rate of change of real balances, because the rate of monetary expansion used to finance the expenditures is completely offset by the rise in the anticipated rate of inflation.

Equation (5.43b) is described graphically by the vectors in figure 5.4(b). When output *per capita* $y(t)$ exceeds capacity output $f(k(t))$, then real balances *per capita* decline, $Dm(t) < 0$. Similarly, when output *per capita* is less than the current capcity output, real balances *per capita* rise, $Dm(t) > 0$. The change in real balances *per capita* (equation (5.43b)) shifts the IS and LM curves (figure 5.4(a)), and thereby changes the level of output *per capita*. This process is described graphically by the movement in the direction of the arrows, along the appropriate curve $m = M(g)$ towards capacity output (figure 5.4(b)).

This is precisely the stabilizing mechanism in Friedman's (1948) proposal, where the money stock is an endogenous variable. Stability depends upon the degree to which the rate of monetary expansion responds to the Okun Gap (τ/m) and the degree of price flexibility (λ) that occurs in the presence of an Okun Gap. In this manner, real balances *per capita* rise when there is an Okun Gap. Aggregate demand is increased, output rises and the Okun Gap is reduced.

The locus of points (y, k) where real balances *per capita* are not changing is described by the full employment curve (FE) in figure 5.5. It is equation (5.44a):

$$y(t) = f(k(t)), \tag{5.44a}$$

with a slope equal to the marginal product of capital

$$\frac{dy(t)}{dk(t)}\bigg|_{Dm\,=\,0} = f'(k(t)).\tag{5.44b}$$

When there is no Okun Gap, $y(t) = f(k(t))$, real balances per unit of effective labor are constant; and, hence, the rate of monetary expansion *per capita* is equal to the rate of inflation. When output is below the FE curve in figure 5.5, then it is to the left of the point $f(k(t))$ in figure 5.4(b). Real balances *per capita* rise. The intersection of the IS – LM curves (figure 5.4(a)) moves to the right, thereby raising the level of income *per capita*. Given the value of the capital intensity, the movement of $y(t)$ to $f(k(t))$ in figure 5.4(b) is described by the vertical vectors in figure 5.5.

Equations (5.38), (5.41a), and (5.43b) constitute a dynamic system in output *per capita* $y(t)$, the capital intensity $k(t)$ and real balances *per capita* $m(t)$. Since my main interest focuses upon output *per capita*

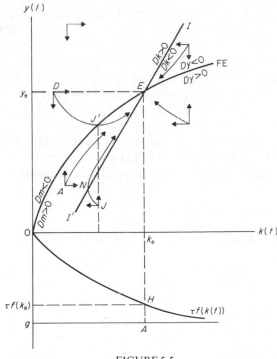

FIGURE 5.5

and the capital intensity, I explicitly consider the time rate of change of output $Dy(t)$. This is done by differentiating the IS – LM solution for output *per capita* (equation (5.38) and substituting equation (5.43b) for the rate of change of real balances *per capita*, to derive

$$Dy = F_k Dk - mF_m\left(\frac{\tau}{m} + \lambda\right)[y - f(k)]. \tag{5.45a}$$

Define the coefficient of $[y - f(k)]$ as h, and treat this coefficient as a function[11] of the tax rate τ and speed of adjustment λ:

$$h \equiv F_m m\left(\frac{\tau}{m} + \lambda\right) > 0. \tag{5.45b}$$

By substituting equation (5.41b) for the time rate of change of the capital intensity into (5.45a) the differential equation (5.46) can be derived for the time rate of change of output *per capita*:

$$Dy = F_k I(k, y; g, \tau, v_c, v_1, n) - h[y - f(k)]. \tag{5.46}$$

Coefficient F_k represents the multiplier effect of a change in the capital intensity upon aggregate demand. It is the sum of several effects. A rise in k (i) raises wealth and hence raises consumption demand and (ii) lowers the marginal product of capital which reduces the rate of change of the capital intensity. Its net effects upon aggregate demand, and the shift of the IS – LM intersection, is ambiguous.

In a stable dynamical system F_k cannot be "too large," as is proved in the appendix to this chapter. It is therefore assumed in the text that F_k is equal to zero. This assumption is consistent with economic stability and facilitates a graphic analysis. The general case is discussed in the appendix. When $F_k = 0$, the differential equation for output *per capita* is

$$Dy(t) = - h[y(t) - f(k(t))]. \tag{5.47}$$

Output *per capita* $y(t)$ converges asymptotically to capacity output *per capita* $f(k(t))$ at speed h.

Table 5.3 is a compact summary of the IS growth model. There are four independent equations and four unknowns which are the focus of interest. Unknowns are: output *per capita* $y(t)$, the capital intensity $k(t)$, real balances *per capita* $m(t)$, and the rate of inflation $\pi(t)$. There are four independent equations: (5.47), (5.41b), (5.48), and *either* (5.38) *or* (5.40), since there are the same equation written in different ways.

TABLE 5.3   *Dynamics and steady state of the IS growth model.*

Dynamics

$Dy(t) = -h[y(t) - f(k(t))]$ (5.47)

$Dk(t) = I(k(t), y(t); g, \tau, v_c, v_I, n) \quad I \equiv (r - i)$ (5.41b)

$y(t) = F(k(t), m(t); g, \tau, v_c, v_I, n)$ (5.38)

or

$m(t) = M(y(t), k(t); g, \tau, v_c, v_I, n) \quad M_{y = 1/F_m}$ (5.40)

$\pi(t) = \dfrac{g - \tau f(k(t))}{m(t)} - n + \lambda[y(t) - f(k(t))].$ (5.48)

Steady state $Dk = 0$

$I(k, y; g, \tau, v_c, v_I, n) = 0 \quad II'$ curve (5.42a)

$\pi = \dfrac{g - \tau f(k)}{m} - n$ (5.49)

$y = f(k) \quad$ FE curve (5.44a)

Symbols: $y(t)$ is output *per capita*; $k(t)$ capital intensity (i.e. capital per effective worker); $m(t)$ real balances *per capita*; $\pi(t)$ rate of inflation; g real government purchases *per capita*; τ tax rate; v_c, v_I exogenous parameters; n growth rate of effective labor; $D \equiv d/dt$.

No artificial distinctions are made in this model between the short, medium and long run. Capital and financial assets change continuously. Policies which attempt to change the Okun Gap $f(k(t)) - y(t)$ have both short- and long-run effects. The rates of monetary expansion and of inflation are endogenous variables.

4.2   The steady-state and dynamic stability conditions

Define the steady state as a situation where the capital intensity is not changing: $Dk = 0$. Several implications of the steady state are drawn from the equations above, and are summarized in the lower part of table 5.2.

1. The rent per unit of capital r is equal to the real rate of interest i. Graphically, the economy is on the II' curve in figure 5.5, based upon equation (5.42a).

2. When the capital intensity is not changing, then output *per capita* is not changing (see equation (5.42a)).

3. When output *per capita* is not changing, actual output is equal to

capacity output. This is implied by equation (5.47) as described by figure 5.4(b).

4. When output *per capita* and the capital intensity are not changing, then real balances *per capita* are not changing (see equation (5.40)). Constant real balances *per capita* imply that the rate of inflation is equal to the rate of monetary expansion *per capita*: $\pi_e = \mu_e - n$.

5. Insofar as output *per capita* is equal to capacity output *per capita*, the actual and anticipated rates of inflation are equal (see equation (5.2)).

6. The inflation tax on real balances DM/pN is equal to the high employment deficit *per capita* $g - \tau f(k) = DM/pN = \mu m$. In the lower half of figure 5.5, the inflation tax *per capita* on real balances is the distance between the line g and real *per capita* tax revenues at full employment $\tau f(k)$. The inflation tax *per capita* on real balances DM/pN represents the goods *per capita* that the government acquires in exchange for the issuance of new money.

7. The correctly anticipated rate of inflation is equal to the rate of monetary expansion *per capita* $\mu - n$, which is equal to the high employment deficit divided by the money stock $[g - \tau f(k)]/m$ less the growth of population n.

Point E in the upper part of figure 5.5, and point H in the lower part, describe the steady state associated with given vector (g, τ, v_c, v_I, n) of control and exogenous variables. At point E, the rent per unit of capital is equal to the real rate of interest, and output is equal to capacity output. As drawn in the lower part of the figure, there is a steady-state real deficit *per capita* $AH = g - \tau f(k_e)$, which is the inflation tax *per capita* on real balances.

In the Keynesian "Rock Bottom" model described in section 3.2 above, budget balance is a condition for equilibrium because the price level is fixed at $p = 1$ or is an algebraic function of output $p = P(y)$. A very different situation prevails here. *Budget balance is most definitely not a condition for equilibrium in the IS growth model. The high employment government deficit determines the rates of monetary expansion and rate of inflation.*

A mathematical statement of the stability conditions is contained in the appendix to this chapter. The literary and graphic presentations in the text draw upon the results contained in the appendix.

Figure 5.5 is drawn to describe the case where the eigenvalues of the dynamical system are negative and real. Three conditions imply that the system is dynamically stable and noncyclical.

First, the short-run dynamical system is stable as described by figure

5.4(b). Given the capital intensity, the proportionate rate of change of real balances is positively related to the Okun Gap, as described by equation (5.43b) above. This requires that the coefficient $h \equiv mF_m[(\tau/m) + \lambda]$ be strictly positive. Such a condition is satisfied, since a parametric rise in real balances *per capita* shifts the IS and LM curves to the right (from IS_0 to IS_1 and from LM_0 to LM_1 in figure 5.4(a).

Secondly, the synthesis Keynes – Wicksell model of money and capacity growth (Stein, 1971: ch. 5, 6) is dynamically stable. A Keynes – Wicksell model of money and capacity growth is one where there are independent savings and investment functions, but output is always at capacity output. Graphically this means that $y(t)$ is always on the FE curve $y(t) = f(k(t))$. Under these conditions, the growth equation (5.41b) becomes

$$Dk(t) = I(k(t), f(k(t))); g, \tau, v_c, v_1, n). \tag{5.50}$$

This Keynes – Wicksell model of money and capacity growth is stable if a rise in the capital intensity $k(t)$ above the equilibrium capital intensity k_e lowers the marginal product of capital below the real rate of interest. Equation (5.51) must be satisfied for the Keynes – Wicksell model of money and capacity growth system to be stable:

$$\left.\frac{dDk(t)}{dk(t)}\right|_{k = k_e} I_k + I_y f' < 0. \tag{5.51}$$

Thirdly, the value of F_k must be sufficiently small. Function F_k is the change in the IS – LM solution for output $y(t)$ that results from a parametric rise in the capital intensity. If F_k is too large, then the system is unstable for the following reason. A rise in capital intensity above the equilibrium lowers the marginal product of capital below the real rate of interest, and the rate of capital formation declines towards the equilibrium. This is the condition $I_k < 0$ described above. If the rise in the capital intensity raises the IS – LM solution for the level of income sufficiently (i.e. F_k is large), then the rate of capital formation is stimulated by a positive marginal propensity to invest. This force $F_k I_y > 0$ (see equations (5.38) and (5.41b)) tends to drive the capital intensity further away from equilibrium.

To guarantee the stability of the system, the curves in figure 5.5 are drawn for $F_k = 0$. Parametric changes in the capital intensity *per se* do not affect the IS – LM solution for the level of income. When $F_k = 0$, the full employment curve FE in figure 5.5 coincides with the locus of points (y, k) along which the level of output does not change (see equations (5.46) and (5.47)).

These three conditions imply that the II' curve is steeper than the FE curve, and that the vectors of motion are as drawn in figure 5.5. Trajectories to the equilibrium E are implied by the vectors in figure 5.5. Output $y(t)$ converges to full employment output $f(k(t))$ at rate h. The capital intensity $k(t)$ converges to k_e, where the marginal product of capital is equal to the real rate of interest. Hence, output $y(t)$ converges to $f(k_e)$.

Tax revenues $\tau f(k_e)$ are less than government purchases g at equilibrium point H as drawn in figure 5.5. Inflation tax on real balances $g - \tau f(k_e)$ is equal to distance HA and is $\mu_e m_e$.

Several trajectories to the equilibrium point $E = (k_e, y_e)$ are drawn in figure 5.5. At point A, there is an Okun Gap, and both income and the capital intensity rise monotonically. Such a situation could be termed a growth recession.

If the economy starts at point J, with a large Okun Gap JJ', the trajectory JNE is followed. Real balances rise as a result of the Okun Gap, and output rises towards capacity output J'. However, the very depressed level of output lowers the marginal product of capital $r(y, k)$ below the real rate of interest. The capital intensity declines, and it is even possible that net investment is negative. In this "Great Depression," capacity output $f(k(t))$ declines along trajectory JN although output $y(t)$ is rising. At point N, the reduction in the capital intensity raises the rent per unit of capital to the real rate of interest, and the capital intensity ceases to decline.[12] Since output at point N is below capacity output, real balances continue to rise. The IS and LM curves in figure 5.4(a) continue to shift to the right, and the IS – LM solution for the level of output increases. As a result of the positive marginal propensity to invest, the rent per unit of capital increases relative to the real rate of interest. The capital intensity rises, and the economy travels along trajectory NE to the steady state. The depression has taken its toll in lost output and high unemployment.

It is possible that the economy is displaced to point D. Output exceeds capacity output, but the rent per unit of capital exceeds the real rate of interest. In this case, the economy follows trajectory $DJ'E$ to the steady state. Output is reduced to capacity output, while capacity output is growing.

4.3   Short- and long-run effects of a countercyclical fiscal policy

Suppose that an exogenous decline in the investment demand schedule (v_1) plunged the economy into a severe depression. Output *per capita* y_0 (figures 5.4(a) and (b)) is substantially below capacity output. The endogenous growth of the money supply control law equation (5.6), and the price flexibility equation (5.2), will return the economy to full employment in the following manner.

As a result of the decline in income below full employment (i.e. the existence of an Okun Gap $f(k_0) - y_0$), tax revenues decline. The larger deficit is financed by money creation, and the rate of monetary expansion rises by $(\tau/m)[f(k_0) - y_0]$. Insofar as the rate of inflation responds to an Okun Gap, in the manner described by equation (5.2), the rate of inflation declines by $\lambda[f(k_0) - y_0]$. Real balances *per capita* rise by $(\tau/m + \lambda)[f(k_0) - y_0]$, and the IS – LM curves in figure 5.4(a) shift to the right. Real income $y(t)$ rises towards $f(k_0)$. Figure 5.4(b) describes the locus of movement of real income *per capita* $y(t)$ and real balances *per capita* $m(t)$ from Z_0 to S_0, resulting from the endogenous rightward shifts of the IS – LM curves in figure 5.4(a). Figure 5.4(b) describes equations (5.47) and (5.40), when the capital intensity is predetermined. The time required for half of the Okun Gap to be closed, denoted by $T(0.5)$, is $0.69/h$, which is inversely proportional to the speed of adjustment $h \equiv [(\tau/m_e) + \lambda]F_m m$. Let us refer to $T(0.5) = 0.69/h$ as the "half-life" of the Okun Gap.[13] The greater the degree of nominal wage and price flexibility λ, the shorter will be the half-life of the Okun Gap. Economies characterized by different institutions determining wages and prices will have different degrees of wage and price flexibility and, consequently, different half-lives of the Okun Gap.

Keynesian impact effects

The half-life $T(0.5)$ may be too long to be socially acceptable; and the Keynesian revolution suggested countercyclical fiscal policy to accelerate the return to full employment. The government may increase its purchase of goods *per capita* by Δg from g_0 to g_1, in order to accelerate the return to full employment. Assume that these demand management expenditures only affect aggregate demand, but do not affect capacity output *per se*. For example, the government hires the unemployed people to work in government offices.

There is an impact effect of the parametric rise in g upon the level of
output, described by equation (5.38) and figures 5.4(a, b). Given the
level of real balances m_0 (figure 5.4(b)), a rise in real government purchases shifts the IS curve from IS_0 to IS_1 (figure 5.4(a)). Short-run
equilibrium moves from z_0 to z_1 (figure 5.4(a)), and the level of income
rises from y_0 to y_1. This impact effect is equal to $F_g \Delta g$. Figure 5.4(b)
illustrates the short-run dynamics. Initially, the relation between real
balances and income is described by curve $M(g_0)$ based upon equation
(5.40). When real government purchases rise from g_0 to g_1, the relation
between m and y (equation (5.40)) shifts from $M(g_0)$ to $M(g_1)$ in figure
5.4(b). The level of output *per capita* associated with real balances m_0
rises from y_0 to y_1. Distance $Z_0 Z_1 = y_0 y_1$ is precisely the Keynesian
impact multiplier $F_g \Delta g$, whereby demand management fiscal policy
can reduce an Okun Gap.

At point Z_1 (figure 5.4(b)), the Okun Gap is $f(k_0) - y_1$. For the
reasons discussed above, real balances *per capita* continue to rise, and
the IS – LM curves continue to shift to the right. The economy travels
at speed h from point Z_1 (figure 5.4(b)) in the direction of the vectors
to point S_1. At short-run equilibrium point S_1, output is equal to
capacity output $f(k_0)$, and real balances *per capita* are m_1^f. Equilibrium
point S_1 in figure 5.4(b) corresponds to point e_1 in figure 5.4(a). At
point e_1, the IS curve IS_2 is based upon real balances m_1^f and real
government purchases g_1; the LM curve $LM(m_1^f)$ is based upon real
balances m_1^f.

In this model, money-financed fiscal policy accelerates the return to
full employment by moving the economy from Z_0 to Z_1 (figure 5.4(b)).
The NCE Policy Ineffectiveness Proposition is not operative here.
The rise in g affects the demand for goods directly by raising aggregate
demand by $F_g \Delta g$. It also raises the rate of monetary expansion (equation (5.6)) and hence the anticipated rate of inflation (equation (5.7)).
The last two effects do indeed cancel each other as a result of the
Asymptotically Rational Expectations hypothesis and the Fisher
effect. It is the first effect $F_g \Delta g$ that shifts the economy from point Z_0
to point Z_1 in the traditional Keynesian manner.

This is as far as Keynesian macroeconomics, embodied in the IS
growth model, describes the economic process. Demand management
fiscal policy and an endogenous rate of monetary growth combine to
eliminate the Okun Gap $f(k(t)) - y(t)$.

During the adjustment of output to the current capacity output
$f(k_0)$, capacity output itself is changing. Moreover, the demand
management fiscal policy which reduces the Okun Gap affects the trajectory of capacity output $f(k(t))$. The IS growth model (tables 5.2 and

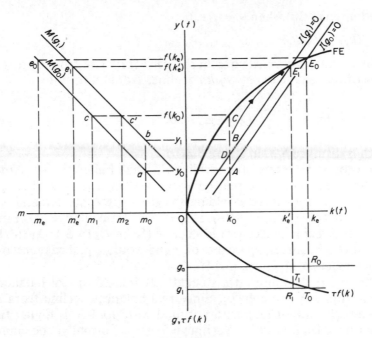

FIGURE 5.6

5.3) permits us to analyze the complete paths of the economy, when demand management policy is undertaken. Figure 5.6, based upon figures 5.4(a, b) and 5.5, illustrates the dynamics in table 5.3 and serves as the basic tool of analysis.

A rise in real government purchases raises the real rate of interest and capacity output
First, it is shown that when real government purchases *per capita* rise from g_0 to g_1, the real rate of interest $i(t)$ at any capacity output $y(t) = f(k(t))$ is increased. The argument is as follows. At any level of income, the real rate of interest $i(t)$ is described by equation (5.52), which is based upon (5.3). It is the LM curve in figure 5.4(a).

$$i(t) = i(y(t), m(t), k(t)). \tag{5.52}$$

At capacity output $y(t) = f(k_0)$, the real rate of interest is

$$i(t) = i(f(k_0), m(t), k_0); \quad i_m < 0. \tag{5.53}$$

As a result of the rise in real government purchases from g_0 to g_1, the medium-run equilibrium real balances decline from S_0 to S_1 in figure 5.4(b). The IS–LM solution for output is equation (5.54), which is based upon (5.38) when $y = f(k_0)$:

$$f(k_0) = F(k_0, m; g, \tau, v_c, v_1, n). \tag{5.54}$$

Since real government purchases *per capita* rise from g_0 to g_1, the value of real balances *per capita* declines from m_0^f to m_1^f:

$$m_1^f - m_0^f = - \frac{F_g}{F_m} (g_1 - g_0) < 0, \tag{5.55}$$

which is distance $S_0 S_1$ in figure 5.4(b).

In economic terms, the decline in real balances *per capita* is explained as follows. If real balances remained at m_0^f, when g rises from g_0 to g_1, then there would be an excess aggregate demand $S_0 R_0$ at capacity output (figure 5.4(b)). Prices would rise relative to the money stock, and real balances would decline (from R_0 to S_1). At the lower level of real balances, aggregate demand would equal capacity output (as described by equation (5.54)).

The real rate of interest i is negatively related to real balances *per capita* (liquidity preference). Since real balances decline from m_0^f to m_1^f, the real rate of interest associated with pont S_1 is higher than it would have been at point S_0 (figure 5.4(b)). Formally, the change in the real rate of interst between points S_0 and S_1 is described by equation (5.56), which is based upon equation (5.53) and (5.55):

$$\Delta i = - i_m \frac{F_g}{F_m} \Delta g > 0. \tag{5.56}$$

Figure 3.1 describes this situation.

The rise in the real rate of interest affects the trajectory of the capital intensity
As a result of the rise in the real rate of interest, the rate of capital formation is affected. Figure 5.6 describes the dynamics in table 5.3. *It is shown that a rise in real government purchases of goods per capita from g_0 to g_1 reduces the steady-state capital intensity, reduces the steady-state capacity output per capita and raises the steady-state rate of inflation.* Graphically, a rise in real government purchases *per capita* raises the II' curve (equation (5.42a)), and the steady state shifts from E_0 to E_1.

The proof is as follows. The rate of change of the capital intensity is equation (5.41a) or (5.41b) repeated here:

$$Dk(t) = \xi[r(k(t), y(t); v_1, \tau) -$$
$$i(y(t), k(t), M(y(t), k(t); g, \tau, v_c, v_1, n))] \qquad (5.41a)$$

$$Dk(t) = I(k(t), y(t); g, \tau, v_c, v_1, n). \qquad (5.41b)$$

It was shown in figure 5.4(b) that a rise in real government purchases lowers the real balances $m(t) = M(y(t), k(t); g, \tau, v_c, v_1, n)$ associated with any IS − LM solution for the level of income $y(t)$. Consequently, the real rate of interest at any level of income is raised. For example, the real rate of interest at point S_1 is higher than it is at S_0 (figure 5.4(b)). The rate of capital formation is adversely affected as described by

$$\left.\frac{\partial Dk(t)}{\partial g}\right|_{y(t), k(t)} = -\xi i_M M_g = I_g < 0. \qquad (5.57)$$

Given the level of income *per capita* $y(t)$ and the capital intensity $k(t)$, a rise in real government purchases *per capita* reduces the rate of capital formation. The $I(g_0) = 0$ curve in figure 5.6 (based upon equation (5.42a)) is the locus of points (y, k) such that $Dk = 0$ when $g = g_0$. If the capital intensity (e.g. k_0) is to remain constant, when the rise in real government purchases raises the real rate of interest, there must be a rise in the level of income by AD to offset this effect. If $I(k, y; g, \tau, v_c, v_1, n) = 0$ for a given k:

$$I_y\Delta y + I_g\Delta g = 0 \qquad (5.58a)$$

and

$$\left.\frac{\partial y}{\partial g}\right|_k = -\frac{I_g}{I_y} > 0. \qquad (5.58b)$$

The positive marginal propensity to invest $I_y\Delta y$ is needed to offset the effect of the rise in the real rate of interest $I_g\Delta g < 0$. Equation (5.58b) states that the $I(g_0) = 0$ curve must shift upwards by $(-I_g/I_y)\Delta g = AD$ to $I(g_1) = 0$, as a result of the rise in real government purchases *per capita*.

The complete dynamic process resulting from a rise in real government purchases per capita
The dynamic process resulting from a rise in real government purchases *per capita* can now be fully described in figure 5.6, based upon table 5.3. The first and fourth quadrants are based upon figure 5.5

and the second quadrant is based upon figure 5.4(b). Upper case letters refer to points in the first quadrant, and lower case letters refer to corresponding points in the second quadrant.

Let there be a large decline in the investment demand schedule (i.e. parameter v_i) which reduced aggregate demand. The economy is in a severe depression at point A. Output y_0 is substantially below the current capacity output $f(k_0)$. The rent per unit of capital is equal to the real rate of interest, and the capital intensity is not rising.

Keynesian demand management fiscal policy is undertaken to restore full employment. Real government purchases of goods *per capita* rise from g_0 to g_1. Aggregate demand is increased, and the IS – LM solution for income rises by the multiplier $F_g \Delta g$ from A to B (or from a to b). Keynesian policy has reduced the Okun Gap from AC to BC. Since the new level of output $y_1 = y_0 + F_g \Delta g$ (at point B or b) is below the current capacity output $f(k_0)$, real balances *per capita* rise. This rise is due to two forces. (i) the gap in income from $f(k_0)$ to y_1 lowers taxes and increases the budget deficit. According to control law equation (5.6), budget deficits are financed through money creation, and the endogenous rate of monetary expansion rises. (ii) According to price change equation (5.2), the existence of an Okun Gap *per se* reduces the rate of inflation. These two factors produce a rise in real balances, as described by equation (5.43b). The economy moves towards capacity output: from b towards c', and from B towards C.

The short-run effects are consistent with Keynesian economics. There is a positive impact effect upon the level of income, $F_g \Delta g = AB = ab$, which reduces the Okun Gap. The resulting rise in income stimulates investment via the positive marginal propensity to invest. Fiscal policy appears to be successful in raising both the level of output and the rate of capital formation.

Activist demand management policy has both long-run and short-run effects. The rise in real government purchases *per capita* lowers real balances *per capita* and thereby raises the real rate of interest associated with any level of income y and capital intensity k. For example, at capacity output $f(k_0)$, the rise in real government purchases reduces real balances from m_1 (associated with point c) to m_2 (associated with point c') in figure 5.6. Therefore, the real rate of interest is higher at point c' than at point c.

The graph of $Dk = I(.) = 0$ shifts up from $I(g_0) = 0$ to $I(g_1) = 0$. The longer-run consequences are that the economy follows trajectory BE_1 rather than a trajectory from A to E_0. Real government purchases of goods *per capita* effectively crowd out real capital formation and raise the rate of inflation. When the economy reaches any capacity output $f(k(t))$, there is less investment *per capita* than would have occurred if the government expenditures remained at g_0. The reduction in the rate of investment is due to the higher real rate of interest resulting from the lower level of real balances. The crowding-out effect of the rise in government expenditures can be measured by distance AD (figure 5.6). This distance is the required rise in real income to raise the rent per unit of capital so that it will equal the real rate of interest. In the steady state, the capital intensity will be k_e' rather than k_e, as a result of the parametric rise in real government expenditures from g_0 to g_1. Output *per capita* converges to $f(k_e')$ rather than to the higher value $f(k_e)$. *One price that is paid for accelerating the return to the current capacity output $f(k_0)$, through the use of demand management policy, is a decline in steady-state capacity output per capita.*

Another cost of demand management policy is that there is a higher steady-state rate of inflation. In the steady state, the rate of inflation π_e is equal to the rate of monetary expansion *per capita* $\mu_e - n$. According to control law equation (5.6), the steady-state rate of monetary expansion is the government budget deficit divided by the money stock. At the steady state, the rate of inflation is described by

$$\pi_e = \frac{g - \tau f(k_e)}{m_e} - n. \tag{5.59}$$

Budget balance is definitely not a condition for equilibrium in the IS growth model, although it is a condition for equilibrium in the "Rock Bottom" model. The deficit is higher at point E_1 than it is at point E_0 because real government expenditures are higher $g_1 > g_0$ and real tax revenues are lower $\tau f(k_e') < \tau f(k_e)$. A surplus $T_0 R_0 = \tau f(k_e) - g_0$ would have been achieved at point E_0; but a deficit $R_1 T_1 = g_1 - \tau f(k_e')$ occurs at point E_1. The inflation tax on real balances $R_1 T_1$ finances the government purchases of goods.

Real balances *per capita* m_e' are lower at point e_1 (corresponding to E_1) than they would have been (m_e) if the economy achieved the steady state at point e_0 (corresponding to E_0). Therefore, the steady-state rate of inflation is higher at realized state (E_1, e_1) than at the unobserved steady-state point (E_0, e_0):

$$\pi_e' = \frac{g_1 - \tau f(k_e')}{m_e'} > \frac{g_0 - \tau f(k_e)}{m_e} = \pi_e. \tag{5.60}$$

points (E_1, e_1)   points (E_0, e_0)

The economic question is whether the short-run gain of reaching the *current* capacity output $f(k_0)$ at a faster rate, by increasing real government purchases, exceeds the costs of: (i) reducing the realized steady-state output *per capita*; (ii) a permanently higher rate of inflation; and (iii) a lower level of real balances *per capita*. Keynesian economics neglects these costs because it does not consider variations in the capital intensity and the rate of inflation. Keynes – Wicksell models of money and capacity growth concentrate upon the growth process and inflation, but assume that output is always equal to capacity output. The IS growth model synthesizes short-run macroeconomics with Keynes – Wicksell models of money and economic growth.

5   Appendix: mathematical analysis of the stability conditions for the IS growth model

Equations (5.47) and (5.41b) in table 5.3 are linearized around the equilibrium point (y_e, k_e) to derive the vector – matrix differential equation

$$\begin{bmatrix} Dy \\ Dk \end{bmatrix} = \begin{bmatrix} -H_y + F_k I_y & H_y f' + F_k I_k \\ I_y & I_k \end{bmatrix} \begin{bmatrix} y - y_e \\ k - k_e \end{bmatrix}, \tag{A5.1}$$

where the entries in the matrix are evaluated at the equilibrium point.

Necessary and sufficient conditions for the asymptotic stability of equilibrium are

$$-H_y + I_k + F_k I_y < 0. \tag{A5.2}$$

$$-H_y [I_k + I_y f'] > 0. \tag{A5.3}$$

The intermediate-run model is stable since

$$H_y \equiv m_e F_m \left(\frac{\tau}{m} + \lambda \right) > 0. \tag{A5.4}$$

Since (A5.4) is satisfied, then (A5.3) is satisfied if

$$I_k + I_y f' < 0 \tag{A5.5}$$

or

$$0 < f'(k_e) < -I_k / I_y. \tag{A5.6}$$

Stability condition (A5.6) implies that, at the equilibrium point (y_e, k_e), the $I(g) = 0$ curve is steeper than the full employment curve FE, and $I_k < 0$.

Since $H_y > 0$, $I_y > 0$ and $I_k < 0$, condition (A5.2) is satisfied if and only if F_k is "sufficiently small" as described by

$$F_k < \frac{H_y - I_k}{I_y}. \tag{A5.7}$$

This is why the discussion in the text assumes that $F_k = 0$.

Assuming that the system is stable, the eigenvalues are real if

$$\left(\frac{-(H_y - I_k)}{I_y} + F_k \right)^2 \geqslant -4 \frac{H_y}{I_y} \left(\frac{I_k}{I_y} + f' \right). \tag{A5.8}$$

The expression on the right-hand side is positive (see (A5.5)). For $F_k = 0$, the eigenvalues are real. For F_k, which satisfies (A5.7) but is close to $(H_y - I_k)/I_y$, the eigenvalues will be a complex pair resulting in a decaying oscillatory behavior about the equilibrium point.

Notes

1   The two Keynes – Wicksell models of money and growth are discussed in Stein (1971) Chapters 3, 4 and 5, 6 respectively.
2   See Infante and Stein (1980). Each variable (e.g. X) is to be understood as having a time index (e.g. $X(t)$), except in the steady state when it is constant. To remind the reader, at certain crucial points, time indices are explicitly stated.
3   See Cargill and Meyer (1977). In their regressions of the nominal rate of interest $P(t)$ upon past rates of inflation $\pi(t)$ of the form

$$P(t) = a + \overset{t}{\Sigma} b(s)\pi(s), \text{ it does not seem that } \overset{t}{\Sigma} b(s) \text{ equals unity.}$$

4   See Stein (1971), chapter 8, especially pp. 245 – 6, for an analysis of Friedman's "Optimum Quantity of Money."
5   Strictly speaking, a "B Regime" does not require that the *constant* rate of monetary expansion μ in $M(t) = M(0) \exp^{(\mu t)}$ be equal to n. However, the assumptions in equations (5.8b) and (5.8c) simplify the analysis without introducing any distortions whatsoever.
6   See Christ (1979) who obtains similar results for a richer model than the "Rock Bottom" model. Christ has been one of the major figures to stress the importance of the government budget constraint. The Tobin – Buiter (1976) model is also unstable, unless the coefficient of adaptive expectations is extremely large. See Niehans (1977).

7   The analysis is based upon Infante and Stein (1976).

8   I am currently studying whether a "B Regime" or constant money growth rule is consistent with economic stability in the general model in table 2.1.

9   Within the context of the "Rock Bottom" model, the same results are obtained if $p = P(y)$, that is, if the price level is a function of real output.

10 Friedman explicitly stated that:

> ... when many prices are moderately rigid, at least against declines, the monetary and fiscal framework described above cannot be expected to lead to reasonably full employment of resources .... (1953: 143)

> The brute face is that a rational economic program for a free-enterprise system (and perhaps even for a collectivist system) must have flexibility of prices (including wages) as one of its cornerstones. (1953: 144)

11 The effects of variations in m upon h are ignored in this linearization.

12 Trajectory JNE captures the argument in Hicks (1950: 119 especially).

13 $T(0.5)$ is the value of t which solves

$$\frac{y(t) - f(k_0)}{y(0) - f(k_0)} = 0.5 = \exp(-ht).$$

CHAPTER 6

Conclusion

1   The strategy to resolve disagreements among macroeconomists

Disagreement among economists takes three forms: (i) disagreements of style, that is, techniques of analysis; (ii) substantive disagreements concerning the controllability of the system and its responses to disturbances; (iii) disagreements concerning the empirical estimates of the structural parameters of the economic system. Although most of the macroeconomic literature is concerned with point (i), concerning literary scenarios, the focus of this book is exclusively upon points (ii) and (iii).

1.1   *Disagreements of style and of substance*

A simple and clear example of disagreement of style concerns the income–expenditure Keynesian approach to the determination of national income in nominal terms as compared to the quantity theory of money approach. The quantity theory approach is equation (6.1): nominal income Y is the product of the money stock M and velocity V

$$Y = MV. \tag{6.1}$$

Equations (6.2)–(6.5) describe the well-known Keynesian approach. Equation (6.2) defines nominal income Y as the sum of consumption C, investment I and government expenditures G. Equation (6.3) is the consumption function, where consumption depends upon disposable income $(1 - \tau)Y$, and τ is the tax rate. Investment, equation (6.4), depends upon income Y and interest rate ρ. Interest rate ρ is determined by the condition that the demand for money is equal to the stock of money. The demand for money depends upon income and the interest rate. The demand for money equation is solved for the interest rate to derive equation (6.5).

$$Y = C + I + G. \tag{6.2}$$

$$C = c(1 - \tau)Y. \tag{6.3}$$

$$I = a_0 + a_1 Y - a_2 \rho. \tag{6.4}$$

$$\rho = b_1 Y - b_2 M. \tag{6.5}$$

The Keynesian system equations (6.2)–(6.5) are easily solved for income Y, and equation (6.6a) is derived:

$$Y = (a_0 + G)F_G + a_2 b_2 F_G M, \tag{6.6a}$$

where

$$F_G = [1 - c(1 - \tau) - a_1 + a_2 b_1]^{-1} > 0 \tag{6.6b}$$

is the "multiplier".

To explain variations in the level of income: (i) quantity theories examine changes in the money stock and velocity; (ii) Keynesians examine shifts in the investment function and changes in government expenditures. The two *styles* are quite different. Whether the two approaches are substantively different cannot be determined simply on the basis of equations (6.1)–(6.6a).

The Keynesian model implies that velocity $V = Y/M$ is equation (6.7), which is obtained by dividing equation (6.6a) by the money stock:

$$V = (a_2 b_2 F_G) + \frac{(a_0 + G)}{M} F_G = V(G,M). \tag{6.7}$$

An implication of the Keynesian model is that velocity is a function $V(G,M)$ which is positively related to government expenditures and negatively related to the stock of money.

Ostensibly, the two approaches are quite different. They do not speak the same language, and seem to disagree about the determinants of nominal income. Nevertheless, there may be no substantive disagreement between the two approaches. Consider the following possibility. Those who use the quantity theory paradigm may claim that velocity depends positively upon the interest rate:

$$V = W(\rho), \qquad W' > 0. \tag{6.8}$$

Moreover, they may accept the view that: (i) a rise in government expenditures financed by bonds lowers bond prices, that is, raises the rate of interest; (ii) a rise in the stock of money raises the demand for bonds and lowers the rate of interest. Users of the quantity theory approach may accept interest rate equation (6.9):

$$\rho = R(G,M) \qquad R_1 > 0, R_2 < 0. \tag{6.9}$$

When interest rate equation (6.9) is substituted into velocity equation (6.8), the resulting velocity function is equation (6.10a). Condition (6.10b) is always assumed.

$$V = W(R(G,M)) = V^*(G,M), \tag{6.10a}$$

$$-1 < \frac{\partial(\ln V^*)}{\partial(\ln M)} < 0. \tag{6.10b}$$

If the quantity theorists believe that the velocity function is V^* in equation (6.10a), then the disagreement with the Keynesians is purely stylistic and not substantive. Both approaches conclude that nominal income can be raised by increases in the money stock or in government expenditures. The Keynesian analysis, equations (6.2)–(6.6a), fully describes the quantity theory approach even though those who use the quantity theory may object that the IS–LM multiplier analysis "is not our story." Such an objection is not substantive and simply reflects stylistic differences. Although the Keynesians and quantity theorists are not speaking the same language, they are saying the same thing about the determinants of nominal income.

A very different situation occurs if the users of the quantity theory claim that velocity is a constant, independent of the stock of money and the level of government expenditures. Then the two approaches are fundamentally different in·*substance*.

Insofar as we want to resolve the disagreement between the Keynesian and quantity theory approaches, it is essential to determine whether the disagreement is stylistic or substantive. The only way to achieve this is to determine the velocity function used by the quantity theory and to compare it with the velocity function implied by the Keynesian approach.

Keynesians, Monetarists and New Classical Economists differ in both style and in substance. Most of the articles concern the stylistic aspects of each school's method of analysis. New Classical Economists discuss the nature of the "unanticipated" disturbances, the measurement of "unanticipated" money growth and the consistency or inconsistency between its price and output equations. Keynesians discuss the wage bargaining process, the role of contracts and the *ad hoc* real shocks. The substantive differences between the schools of thought concern the efficacy of demand management, the social cost of reducing an inflation, and the inflationary implications of a rise in the rate of monetary expansion when there are unemployed resources.

The NCE Policy Ineffectiveness Proposition contradicts Keynesian demand management policy. Monetarist propositions [M1] − [M3] in chapter 1 contradict both Keynesian economics and NCE. These substantive differences concern the dynamics of the economy between steady states; but there is no disagreement among the three schools of thought concerning the properties of the steady state. How can these differences be resolved?

New Classical Economists often ask whether the ratio of output $y(t)$ to capacity output $f(k(t))$ is affected by "unanticipated" money growth $\mu(t) - E_{t-1}\mu(t)$ in equation (6.11a), or by money growth $\mu(t)$ *per se* in equation (6.12). They compare (Barro, 1978: 556) the explanatory powers of equations (6.11a) and (6.12):

$$\frac{y(t)}{f(k(t))} = a_0 + \sum_{i=0}^{n} a_i [\mu(t-i) - E_{t-i-1}\mu(t-i)] . \tag{6.11a}$$

$$\frac{y(t)}{f(k(t))} = b_0 + \sum_{i=0}^{n} b_i \mu(t-i). \tag{6.12}$$

This "test" is incapable of resolving any substantive disputes for several reasons. First, all schools of thought agree that, in the steady state, money growth cannot affect the ratio of actual to capacity output. Keynesians, Monetarists and New Classical Economists agree that

$\sum_{i=0}^{\infty} b_i$, the sum of the coefficients b_i in (6.12), is zero.

Secondly, if, as is usually the case, the "expected" money growth $E_{t-1}\mu(t)$ is a function of past rates of money growth, as described by (6.11b), the equations (6.11a) and (6.12) are not substantively different:

$$E_{t-1}\mu(t) = \sum_{i=1}^{m} \gamma(i) \ \mu(t-i). \tag{6.11b}$$

Moreover, equations (6.11a) and (6.11b) imply that the Policy Ineffectiveness Proposition is not valid. A change in the rate of monetary expansion would then affect expected money growth with a lag (equation (6.11b)). In the interim, until expected money growth catches up to the actual money growth, there is "unanticipated" money growth, and demand management policy is effective.

The approach taken in this book has been to formulate a general dynamic growth model which can imply the equations of motion, that is, the *substance*, of each school of thought, depending upon the particular parameter specifications. Thus the NCE, Monetarist and Keynesian dynamic unemployment and inflation equations are derived as special cases. A variable which is crucial to the substance of each school of thought will manifest itself in the resulting equation of motion. In this way, the different scenarios which characterize the different schools of thought are replaced by different substantive dynamic equations. Substantive, not stylistic, differences are the focus of my analysis.

1.2 *Disagreements concerning estimates of parameters*

Economists also disagree whether, as an empirical "fact," variable X_2 has a significant effect upon variable X_1. For example, does the rate of monetary expansion in year $t-1$ have a significant effect upon the rate of inflation in year t? This disagreement concerning the empirical estimates of parameters stems from the differences in models used to test alternative hypotheses. If group A simply regresses X_1 on X_2 then dX_1/dX_2 is estimated by regression coefficient b_{12}:

$$b_{ij} = \frac{\text{cov } (X_i, X_j)}{\text{var } X_j}. \tag{6.13}$$

Group B may believe that it is variable X_3 not X_2 that affects variable X_1. Then the relevant regression coefficient to test the view of group A is $b_{12\ 3}$, which measures the partial effect of X_2 upon X_1, that is, $\partial X_2/\partial X_1 \mid_{x_3}$, where

$$b_{12.3} = \frac{b_{12} \text{ var } X_2 - b_{13}b_{23} \text{ var } X_3}{\text{var } X_2 - b_{23}^2 \text{ var } X_3}. \tag{6.14}$$

Group A may claim that b_{12} is significantly positive and hence their hypothesis, that X_2 positively affects X_1, is consistent with the data. Group B may claim that $b_{12\ 3}$ is not significantly different from zero, and hence X_2 has no effect upon X_1.

In general, the estimated effect $\beta_i = \partial Y/\partial X_i$ of variable X_i upon variable $Y \equiv X_1$ depends upon the other explanatory variables in the regression

$$Y = \beta_1 + \beta_2 X_2 + \beta_3 X_3 + \ldots + \beta_n X_n. \tag{6.15}$$

The reason is that the ordinary least squares (OLS) estimate of β_i is based upon equation (6.16) and depends upon the other variables that are in the columns of matrix X of observations:

$$\beta = (X'X)^{-1}X'Y, \tag{6.16}$$

where β is a column vector of β_i.

Consequently, the "facts" do *not* speak for themselves. The parameter estimates β_i of the population parameter $\beta_i = \partial Y/\partial X_i$ depend upon the other variables which are taken into account in obtaining estimates of β_i. Estimate b_{12} in (6.13) may be positive, and estimate $b_{12\ 3}$ in (6.14) may be negative. The model used to test a hypothesis fundamentally affects the parameter estimates.

Therefore, empirical analysis must be conducted within the framework of a general model which includes the substantive variables of each school of thought. It is not useful to ask whether the hypothesis of school A is consistent with the data. The crucial question is whether the data are consistent with hypothesis A *relative* to hypothesis B.

1.3   *Resolution of disagreements*

My orientation is to focus upon substantive disagreements and not on stylistic (scenario) differences. The essence of a school of thought is its dynamic equations concerning the unemployment rate, ratio of actual to capacity output, rate of inflation, rate of change of the capital intensity and real balances *per capita*. If two groups obtain the same equations for the trajectories of these variables (e.g. see equations (6.7) and (6.10a) or (6.11a)–(6.11b) and (6.12), then there are no substantive differences between them concerning the controllability of the system and response to disturbances. To be sure, their scenarios differ; but there is a direct correspondence between the two scenarios. Each is describing the same phenomenon, but in different languages.

For this reason, I construct a general model (chapter 2) which can imply any one of the three schools of thought: Keynesian, Monetarist or the New Classical Economics, depending upon the specification of crucial parameters (chapter 3). This model must be dynamic, because all of the disagreement concerns the transition between steady states. All three schools of thought agree (chapter 3, section 2) that, in the steady state, the equilibrium rate of unemployment is independent of the monetary policies followed, and the rate of inflation is closely tied to the rate of monetary expansion.

Moreover, the parameter estimates of $\partial Y/\partial X_i$ depend upon the other variables which are considered in the model. Since my model is sufficiently general to contain each school of thought as a special case, I am not ignoring variables which one school of thought deems to be important and another school deems to be unimportant. Usually, a group will claim that b_{12} in equation (6.13) is significantly positive; and it will accept that hypothesis if b_{12} is significantly different from zero at the 5 per cent level of significance. Insofar as I consider a general model which can imply any school of thought, I test (chapter 4) whether $b_{123} \ldots n$ is positive, where $X_3, X_4, \ldots, X_n$ are of significance to rival schools of thought.

. My conclusions, concerning the differences among the schools of thought, are as follows.

(i) The substantive difference between the NCE and the Monetarist gospels stems from the use of the Muth Rational Expectations hypothesis (MRE) by the former, and the Asymptotically Rational Expectations hypothesis (ARE) by the latter, as the determinant of the *risk adjusted anticipated price* which guides demand and supply decisions.

(ii) The parameter specifications that generate either Monetarist or Keynesian results are as follows. (a) Monetarist results are obtained if the relevant variable for the rate of inflation is the Keynesian excess demand for goods. Keynesian results are obtained if the relevant variable for the rate of inflation is the Okun Gap between actual and capacity output. (b) Monetarist results are obtained if a rising ratio of debt to money, resulting from continuing budget deficits, raises the real rate of interest and adversely affects investment. This is the crowding-out effect which dominates the wealth effect in the consumption function. Eventually, excess aggregate demand is lowered by the rise in the debt−money ratio. Keynesian results are obtained if a rising stock of debt, given the money stock, does not lower excess aggregate demand.

The Monetarist gospel is consistent with the macroeconomic data, whereas the Keynesian and the New Classical Economics gospels are inconsistent with the data (chapter 4). In section 2 below, I explain how the Monetarist hypothesis explains the paradox of stagflation, the phenomenon which led to the disenchantment with Keynesian economics.

2 The paradox of stagflation

Disenchantment with Keynesian economics developed during the post-1968 period when the rate of growth of output declined, the rate of inflation increased and the unemployment rate rose (see table 1.1 and figure 1.1). This "paradox" of stagflation is inconsistent with the tenet of Keynesian economics ([K4] in chapter 1) that cyclical movements in prices and output relative to trend are positively correlated. A search occurred for a more satisfactory theory of macroeconomics which can explain the paradox of stagflation.

It is shown in chapter 4 that neither New Classical Economics nor Keynesian economics is capable of explaining the observed trajectories of the unemployment and inflation rates. The Monetarist analysis in this book explains the phenomenon of stagflation as the result of two policies. First, large *high employment deficits* in the post-1967 period produced high rates of monetary expansion, whereas there were *high employment surpluses* from 1957 to 1966. The rate of inflation converges asymptotically to the rate of monetary expansion with a "half-life" of one year. After five years, the rate of inflation is approximately equal to the constant rate of monetary expansion. Therefore, the high rate of inflation is ultimately due to a run of large high employment deficits. Secondly, Keynesian demand management policy, which was accepted by Presidents[1] Kennedy, Johnson, Nixon, Ford and Carter, led the government: (i) to raise substantially the high employment deficit and the rate of monetary expansion when the unemployment rate was high; and (ii) to lower substantially the rate of monetary expansion when the rate of inflation was too high. These policies raised the rate of inflation when unemployment was high, and then raised the unemployment rate when the rate of inflation was too high.

2.1   High employment deficits, rates of monetary expansion and inflation

The first two columns in table 6.1 describe the average ratio[2] of the high employment deficit as a fraction of the money supply $F^H(t)/M(t)$ and the average rates of monetary expansion $\mu(t+1)$ from year t to year $t+1$. It was shown in chapter 2 (equations (2.49a), (2.49c)) that approximately two-thirds of the growth of the money supply from year t to year $t+1$ is explained by the *high employment* deficit to the money stock $F^H(t)/M(t)$ in year t.

There is no relation between the *actual* deficit $F(t)$ and the rate of monetary expansion, because the actual deficit is a dependent variable. When there is a decline in economic activity, the actual deficit rises relative to the high employment deficit, but the money multiplier also declines. The rise in the actual deficit above the high employment deficit tends to raise the rate of monetary growth, but the decline in the money multiplier tends to reduce the rate of monetary growth. These two effects tend to cancel each other. Therefore, the *high employment deficit* is the only systematic factor determining the rate of monetary growth. Given the high employment deficit $F^H(t)/M(t)$, there is no relation between the actual deficit $F(t)/M(t)$ and the rate of monetary expansion. This hypothesis is consistent with regression equation (6.17), which is based upon the sample period t for 1957 through 1979:

$$\mu(t+1) = \quad 4.25 \quad + \quad 0.365F^{H}(t)/M(t) + \quad 0.00F(t)/M(t). \quad (6.17)$$
$$(t=) \qquad (10.98) \quad (3.85) \qquad\qquad (0.00)$$
$$R^2 = 0.63; \quad DW = 1.58; \quad SE = 1.42$$

The relation between the high employment deficit and the rate of monetary expansion in the subsequent year reflects the policy of the monetary authority in financing the high employment deficit. When the high employment deficit is financed by bonds, then the real rate of interest tends to increase. The less willing the monetary authority is to permit interest rates to vary when the government has to finance its deficit, the greater the fraction financed by money; and the larger is the coefficient relating the rate of monetary expansion $\mu(t+1)$ to the previous year's ratio of the high employment deficit to the money stock.

The mean ratio of the high employment deficit to the money stock increased substantially from the 1957–66 period to the 1967–79 period, with no perceptible rise in the standard deviation. On average, there were high employment surpluses during 1959–66 and high employment deficits during 1967–77. The Vietnam War was responsible for the high employment deficits during 1967–73 and domestic considerations were responsible for the high employment deficits during 1974–79. As a consequence of the rise in $F^{H}(t)/M(t)$ by seven percentage points (from -2.24 to 4.72 per cent), the mean annual rate of monetary expansion $\mu(t+1)$ rose from 2.9 per cent per annum during 1958–67 to 6.37 per cent per annum during 1968–80. There was no perceptible difference in the variability (standard deviation) of money growth during the two periods. The columns μ and π in table 6.1 contain the compound annual rate of monetary expansion and of inflation between the initial and terminal dates.

A comparison of the μ and π columns illustrates the argument in chapter 4 that the rate of price inflation converges to the rate of monetary expansion with a "half-life" of one year. Equation (6.18) is equation (4.45), which is a closed form solution for the annual rate of inflation $\pi(t)$ in terms of the constant rate of monetary expansion μ from year $t = 0$ to the present:

$$\pi(t) = (0.5)^t\pi(0) + \mu[1 - (0.5)^t]. \tag{6.18}$$

After five years, the rate of inflation $\pi(5)$ is approximately equal to the constant rate of monetary expansion μ. Equation (6.19) is equation (4.46e):

$$\pi(5)/\mu = 0.97 + 0.03\pi(0)/\mu. \tag{6.19}$$

TABLE 6.1 *Average high employment deficit to the money stock, average rate of monetary expansion, compound rates of monetary expansion and inflation: 1956–80.*

Period t	$F^H(t)/M(t)$ (% p.a.)	$\mu(t+1)$ (% p.a.)	Period t	μ (% p.a.)	π (% p.a.)	ρ (% p.a.)
1. 1957–66						
Mean	−2.24	2.91	1956–67	2.7	2.1	4.34
Standard deviation	(3.35)	(1.5)				
2. 1967–79						
Mean	4.72	6.37	1968–80	6.3	6.6	7.77†
Standard deviation	(3.5)	(1.35)				

Symbols: $F^H(t)$ is the high employment deficit (+) or surplus (−) in year t; $M(t)$ is the M1B money stock in year t; $\mu(t+1)$ is the rate of monetary expansion from year t to year $t+1$. The columns μ and π are the compound rates of growth of money and of the GNP deflator from the initial and terminal dates. Column ρ is the A_{aa} corporate bond yield as a yearly average. †denotes 1967–80.

A comparison of the μ and π columns is consistent with equation (6.19). Insofar as the trend rate of monetary expansion was higher in the 1967–79 period than in the 1957–66 period, there was a higher rate of inflation during the recessions of the second period than during the recessions of the first period. Moreover, on average the nominal long-term interest rates ρ (Aaa corporate bond yields) were higher in the second period when there was more inflation than they were in the less inflationary period. Nominal long-term interest rates rose on average by 3.5 percentage points when the compound rate of inflation rose by 4.5 percentage points. Long-range predictions of rates of inflation, and of nominal rates of interest, which are not long-range predictions of the rate of monetary expansion, have no scientific validity (i.e. explanatory power).

2.2 Stagflation results from the demand management policies followed

The philosophy of Keynesian demand management policy, which was accepted by Presidents Kennedy, Johnson, Nixon, Ford and Carter, produced the stagflation. The Nixon Council of Economic Advisers based its outlook for 1972 upon the same Keynesian demand management policy that was articulated by Arthur Okun (see chapter 1). In 1971, the unemployment rate was 5.9 per cent and the inflation rate was 5.1 per cent per annum. Nixon's Council analyzed the situation as follows.

There are several reasons for expecting a significantly faster rate of increase of GNP from 1971 to 1972 than was experienced from 1970 to 1971 . . . .

Federal budget policies will contribute to the increase in GNP in 1972 through tax reductions that stimulate both consumption and investment, as well as through increases in transfer for payments to individuals, increased grants to state and local governments, and increases in its own purchases . . . .

The outlays that would be made at full employment would exceed revenues that would be collected at full employment $[F^H(t)]$ by about \$8.1 billion in fiscal 1972.

The role of monetary policy in the expansion ahead will be to provide for the increase of liquidity to support increases in activity and income.

The prospect is that we will have in 1972 not only a more rapid increase of GNP than in 1971 but also a slower rate of inflation. There are two reasons for expecting a slower rate of inflation. One is the accumulation effect of the continued operation of the economy below normal rates of employment and plant utilization, even though these operating rates will be rising in 1972. The other is the effect of the price–wage–rent control system. (Council of Economic Advisers, 1972: 25–6)

This is precisely Keynesian demand management designed to reduce the unemployment rate. A rise in the high employment deficit shifts the IS curve to the right. An accommodative monetary policy keeps the LM curve relatively horizontal. Output and employment are expected to rise. An unemployment rate in excess of the equilibrium rate, and the wage and price controls, keep nominal unit labor costs and prices relatively constant. Output is supposed to rise without increasing the rate of inflation.

My monetarist explanation of stagflation is fundamentally different from either the Keynesian or the New Classical Economics accounts. The stagflation phenomenon of: (i) rising inflation in the presence of excess capacity and high unemployment and (ii) rising unemployment with high inflation is explained as follows.

When the unemployment rate is "too high," Keynesian demand management policy advocates that the government raise the high employment deficit. A subsequent rise occurs in the rate of monetary expansion, because the monetary authority does not want a bond-financed deficit to raise real interest rates and abort a recovery.

At the current level of output, the Keynesian excess demand for goods $(C + I + G - Y)$ is increased. The rise in real government purchases of goods (G) increases aggregate demand directly. Real balances rise with the rate of monetary expansion, because prices change differentially. Consumption (C) and investment (I) are thereby stimulated. The IS and LM curves shift to the right, and the Keynesian excess demand for goods is raised.

The main determinants of the *change* in the rate of inflation are: (i) the change in the Keynesian excess demand for goods; and (ii) the change in the risk-adjusted anticipated rate of inflation. The current value of the Okun Gap or unemployment rate does not significantly affect the change in the rate of inflation.

The asymptotically rational (risk-adjusted) anticipated rate of inflation is raised *differentially* towards the higher rate of monetary expansion, for two reasons. (a) There is a lag between the current higher rate of monetary expansion $\mu(t)$ and the expected longer-run rate of monetary expansion $E\mu$, which determines the expected steady-state rate of inflation $E\pi$. The length n of this lag depends upon the variance of the rate of monetary expansion $\sigma^2(\mu)$, the confidence level that the public requires before it revises its estimate of the expected rate of monetary expansion $t(Pr)$ and the degree of accuracy that the public requires between the observed sample means of the rate of monetary expansion $\bar{\mu}$ and the unknown longer-run average rate of monetary expansion $E\mu$. Equation (6.20), describing the lag n between the announced change in policy and the public's acceptance, is equation (3.46b):

$$n = \frac{\sigma^2(\mu)\ t(Pr)^2}{(\bar{\mu} - E\mu)^2}. \tag{6.20}$$

There are good reasons for being uncertain about the expected rate of monetary expansion $E\mu$. From 1962 through 1971, the standard deviation $\sigma(\mu)$ of the annual rate of monetary expansion was 34 per cent of its mean.

(b) Another lag exists between the expected price $E_t p(t + 1)$ and the risk-adjusted effective anticipated price which guides firms' input and output decisions. The change in output $q(t)$, and the demand for productive services, resulting from a change in the expected price is inversely related to the variance of the price $\sigma^2(p)$ and the coefficient α of absolute risk aversion. Variable c is the slope of the marginal cost curve. Equation (6.21) is equation (2.60), derived from an expected utility maximization process:

$$\frac{dq(t)}{dE_t p(t+1)} = \frac{1}{\alpha\sigma^2(p) + c}. \tag{6.21}$$

There is considerable price uncertainty. From 1962 through 1971, the standard deviation of the annual rate of inflation was 47 per cent of the mean annual rate.

For reasons (a) and (b), the risk-adjusted anticipated rate of inflation, which guides supply and demand decisions, converges differentially (slowly) to the current rate of monetary expansion.

It was proved in chapter 3 (equations (3.55) and (3.56)) that, under these conditions, when there is a rise in the rate of monetary expansion above the current rate of inflation, the actual rate of inflation rises faster than the risk adjusted effective anticipated rate of inflation (3.54). Real unit labor costs decline, since the growth of nominal unit labor costs is less than the rate of inflation. The excess demand for labor rises in response to the decline in real unit labor costs, and the unemployment rate declines. Equation (2.20) quantifies this relation.

The estimated dynamic equation for the unemployment rate, equation (6.22), is equation (4.13). The change in the unemployment rate $U(t+1) - U(t)$ from year t to year $t+1$ depends upon (i) the rate of monetary expansion less the rate of inflation $\mu(t) - \pi(t)$ from year $t-1$ to year t and (ii) the deviation of the unemployment rate in year t from the estimated equilibrium rate $U(t) - 5.8$. The first variable reflects the upward shift of the aggregate demand curve for goods resulting from the rise in real balances, and the degree of anticipated inflation. The second variable reflects the change in nominal unit labor costs that occurs when the unemployment rate is not at its equilibrium rate.

$$[U(t+1) - 5.8] = 0.4[U(t) - 5.8] - 0.4[\mu(t) - \pi(t)]. \tag{6.22}$$

When the unemployment rate exceeds the equilibrium rate, and the rate of monetary expansion exceeds the rate of inflation, the Keynesian excess demand for goods rises and real unit labor costs decline. Firms increase their demand for labor, and the unemployment rate declines.

The rise in the Keynesian excess demand for goods which results from the rise in real balances $\mu(t) - \pi(t)$, as well as the rise in the risk-adjusted anticipated rate of inflation, raise the rate of inflation from its current level. The *change* in the rate of inflation of the GNP deflator from year t to year $t+1$ is described by equation (6.23a), which is based upon equation (4.41). The rise in the rate of inflation is relatively independent of the initial slack in the economy, but it depends upon the change in the Keynesian excess demand for goods:

$$\pi(t+1) - \pi(t) = 0.5[\mu(t) - \pi(t)] \tag{6.23a}$$

or

$$\pi(t+1) = 0.5\pi(t) + 0.5\mu(t). \tag{6.23b}$$

When there is a positive Keynesian excess demand for goods in the macroeconomy, the rate of price change differs by markets. In auction markets, and in the markets for basic and intermediate materials (such as agricultural products and metals) where the supplies are relatively inelastic, the major impact of the Keynesian excess demand for goods is upon price. In markets for finished goods, the labor input is of relatively greater importance than it is in the markets for basic and intermediate materials, and the supply is more elastic. Hence, the speed of price response in the markets for finished goods is less than in markets for materials.

However, the output of the sector producing materials is an input to the finished goods sector. Increases in the prices of materials are transmitted to the markets for finished goods as cost increases. The expansion of output at all stages resulting from the rise in the Keynesian excess demand for goods, which was produced by the rise in the rate of monetary expansion above the current rate of inflation, leads to a tightening of the macro labor market. As a result, there is a rise in nominal unit labor costs as nominal wages rise, more overtime occurs and less efficient workers are employed.

Equation (6.24a) refers to the rate of inflation of the *producer price index for consumer foods* $\pi_1(t)$ from year $t-1$ to year t, estimated over the period 1963–80:

$$\pi_1(t) - \pi_1(t-1) = 0.13 + 0.78[\mu(t-1) - \pi_1(t-1)]; \quad R^2 = 0.43.$$
$$(t=) \qquad\qquad\qquad\qquad (3.5) \qquad\qquad\qquad\qquad\qquad (6.24a)$$

In both equations (6.23a) and (6.24a), each rate of inflation converges to the rate of monetary expansion μ. However, the speed of response is faster for the producer price index for consumer foods than for the GNP deflator. After one year, about half of the effect occurs with respect to the GNP deflator, but about 80 per cent of the effect occurs with the producer price index for consumer foods.

Very similar results occur for the rates of inflation of the price index of finished goods, the price index of intermediate goods and the index of unit labor costs.[3] All of these rates of inflation converge to the driving force — the rate of monetary expansion.

During this phase of the stagflation process, *the rate of inflation rises while there is an unemployment rate in excess of the equilibrium rate.* However, the unemployment rate declines, while the rate of inflation increases.

Appalled by the high and rising inflation, which is erroneously attributed to "supply shocks" and other *ad hoc* factors, the monetary authority announces and implements a policy to reduce the rate of monetary expansion. As a rule, the monetary authority is responsive to the wishes of the Administration.

The decline in the rate of monetary expansion starts from a higher average level than prevailed before the expansionary demand management policy was implemented. Both the unemployment rate (equation (6.22)) and the *changes* in the rate of inflation (equation (6.23a)) are affected by the decline in the rate of monetary expansion. The scenario is the reverse of the one described earlier. Since prices change differentially, real balances decline. The real rate of interest rises, and the Keynesian excess demand for goods (at the current level of output) declines. The impact upon the rate of inflation is greatest upon the prices of raw materials and intermediate goods; consumer goods prices respond at a slower rate. Moreover, the asymptotically rational anticipated (risk-adjusted) rate of inflation responds slowly to the decline in the rate of monetary expansion, for the reasons cited in connection with equations (6.20) and (6.21) above. Since the anticipated rate of inflation declines by less than the actual rate of inflation, nominal unit labor costs rise at a faster rate than prices. The wage bargaining process is more closely geared to the recent history of the rate of inflation than to the current rate of monetary expansion. Real unit labor costs rise, and the unemployment rate increases. Equation (6.22) describes how the unemployment rate responds to a decline in the rate of monetary expansion.

Real balances continue to decline; and the resulting rise in real rates of interest produces a downward shift in the aggregate demand for goods curve. Both the decline in the Keynesian excess demand, and the gradual decline in the asymptotically rational (risk-adjusted) anticipated rate of inflation, interact to reduce the actual rate of inflation.

The inflation rate declines monotonically (see equation (6.23a)) to the new rate of monetary expansion, but prices continue to rise during the recession. The unemployment rate rises for a couple of years, and then it converges to the equilibrium rate of unemployment of about 5.8 per cent (see table 4.15 for an example of the trajectories). *During the first two years of the monetary deceleration, unemployment rises while inflation is still high but declining. This is the stagflation phenomenon, implied by equations (6.22) and (6.23a), which seems paradoxical.*

Since the inflation seems to be abating, the government is urged to reverse the rising unemployment. A reversal of monetary policy and a rise in the rate of monetary expansion is advocated by the public. A democratically elected government is generally sensitive to such pleas, and the restrictive monetary policy is generally reversed. Thereby, we return to the first part of the stagflation process described above.

Stagflation is the result of demand management policies which focus exclusively upon either the high rate of unemployment or upon the high rate of inflation, depending upon which seems to be the more serious problem of the moment. *The dynamic process (equations (6.22), (6.23a)) implies that these demand management policies produce a high trend rate of inflation and cycles in the unemployment rate.* This is my monetarist explanation of the paradox of stagflation, which leads to the disillusionment with Keynesian economics.

Chapter 1 described the polarization of views in macroeconomics. The theme of this book is that a synthesis of the two poles, which I define as Monetarism, is closer to the truth. It is appropriate to conclude with the views of a great economist and philosopher.

The beliefs which we have most warrant for have no safeguard to rest on, but a standing invitation for the whole world to prove them unfounded.

He who knows only his own side of the case knows little of that. His reasons may be good, and no one may have been able to refute them. But if he is equally unable to refute the reasons on the opposite side; if he does not so much as know what they are, he has no ground for preferring either opinion. (J.S. Mill, *On Liberty*)

Notes

1   See R.E. Weintraub (1981a, 1978).
2   The data are from table 2.6.
3   John Van Huyck applied my inflation equation (4.31)

$$\pi(t) = a\pi(t-1) + (1-a)\mu(t-1)$$

to: (6.24b) the rate of inflation of the price index of finished goods $\pi_2(t)$; (6.24c) the rate of inflation of the price index of intermediate goods $\pi_3(t)$; and (6.24d) the rate of inflation of unit labor costs $\omega(t)$, for the period 1950–80. His results are as follows:

$$\pi_2(t) = -0.002 + 0.47\pi_2(t-1) + 0.7\mu(t-1); \qquad (6.24b)$$
$$(t=) \quad (-0.47) \quad (2.86) \quad\quad (2.44)$$
$$\bar{R}^2 = 0.46; \quad DW = 1.74$$

$$\pi_3(t) = -0.006 + 0.37\pi_3(t-1) + 0.8\mu(t-1); \qquad (6.24c)$$
$$(t=) \quad (-0.39) \quad (2.11) \quad\quad (2.25)$$
$$\bar{R}^2 = 0.38; \quad DW = 1.84$$

$$\omega(t) = -0.003 + 0.29\omega(t-1) + 0.8\mu(t-1); \qquad (6.24d)$$
$$(t=) \quad (-0.36) \quad (1.86) \quad\quad (3.84)$$
$$\bar{R}^2 = 0.51; \quad DW - 2.3$$

References

Andersen, L. and Carlson, K. 1970: A monetarist model for economic stabilization. Federal Reserve Bank of St Louis. *Review*, 52, No. 4.

Barro, Robert 1978: Unanticipated money, output and the price level in the United States. *Journal of Political Economy*, 86, pp. 549–80.

Blinder, Alan S. and Solow, Robert M. 1973: Does fiscal policy matter? *Journal of Public Economics*, 2, pp. 319–37.

Blinder, Alan S. and Solow, Robert M. 1974: Analytical foundations of fiscal policy in *The Economics of Public Finance*. Washington, DC: Brookings Institution.

Brunner, Karl 1970: The monetarist revolution in monetary theory. *Weltwirtschaftliches Archiv*, 105, No. 1.

Brunner, Karl and Meltzer, Allan H. 1964: The Federal Reserve's attachment to the free reserve concept. Subcommittee on Domestic Finance, Committee on Banking and Currency, House of Representatives, Washington, DC, May 7.

Brunner, Karl and Meltzer, Allan H. 1971: Why did monetary policy fail in the 'thirties'? July, draft.

Butkiewicz, James L. 1981: The impact of debt finance on aggregate demand. *Journal of Macroeconomics*, 3, No. 1, pp. 77–90.

Cagan, Phillip 1979: *Persistent Inflation*. New York: Columbia University Press.

Cargill, Thomas F. and Meyer, Robert A. 1977: Intertemporal stability of the relations between interest rates and price changes. *Journal of Finance*, 32.

Carlson, Keith 1978: Inflation, unemployment, and money: comparing the evidence from two simple models. Federal Reserve Bank of St Louis. *Review*, 60, No. 9, pp. 2–6.

Carlson, Keith 1980: Technical notes for estimates of the high employment budget. Federal Reserve Bank of St Louis (unpublished memorandum).

Christ, Carl F. 1979: On fiscal and monetary policies and the government budget constraint. *American Economic Review*, 69, pp. 526–38.

Council of Economic Advisers, *see* US Government.

Creamer, Daniel 1950: Behavior of wage rates during business cycles. Occasional Paper 34, National Bureau of Economic Research, New York.

Cyert, Richard M. and DeGroot, Morris H. 1974: Rational expectations and Bayesian analysis. *Journal of Political Economy*, 82(3).

Economic Report of the President, *see* US Government.

Friedman, Milton 1948: A monetary and fiscal framework for economic stability. *American Economic Review*, 38, pp. 245–64; also in 1953: *Essays in Positive Economics*. Chicago: University of Chicago Press, pp. 133–56.

Friedman, Milton 1970: *The Counter-revolution in Monetary Theory*, London: Institute for Economic Affairs.

Friedman, Milton 1974: A theoretical framework for monetary analysis. In Gordon, Robert (ed.), *Milton Friedman's Monetary Framework*. Chicago: University of Chicago Press.

Friedman, Milton and Schwartz, A.J. 1963: *A Monetary History of the United States*. Princeton, NJ: Princeton University Press.

Gordon, Robert J. 1980: Postwar macroeconomics: the evolution of events and ideas. In Feldstein, Martin (ed.), *The American Economy*. Chicago: University of Chicago Press, pp. 101–62.

Hanson, James A. 1980: The short-run relation between growth and inflation in Latin America. *American Economic Review*, 70(5), pp. 972–89.

Hempel, Carl G. and Oppenheim, Paul 1948: Studies in the logic of explanation. *Philosophy of Science*, 15(2), pp. 135–75.

Hicks, J.R. 1950: *A Contribution to the Theory of the Trade Cycle*. Oxford: Clarendon Press.

Hultgren, Thor 1960: Changes in labor cost during cycles in production and business. Occasional Paper 74, National Bureau of Economic Research, New York.

Infante, E.F. and Stein, J.L. 1973: Optimal growth with robust feedback control. *Review of Economic Studies*, 40.

Infante, E.F. and Stein, J.L. 1976: Does fiscal policy matter? *Journal of Monetary Economics*, 2, pp. 473–500.

Infante, E.F. and Stein, J.L. 1980: Money financed fiscal policy in a growing economy. *Journal of Political Economy*, 88, pp. 259–87.

Kane, Edward J. 1980: Politics and fed policymaking. *Journal of Monetary Economics*, 6, pp. 199–211.

Keynes, J.M. 1923: *A Tract on Monetary Reform*. London: Macmillan.

Keynes, J.M. 1930: *A Treatise on Money*. London: Macmillan. Reprinted 1950.

Lucas, Robert E. 1972: Expectations, the neutrality of money. *Journal of Economic Theory*, 4, pp. 103–24.

Lucas, Robert E. 1973: Some international evidence on the output–inflation tradeoffs. *American Economic Review*, 63, 3, pp. 326–34.

Lucas, Robert E. 1976: Econometric policy evaluation: a critique. *Journal of Monetary Economics*, 2, Supplement, pp. 19–46.

Lucas, Robert E. and Sargent, Thomas J. 1978: After Keynesian macro-economics. Federal Reserve Bank of Boston, *After the Phillips Curve*, Conference Series No. 19.

Maital, Shlomo 1979: Inflation expectations in the monetarist black box. *American Economic Review*, 69, 3, pp. 429–34.

Makin, John 1980: Anticipated money does matter. University of Washington Discussion Paper 80-1.

Mayer, Thomas 1978: *The Structure of Monetarism*. New York: W.W. Norton.

McCallum, Bennett T. 1979: On the observational inequivalence of classical and Keynesian models. *Journal of Political Economy*, 87, 2, pp. 395–402.

McCallum, Bennett T. 1980: Rational expectations and macroeconomic stabilization policy. *Journal of Money, Credit and Banking*, 12, 4, Part 2, pp. 716–46.

McCallum, Bennett T. and Whitaker, J.K. 1979: The effectiveness of fiscal feedback rules and automatic stabilizers under rational expectations. *Journal of Monetary Economics*, 5, pp. 171–86.

Meyer, L. and Rasche, R. 1980: On the costs and benefits of anti-inflation policies: Federal Reserve Bank of St Louis. *Review*, 62, No. 2, pp. 3–14.

Meyer, L. and Webster, Charles 1981: On the real effects of imprecise monetary control. Conference on *Improving Money Stock Control*, Federal Reserve Bank of St Louis and Center for the Study of American Business, Washington University, October 31.

Mitchell, Wesley C. 1960: Business cycles and their causes. Berkeley and Los Angeles: University of California Press (4th printing; paper).

Modigliani, F. and Papademos, L. 1975: Targets for monetary policy in the coming year. *Brookings Papers*, 1, pp. 141–63.

Modigliani, F. and Papademos, L. 1976: Monetary policy for the coming quarters. Federal Reserve Bank of Boston. *New England Economic Review*, March/April.

Muth, John F. 1961: Rational expectations and the theory of price movements. *Econometrica*, 29, pp. 315–35.

Niehans, Jürg 1977: A comment on stabilization paradoxes. In *Quantitative Wirtschaftsforschung*. Albach, Horst (ed.), Tübingen: Mohr.

Okun, Arthur M. 1970: *The Political Economy of Prosperity*. New York: W.W. Norton.

Perry, George L. 1978: Slowing the wage price spiral: the macroeconomic view. *Brookings Papers on Economic Activity*, 2, pp. 259–91.

Purvis, Douglas 1980: Monetarism: a review. *Canadian Journal of Economics*, 13, 1.

Sargent, Thomas J. 1973: Rational expectations, the real rate of interest, and the natural rate of unemployment. *Brookings Papers on Economic Activity*, 2, pp. 429–72.

Sargent, Thomas J. 1976a: A classical macroeconometric model for the United States. *Journal of Political Economy*, 84, 21, pp. 207–37.

Sargent, Thomas J. 1976b: The observational equivalence of natural and unnatural rate theories of macroeconomics. *Journal of Political Economy*, 84, 3, pp. 631–40.

Sargent, Thomas J. and Wallace, Neil 1975: Rational expectations, the optimum monetary instrument, and the optimal money supply rule. *Journal of Political Economy*, 83, pp. 241–54.

Sheffrin, S.M. 1979: Unanticipated money growth and output fluctuations. *Economic Inquiry*.

Stein, J.L. 1962: The nature and efficiency of the foreign exchange market. Essays in International Finance, No. 40, Princeton University.

Stein, J.L. 1971: *Money and Capacity Growth*. New York: Columbia University Press.

Stein, J.L. 1974: Unemployment, inflation and monetarism. *American Economic Review*, 64, 6, pp. 867–87.

Stein, J.L. 1976: Inside the monetarist black box. In Stein, J.L. (ed.), *Monetarism*. Amsterdam: North-Holland.

Stein, J.L. 1978: Inflation, employment and stagflation. *Journal of Monetary Economics*, 4, pp. 193–228.

Stein, J.L. 1979: Spot, forward and futures. In Levy, Haim (ed.), *Research in Finance*, 1, JAI Press, Greenwich, Connecticut, pp. 225–310.

Stein, J.L. and Infante, Ettore F. 1973: Optimal stabilization. *Journal of Money, Credit and Banking*, 5, No. 1, Part 2, pp. 525–62. (See also Infante and Stein.)

Stephens, J. Kirker 1980: An empirical note on some monetarist propositions: comment. *Southern Economic Journal*, 47, 4, pp. 1237–43.

Swamy, P.A.V.B., Barth, J.R. and Tinsley, P.A. 1980: The rational expectations approach to economic modelling. Special Studies Paper, No. 143, Federal Reserve Board.

Taylor, John B. 1975: Monetary policy during a transition to rational expectations. *Journal of Political Economy*, 83, 5, pp. 1009–21.

Taylor, John B. 1979: Staggered wage setting in a macro model. *American Economic Review*, 69, 2, pp. 108–13.

Tobin, James 1969: A general equilibrium approach to monetary theory. *Journal of Money, Credit and Banking*, 1, 1.

Tobin, James 1975: Monetary policy, inflation and unemployment. Papers on Monetary Economics, Bank of Australia.

Tobin, James 1977: How dead is Keynes? *Economic Inquiry*, 15, pp. 459–88.

Tobin, James 1980: *Asset Accumulation and Economic Activity*. Chicago: University of Chicago Press and Oxford: Basil Blackwell.

Tobin, James and Buiter, Willem 1976: Long-run effects of fiscal and monetary policy on aggregate demand. In Stein, J.L. (ed.), *Monetarism*. Amsterdam: North-Holland.

US Department of Commerce, Bureau of Economic Analysis 1973: *Long-term Economic Growth, 1860–1970*. Washington, DC.

US Government, *Economic Report of the President*, together with the *Annual Report of the Council of Economic Advisers*. US Government Printing

Office, Washington, DC.

Weintraub, Robert E. 1978: Congressional supervision of monetary policy. *Journal of Monetary Economics*, 4, pp. 341–62.

Weintraub, Robert E. 1981a: Political economy of inflation. In Brunner, Karl, *et al.*, *The Political Economy of Inflation*. Center for Research in Government Policy and Business, Graduate School of Management, University of Rochester, Center Symposia Series CS-9, pp. 37–72.

Weintraub, Robert E. 1981b: Deficits: their impact on inflation and growth. Staff Study, Subcommittee on Monetary and Fiscal Policy of the Joint Economic Committee, Congress of the United States, July 30, US Government Printing Office.

Weintraub, S. 1978–9: The missing theory of money wages. *Journal of Post Keynesian Economics*, Winter, 1, 2, pp. 59–78.

Index

225